Muslim, Trader, Nomad, Spy

The New Cold War History

Odd Arne Westad, editor

This series focuses on new interpretations of the Cold War era made possible by the opening of Soviet, East European, Chinese, and other archives. Books in the series based on multilingual and multiarchival research incorporate interdisciplinary insights and new conceptual frameworks that place historical scholarship in a broad, international context.

Muslim, Trader, Nomad, Spy

China's Cold War and the People
of the Tibetan Borderlands

SULMAAN WASIF KHAN

The University of North Carolina Press CHAPEL HILL

Jacket illustration: © Depositphotos.com/bhairav

Complete cataloging information can be obtained online
at the Library of Congress catalog website.
ISBN 978-1-4696-2110-4 (cloth: alk. paper)
ISBN 978-1-4696-3075-5 (pbk.: alk. paper)
ISBN 978-1-4696-2111-1 (ebook)

For ABK,

fellow wanderer.

And for my parents,

Zeba and Wasif,

who gave me the gift

of books.

Contents

Maps

Acknowledgments

Every now and then, I find myself grinning at the memory of a chuckle. The chuckle mixes amusement and pride—generally provoked by an irreverent question, or a sharp, uncompromising turn of phrase—and it belongs to John Gaddis. I hope John chuckles when he reads this book, for his fingerprints are all over it. It was John who first inspired me to enter academe, with his integrity as a historian and his compassion as a teacher. Integrity and compassion alike made this a much better dissertation and book. It was, as always, an adventure working with him, and it is John's favorite approbation—"That's quite remarkable"—that I aim for, whether writing or teaching.

Paul Kennedy brought his immense knowledge of international history to this project. I will forever treasure our rambles across the salt marshes, looking for eagles and discussing empire. Peter Perdue insisted that the study of modern China's foreign relations could and should begin with at least the Qing; the length and breadth of perspective he brought to my graduate education proved invaluable. Peter also reminded me of the need to convey a sense of Tibet's vastness as I wrote. Odd Arne Westad, that marvelous scholar of China's Cold War, gave generously of his time: first as an external reader for my dissertation, and then as the editor of the New Cold War History series. Arne showed me how much anthropology had to offer; for that and for lunch at the Granta I will always be grateful.

Several other people in New Haven provided advice and support. Charlie Hill first taught me to write and self-edit. It was Charlie who explained the importance of the United Nations to me, and it was Charlie who knew what Chiang truly wanted in Tibet, even without seeing the Generalissimo's diaries. Daniel Headrick braved the entire manuscript in draft and offered excellent suggestions. So too did Jonathan Spence, whose question, "What was it like to be there?", became a clarion call. Anne Fadiman reminded me that "academic writing" did not *have* to be different from "writing writing"—an insight that made the work on this book much more fun. Tim Snyder's incandescent series of lectures on Eastern Europe taught me how to think about ideology. Adam Tooze intervened at a crucial moment with crucial advice: "Work on it every day." (I settled, I confess, for five days a week.)

This work was funded by the Smith Richardson Foundation, the Council on East Asian Studies, and International Security Studies (ISS) at Yale. ISS, in addition to pouring enormous amounts of money into this project, offered a colloquium where I could be confronted with challenging questions, more free coffee than even I could drink, and, above all, wonderful company. Fortunate is the person who can count Igor Biryukov, Ann Carter-Drier, and Kathleen Galo Murphy as friends; Kathleen ran a few dozen printouts of this manuscript, and, by cat-sitting, made sure I could head off to Taiwan. Some of my happiest afternoons (and the second chapter of this book) came from arguing with Ryan Irwin about the UN. Tracy Jackson's friendship has been a boon since I first went to work for her at Koffee Too? (the best café that ever existed; now, alas, no more); it ensured that I could travel without worrying about practicalities back home. I am indebted to her, Lee, Chloe, and Alyssa. I could never tire of sharing café space with John Merriman and Jim Silk. Jim's leads in Nepal were useful and his company was invariably stimulating. Toni Dorfman has been a second mother to me; her gift of unabashed laughter is contagious, and I learned much from her discussions of theater. Cynthia Farrar did me a favor when she talked me out of law school and another when she dined with me the night after the great snowstorm in Boston. I could not have continued to write without a weekly excursion around East Rock in the company of Ranger Dan Barvir. Bill Lyle made sure that "his book" was on schedule, halting his poodles every time we ran into one another and fixing me with a gimlet eye to ask just where it was. He was the best one could hope for in a neighbor. Susie Jakes, Zhang Taisu, Kate Epstein, Michael Morgan, Carolyne Davidson, Aaron O'Connell, Schuyler Schouten, Chris Miller, Charlie Laderman, and Victor McFarland made Yale fun. Lien-Hang Nguyen, who first taught me Southeast Asian history, took it upon herself to give me a tutorial in publishing; she remains a superb teacher and friend. Sara Shneiderman and Rana Mitter provided valuable feedback.

I could not have started this book without the financial and logistical help of Christian Ostermann and his team at the Cold War International History Project (CWIHP). I owe Christian for many things, but above all, for his friendship—for the discussions on Markus Wolf and bamboo groves in Istanbul and Shanghai. CWIHP hosted a memorable discussion on Tibet and the Cold War; my thanks for that to Kristina Terzieva and Allison Lyalikov. Shortly after that workshop, John Kenneth Knaus spent a memorable few hours with me, recalling his work with Tibetans.

Xu Laoshi's excellent lessons took me to the point where I could read freely in Chinese archives. Xiao Gan and Li Dongyan made sure I ate well and in good company whenever I returned to Beijing. I would never have gotten anywhere in China without the help of two true scholars: Li Danhui and Shen Zhihua. They were patient with my bumbling; they gave freely of their own immense store of information. Li Danhui, in particular, held my research to a high standard; I will never forget the day she came up to me and said, "What you found was interesting." The Foreign Ministry Archives in Beijing are the only archives I know of where a visiting researcher could be scolded for not wearing an overcoat on a cold day ("Young people these days!" was how I was eventually dismissed, with a PLA overcoat thrust upon my shoulders) or be given watermelon in the summer. My thanks to Zhang Sulin, Xiao Ying, and above all, the effervescent and charming Hao Weihua. Archivists in Chongqing, Xining, Taiwan, Britain, and California all did much to help.

One does not often get to thank anonymous readers in person—but mine revealed themselves. It was appropriate that one of them would be Liu Xiaoyuan, who, since our first encounter in Beijing, has been a teacher and guide. His knowledge of China's frontiers and ethnopolitics enriched this book immensely. Chen Jian told me of his role in reading the manuscript with a booming laugh. When I was first presenting a part of what became chapter 3, it was Chen Jian who told me that there was much more to the story than I thought, thereby causing me to widen the scope of this book dramatically. The revisions both these scholars demanded improved my work immensely. My thanks to them and to the team at the University of North Carolina Press, especially Chuck Grench, Paul Betz, Katherine Fisher, Lucas Church, Alison Shay, and Sara Jo Cohen. Kelly Sandefer of Beehive Mapping was a wonder in bringing the maps in this book to life; it was a pleasure working with her.

Lin Hsiao-ting charted my course for Taiwan and for Hoover (where his guidance on sources was indispensable). In Taiwan, Wenlung Wang made archival navigation easy. CJ Huang's company there was as welcome and as eye-opening as it had been in New Haven. Staying with Abraham and Miriam Bar was one of the best parts of being in California; I am grateful to their daughter Noa and to my sister Maryam for putting me in touch with them, and to Maryam for much else, especially the bursts of generosity and the entertainment. For help in Nepal, my thanks to Nina Smith, John Ackerly, Lobsang, Maya and Rinku Gurung, and especially Shyam Chokani; Shyam's hospitality alone provides a compelling reason to return. For a couch to crash on in D.C., thanks to Justine Isola and Christopher Oropeza. Zaka Shafiq, who introduced me to Sultan Khan, took me on an unforgettable trip along the Karachi coast. For several stimulating exchanges on Tibet and China, my thanks to Simon Long. There are other people whom I wish to thank, but who preferred to remain anonymous.

John Curtis Perry's invitation to give a talk at the Fletcher School at Tufts led me through a blizzard to a delightful job. Kelly Sims Gallagher, Dan Drezner, Ian Johnstone, Jim Stavridis, Michael Klein, Yoon Lee, Jonathan Brookfield, Toni Chayes, Michael Glennon, Richard Shultz, Jennifer Weingarden Lowrey, Michelle Frankfort, Nora McMillan, and Joel Trachtman have been marvelous colleagues. Lupita Ervin, whose efficiency is formidable, made sure that I got back from China and could focus on my work. Ellen McDonald solved a mystery I thought I would have to give up on by opening the door to Shen Shumei's non-Chinese name. The sheer breadth of Ellen's reading amazes me; it is surpassed only by her generosity as a friend. Cyndi Rubino rescued me from a computer meltdown, as did Ian Dinwoodie. Carolyn Talmadge answered my questions about cartography with patience and kindness.

My grandparents made trips to Lahore worth it. My grandfather, M. A. Khan, first explained Nehru to me and told me of the Tibetan traders striding down to Simla; I only wish he had lived to read this. My parents gave me the gift of books—which is why I could contemplate writing one of my own. My mother, Zeba Aziz, forbore to remind me that her work as a cancer specialist was a little harder than mine. My father, Wasif Khan, made sure that I knew that I could finish faster and was only dragging the dissertation out. Koshka the cat kept this book on track, whether by chewing through a computer charger just before a research trip, cutting and pasting in Word, or sprawling full-length on the particular document I happened to need at the time. Any mistakes in this book remain, of course, my own.

The best thing that ever happened to me was meeting Anna Beth Keim in Lhasa. Anna Beth's own excellence as a translator and writer meant she was my first port of call when I ran into trouble. She has traveled with me from the Barkhor to Cambridge, making each stop along the way a magical one. She is home.

A Note on Sources

This book relies heavily on newly declassified materials from the archives of the Foreign Ministry of the People's Republic of China (FMPRC) in Beijing. I conducted research in these archives at various points between 2006 and 2012. In the summer of 2013, I returned to Beijing to find that all the documents used here—along with many others—had been reclassified.

Access to provincial, municipal, and local archives in mainland China remains unpredictable. For the communist period in particular, foreign researchers still find it difficult to gain archival access. Nevertheless, I was fortunate enough to obtain some documents in the Chongqing Municipal Archives (CQA). The documents on the boundary commission used in chapter 1 are drawn from a variety of provincial archives (identified in the notes and bibliography); these were given to me by a Chinese scholar who asked to remain anonymous.

Cast of Characters (in Order of Appearance)

Yang Gongsu: Chinese diplomat, dispatched to Tibet in 1951. Found out firsthand just how hard it could be to distinguish between domestic and foreign affairs.

Chiang Kai-shek: Defeated Nationalist leader, ruling over Taiwan. Saw an opportunity to take back the mainland in the Tibetan rebellion.

Mao Zedong: Chairman of the PRC. Moved from promising Tibet self-determination to declaring it was a part of China.

Dalai Lama: The most important figure in the Tibetan religion. Moved from wishing to join the Communist Party to running a government in exile in India.

Panchen Lama: One of the most powerful figures in the Tibetan laity. Became a crucial source of support for Chinese policy in Tibet.

Ngabo Ngawang Jigme: High-ranking Tibetan official who surrendered to the PRC and encouraged the Dalai Lama to negotiate with the Chinese.

Peng Dehuai: One of Mao's ablest generals; first asked to oversee the PLA's assault on Tibet.

Deng Xiaoping: Helped negotiate the Seventeen-Point Agreement—an experience he would draw on in his later years.

Zhou Enlai: China's capable, smooth foreign minister. Could cajole the Dalai Lama, soothe ruffled feathers in Nepal, and defend China's claims before all and sundry.

Jawaharlal Nehru: Prime minister of India. Prided himself on his understanding of the new, postcolonial world, only to be humbled by the Sino-Indian war.

Gyalo Thondup: Dalai Lama's brother. Would work furiously for Tibetan independence long before his brother fled to India.

John Kenneth Knaus: CIA agent, who helped Gyalo in his quest.

Jayprakash Narayan: Indian intellectual who sought to get the
international community behind Tibet's quest for independence.
Chang Kuo-sin: Hong Kong journalist with ties to the Guomindang.
Ensured that Tibet was not treated as an independent country at
the Afro-Asian Convention on Tibet.
Ciren, Asuo, and Chenbo: Three Tibetans from Dingri, who found
themselves in trouble when a propaganda mission to Nepal
went wrong.
A. B. Basnyat: Nepali consul in Lhasa; awoke one day to find
himself under attack.
Qiangba Luozhuo: Both Nepali and Tibetan by blood, he opted for
Nepali citizenship but helped organize resistance to the PRC.
A Wang Jinba: Hailing from Sikkim, he used his status as a senior
monk to make protective icons for Tibetan rebels.
B. P. Koirala: Nepal's prime minister. Began negotiations with Zhou
Enlai on the Sino-Nepali boundary, but would be out of office
before he had a chance to finish them.
Ma Tengbiao: Also known as Lokchung Tinglai or Kaku, the man
from Qinghai coordinated various Tibetan resistance groups.
Wang Shengfu: An associate of Ma's, who helped with Tibetan
relief efforts.
Ismail: A Muslim who worked with Ma to circulate pamphlets
against land reform.
Chou Shu: Originally from Jiangsu, she was married to a Guomindang
agent in Calcutta. Arrived in Kathmandu just before Zhou in the
company of a mysterious American named Backman.
Pan Zili: Chinese ambassador to India, who was also in charge of
dealings with Nepal until a Chinese diplomatic mission was
opened there.
Suonan Daji: Official in Ali, who wanted Sino-Indian trade in Tibet
to grow.
Sangzheng Duojie Pamu: A Living Buddha, she sought assistance to
make her way back to China after being brought to India by force.
Huang Mou and Chen Cai: Intelligence agents of the Republic of
China, operating in India.
R. K. Nehru: Indian diplomat who argued that China and Pakistan
could not negotiate a boundary because they were discussing

Indian territory, before approaching Ambassador Pan on behalf of G. N. Taring, a Tibetan woman who had left her children behind.

Hamite: A Tibetan Muslim who had traveled back and forth from India several times. Learned how to operate a telegraph from Reginald Fox.

Reginald Fox: Former British agent; settled in Tibet where he had ties to the resistance.

S. Sinha: Indian diplomat and student of Chinese history; tried desperately to renew the Sino-Indian trade agreement.

Ye Chengzhang: Chinese diplomat; rejected Sinha's plea.

Basang Ciren: Tibetan trader who tried and failed to get grain from Nepal.

Chronology of Main Events

October 1, 1949: Mao Zedong proclaims the People's Republic of China.

1950: The PLA enters Tibet. The Korean War breaks out.

May 23, 1951: Conclusion of the Seventeen-Point Agreement between China and Tibet. Some resistance to Chinese rule remains in various parts of the Tibetan plateau, but relations are, by and large, peaceful. The agreement allows the Panchen Lama to return to Tibet.

1954: China and India sign an agreement on trade in Tibet, based on the five principles of peaceful coexistence. Zhou and Nehru visit each other's countries, celebrating the achievement.

April 1955: The Afro-Asian conference is held in Bandung.

1956: Khamba rebellion intensifies. Mao abandons plans to implement reform in Tibet.

1958: Mao Zedong launches the Great Leap Forward.

March 1959: The Dalai Lama flees from Lhasa and makes his way to India, repudiating the Seventeen-Point Agreement along the way.

May Day, 1959: In Beijing, the Panchen Lama reassures diplomats from the Soviet Union and Eastern Europe that all is well in Tibet.

June 1959: Gradual land reform is introduced in Tibet.

September 28, 1959: Malaya and Ireland move to discuss Tibet at the fourteenth session of the UN General Assembly. The Tibetan question continues to arise at the UN in subsequent years.

1960: Afro-Asian Convention on Tibet.

March 1960: Nepali Prime Minister B. P. Koirala visits China.

April 1960: Zhou Enlai visits Nepal. The two sides agree that troops will avoid coming within twenty kilometers of an as yet undemarcated boundary. Zhou also visits India, where his proposal to resolve a boundary dispute is rejected by Jawaharlal Nehru.

June 1960: PLA troops open fire on Nepalis; the exact location remains unclear. Zhou moves to resolve the matter swiftly. Nepal accepts the PRC's offered compensation.

1961: China and Nepal conclude a final treaty demarcating their boundary.

June 1962: The trade in Tibet stutters to a halt, exacerbating food shortages.

October 1962: Outbreak of the Sino-Indian border war. The PRC easily defeats India, then withdraws to its customary position.

December 1962: Ceylon, Indonesia, Burma, Egypt, Cambodia, and Ghana gather in Colombo to seek means of reconciling China and India. Beijing rejects the proposals these countries offer in 1963.

March 2, 1963: Conclusion of Sino-Pakistani boundary agreement.

Muslim, Trader, Nomad, Spy

Prologue

It was the birds that broke his heart.

When the People's Liberation Army flooded Lhasa in 1959, food grew scarce; the city was not equipped to supply so many people. Food prices rose, and the soldiers ordered people to start killing animals: yaks, dogs, and birds. There was a lake behind the Potala Palace where black-necked cranes—the black-necked cranes that so many Tibetans saw as symbols of peace—used to nest. These had been slaughtered. He had been told that he too must bring in his share of food. So he and his friends had somehow caught six nestlings, and put them on the ground. But then, they had not known how to kill them; they had never killed before. Finally, someone had produced a rock—but this he would rather not remember. The soldiers later told him that the birds were not large enough anyway.

Now he is climbing among the mountains, along paths unknown to the soldiers. Below, he can see the Lhasa River and how the geese are gone. The snow is thick, but in Tibet, the sun blazes hard and keeps you warm.

He pulls out his radio, and starts fumbling for the station he wants. The broadcast is in Tibetan, but it comes from Taiwan. Chiang Kai-shek, leader of the Guomindang in the republic, is urging the Tibetan people to rebel against the People's Republic of China (PRC).[1]

■ The soldiers did not see the boy in the mountains that day. But as the stories told in this book show, the non-state actors who peopled the Tibetan frontier had a dramatic impact on the nature and diplomacy of the PRC. The nomads in search of grasslands for their herds, the traders swapping goods and gossip in the markets of the Himalayas, the spies who brought anticommunist propaganda to what the PRC saw as its sovereign territory, the people caught in the maelstrom of rebellion and counterinsurgency: these characters rarely take center stage in stories of Cold War China—partly because they seem too remote from the ideological contests of the time, partly because they remain difficult to study. And yet between 1959, when the Dalai Lama fled into exile, and 1962, when the Sino-Indian entente came to a bitter end, the fourth world—that stateless realm of nomadic tribes and hamlets strung along the peaks, far from the reach of central authorities—weighed heavily on the official mind of the PRC.[2] In this vast, mountainous stretch of land so far removed from China proper, the state was weak in several crucial respects; the flood of local crises that confronted the PRC in 1959 showed how deep and dangerous that weakness ran. Suddenly, Beijing found itself compelled to defend its sovereign claims before the world while excluded from the United Nations. It had to bring the borderlands under control without alienating its neighbors—all the while not knowing the full extent of its realm. It had to police its citizens, but in doing so, it had to distinguish them from foreigners—a distinction which the citizens themselves had not dreamt of. (These symptoms of state weakness existed along other frontiers as well—it would be interesting, if sources were available, to see how the developments charted in this study compare to Kazakh movements across the Sino-Soviet border in Xinjiang—but it was in Tibet that events first revealed how dangerous such weakness could be to the PRC. In and of itself, state weakness was not a problem; it was when insurgency broke out that weakness became a cause for concern.) Could the state regulate the movements of people and goods across mountain passes it was only just learning to name, or stanch the flow of ideas, rumors, whispers of impending doom that came with those movements? Out in the Tibetan borderlands, the Chinese state lacked the capacities to enforce its will.

This book shows too how, in addressing that weakness, the PRC shifted from empire-lite to a harder, heavier imperial formation. That the PRC was an empire seems obvious. For all its anti-imperial rhetoric—possibly no country other than the United States has been as vocal in its opposition to empire while being one—the Chinese government ruled vast territories that were ethnically, linguistically, and religiously different; it imposed its rule by a combination of blandishment and force, typical of empires. Mao Zedong took China to territorial limits it had not seen since the glory days of the Qing dynasty—a dynasty that was, as historians recognize, an imperial one. The PRC saw itself as creating a multination state, which it did; the multination state it created, however, was also an imperial formation. I use the terms "empire" and "imperialism" in this book neutrally, free of any moral charge.[3] "Empire-lite" describes an empire that rules by allowing local autonomy and mores to flourish, even while asserting control over functions such as foreign policy and defense. Despite a low-intensity conflict in eastern Tibet, for much of the fifties, Mao's China sought to govern Tibet with a light touch. There was room for Tibetan autonomy, for religious independence, and Mao himself emphasized the need to guard against "Han chauvinism." He encouraged cross-border exchange—Tibet at this point was a multinational entrepôt, where one could hear the clamor of several different languages and find goods from far afield—realizing perhaps that it was difficult to control and that the benefits it brought kept Tibet stable. The system of governance in Tibet was different—was supposed to be different—from that in the rest of the country: Tibet had a non-socialist economy, religious freedom, and assurances that major reform would be undertaken only with local consent. 1959 changed that; Tibet would henceforth be governed in much the same way as any other Chinese region. The change manifested itself in numerous ways. Lamas found themselves watched more closely by the government, even though religious freedom remained intact, at least in theory, for a while. The lines separating countries were defined more clearly; so too were the lines separating those countries' citizens. And the agreement that had kept Tibet immune to Chinese reform would be, finally, irrevocably undone. The strength of the Chinese state in the region grew dramatically—and it told upon the easy movement and cosmopolitanism that had been the hallmark of life in the borderlands. Developments on the Tibetan frontier triggered a transformation in the structure of the PRC.

This transformation had a dramatic impact on China's foreign relations. The fourth world, after all, cut across third world states; the non-state actors whom the PRC found so dangerous could and did cross easily to Nepal or India and back. China's relations with its Himalayan neighbors had been forged in the age of empire-lite; they were based on the idea that people and goods were free to move across boundaries which had yet to be demarcated. As China shifted to a harder imperial model, its relations with its neighbors had to shift too. Lines would have to be drawn more sharply, stating where China ended and the rest of the world—the world beyond Chinese Communist Party (CCP) jurisdiction—began. And the neighbors, like everyone else, would have to show where they stood on the Tibetan issue, whether they were true friends to China in its hour of crisis.

There was nothing inevitable about their reactions. As the twists and turns in the Sino-Nepali relationship showed, states could move from friendship to suspicion and back again. Chinese perceptions that India was exploiting the Tibetan crisis were formed early, but PRC diplomats made repeated efforts to reach a modus vivendi with New Delhi. The failure to do so was due to the perceived ties between the Indian government and the Tibetan rebels. That failure, in turn, would undo the movement for third world unity that China and India had championed throughout the fifties.[4]

For China's third world policy, based on the five principles of peaceful coexistence, had emerged as a result of a Sino-Indian agreement on trade in Tibet, concluded in 1954. The resulting Sino-Indian entente was heralded by Beijing as a shining model for the rest of the third world. The influence of the Tibetan frontier on Sino-Indian relations put an end to that policy. Gone were the days when Beijing and New Delhi would come together to preach the gospel of Afro-Asian unity; Beijing instead reached out to Nepal and Pakistan, heightening Indian suspicions of Chinese policy. The third world was fractured, realigned, thereby changing the course of the Cold War. We tend to think of the Cold War era as state-centric, but these were changes triggered by non-state actors moving uncontrolled across states, far from central governments who spoke of third world unity and the postcolonial age.

■ These arguments—that the Chinese state was weak in the Tibetan borderlands; that addressing that weakness caused the PRC to change from empire-lite to a harder imperial formation; and that the transition brought about a shift in Chinese foreign policy during the Cold War—mark a sharp departure from several existing historiographical paths. This book was written primarily as a contribution to the literature on Chinese foreign policy during the Cold War; it also challenges understandings of Cold War international history and the comparative history of empires.

A flood of new sources is transforming the field of Chinese foreign relations, and there has been some remarkable work based on recently declassified materials from the PRC. This work, however, has largely been devoted to debating the importance or irrelevance of ideology to topics such as the Korean War, the Sino-American relationship, the Bandung and Geneva conferences, and the Sino-Soviet split. The links between domestic politics and foreign policy are sometimes explored, but focusing on decisions made in Beijing, rather than on ones in the more remote corners of the PRC. To a large degree, the importance of China's frontiers and border peoples to its foreign policy has been neglected. Some excellent literature on Tibet exists, but it does not, as a general rule, explore the ramifications for broader Chinese grand strategy.[5] In treating the Tibetan borderlands as seriously as the PRC did, this book brings to light a key source of Chinese conduct, as well as a more nuanced picture of what the Chinese state was.

The state-centrism that marks studies of China's Cold War has been, to a surprising extent, true of Cold War history in general. The "new Cold War history," to use John Gaddis's famous coinage, has been new in being multiarchival, but it has by and large taken the nation-state for granted, whether in the Soviet bloc or in the third world.[6] The fourth world has been absent from the field. This is a major gap in our understanding of international history during the Cold War, for non-state actors mattered to states still trying to define themselves. The new Cold War history can and should venture into the fourth world; as the Tibetan case shows, events there could often be of vital importance.

A third world state subsuming the fourth world constitutes a form of empire. The description of the PRC as an empire is no longer unprecedented—Odd Arne Westad and Carole McGranahan provide different but excellent accounts of that empire—but it is not one fully comprehended by historians who write of the late twentieth century as the age of decolonization. The decline of western empires and the emergence of third world states meant that a new form of imperialism came into being in many places—a form that merits as much thorough exploration as the older British, French, or Qing empires. The relationship between state and empire remains unclear; we need to look far more skeptically than we have thus far at the claim that independence meant an end to imperialism. That states like China and India contained multiple ethnicities—often by force—means that concepts of imperialism are well worth applying to the latter half of the twentieth century. This book is, to my knowledge, the first to explore the nature and transformations of the PRC as an empire, in the manner of imperial histories like those of Ronald Robinson and John Gallagher, Bernard Porter, and Charles Maier.[7] Those works certainly deepened my understanding of events in the Tibetan borderlands; this book, in turn, should be a useful addition to the literature on comparative imperialism. Empires did not die away in the postwar world; we have only begun to write the next chapter in their long histories.

The book's significance, moreover, goes beyond the field of history. It offers anthropologists a case study in the problems of state formation and transnational movements (those working on Tibet will find here the historical background to many of the issues that lie at the heart of their research). It offers geographers a close look at attempts to draw boundaries in the Himalayas. It illustrates the difficulties of counterinsurgency in a mountainous, cosmopolitan realm—something that should interest scholars of international security and politics.[8]

▨ In documenting the fourth world's impact on the third, this book has drawn on several sources. The core collection is the recently declassified material in the archives of the Foreign Ministry of the People's Republic of China (FMPRC), previously untapped by scholars. The archives are bursting with reports from Chinese officials stationed on the frontier: reports of spycraft and starvation, nomads claiming territory on behalf of the Indian government and simmering unease among Tibetan Muslims. They also contain memoranda of conversations between top Chinese officials and their counter-parts, reports from diplomats abroad, and reflections on the problem of the Tibetan issue being brought up at the United Nations. Drawing on these documents, one can begin to understand how the borderlands shaped PRC policy.

The materials in the FMPRC raise many questions that go beyond Beijing—and I have not been able to answer all of them. There is nothing in this book about why Indian policymakers responded to the Tibetan crisis the way they did, or how the convulsions in Nepali politics managed to leave policy toward China unchanged, or just what a Soviet lama in Tibet might have been up to. But some trails I could follow—and they led in interesting directions. The archives in Taiwan and Chiang Kai-shek's diaries held at the Hoover Institution shed light on Taiwan's connections with Tibet—connections that both helped and hindered Beijing's cause. British officials were shrewd observers, with astonishing intellectual resources in South Asia long after the Raj vanished; the holdings of the British archives at Kew were invaluable for understanding developments in Nepal, India, and, perhaps most interestingly, in the United Nations.

I also consulted various other printed materials—principally official histories and gazetteers, as well as memoirs by officials. Fascinating and instructive though they are, I have been wary of relying on these materials too much: they are heavily redacted (often covering the same material one can locate in the archives, but without the full detail and the back-and-forth the original documents offer) and sometimes outright inaccurate.[9] I have, therefore, cited them only when I must, and then with the utmost caution.

One further source is worth mentioning here: interviews with the handful of survivors left. Memory is not objective, but the events discussed in this book were deeply felt. Talking to old Tibetans in the back alleys of Kathmandu is the best way to get a sense of that fundamental question: What was it like to be there?

■ What was it like to be there? What was it like to live in a hamlet strung along a mountain, to make your way through a pass, carrying salt that you would trade for grain? What was it like to be told that you were now part of a state and that the state would take care of you, even as life continued in its old stateless ways? And what was it like to come in to govern this place where the altitudes made you ill, where the languages and the food and the faiths were not what you had known, where people from abroad mingled freely with your subjects, in plain sight as well as in secret gatherings that you could not dream of, let alone reach?

The Road to Lhasa

Sky Burial

In 1951, Yang Gongsu received orders to move to Lhasa. The People's Republic of China was knitting Tibet into its sovereign territory, and as part of this process, the Foreign Ministry needed more diplomats to staff that distant borderland. So Yang and some of his colleagues made their way to Chengdu.[1] From Chengdu, they began the long, uncomfortable journey northwestward to Tibet. The green plains gave way to mountains. Some of the mountains were thick with forests of spruce, larch, and pine; others were a bare, rusty red. When the day was clear, they could see glaciers in the distance; the closer peaks, with their caps of snow, were reflected in the blue river beside them. Now and then, the low, howling cry of a wolf would break in upon the night.

The highway—it was not so much a highway, really, as a rock-strewn track along which a powerful vehicle could bump and bounce—ended in Ganzi, a town at an altitude of some four thousand meters. In the strange cartography of the PRC, Ganzi was categorized in the province of Xikang, separate from what the Chinese state considered the locality of Tibet, but the people swaggering around the streets were Khambas—eastern Tibetans—and their religious allegiance lay with the Dalai Lama. And it was in Ganzi that Yang Gongsu saw his first sky burial. A death had occurred and the locals set about burying the body according to Tibetan custom, while the Chinese newcomers watched from a distance. On a mountain slope, the lama presiding over the funeral chopped the corpse into pieces, muttering prayers as he did so. Then he stepped back, and the vultures that had gathered in anticipation—"gray, yellow vultures as large as a small cow," Yang would remember—descended on the body. When they had eaten the flesh, the lama ground the bones and the skull, so that the vultures could eat those too. Nothing was left. After returning, Yang recalled: "Many comrades threw up and could not eat their food. I too felt very nauseated. According to what the Tibetan people said, this [the sky burial] was very natural. The person was returning whence he had come. He had already ascended to heaven, and they wished him good fortune in the life to come."[2] In Yang's bemusement at how natural the sky burial was to the Tibetans, in his recollections of his own queasiness, one hears an old note: that of a traveler caught in a strange, disquieting land. These people were not his people, their ways not his ways.

Yet he was being asked and trained to respect their customs. In telling the story of how the PRC set about state-building in the Tibetan borderlands, one is struck by how much central authorities relied on local collaboration—something that required respect for local mores. In the early fifties, Beijing sought to perpetuate its rule in Tibet by giving Tibetans a loose rein. PRC governance of Tibet formed an imperial structure, but it was empire-lite.[3] And because Tibet was a frontier region where the line between East and South Asia blurred, sovereignty over Tibet required a foreign policy. Largely unremarked by scholarly accounts of the Chinese conquest of the region, the Tibetan frontier became a key source of Chinese foreign policy, one that would provide Beijing with a template for dealing with the Cold War in the third world.[4]

The View from Beijing

The borderlands that Yang had come to govern were vast. They rolled out over an area four times the size of France, embracing alpine grasslands and Himalayan desert, mountains and great saline lakes. There were valleys unconnected except by nomads and their yaks; if you ascended a peak, you could look out over miles and miles of emptiness and rock. The sheerness of the slopes and the snow that blocked the passes meant that travel was hard; it took Yang more than twenty days to make the relatively short trip from Ganzi to Chamdo.

Perhaps it was this forbidding geography that made it difficult for Tibet to function like a nation-state. Even at the peak of its power in the eighth century, when the Tibetan empire had struggled for mastery of east-central Asia with the Tang Dynasty and the Uighurs of Xinjiang, the Tibetan plateau looked more like a collection of small fiefdoms than a cohesive national power; local valleys had their own chieftains and life went on largely unimpeded by centralized authority.[5] When the Mongols swept across Eurasia, they conquered China proper, Tibet, and a host of other places: this unification in the form of the Yuan dynasty would later form the basis for Chinese claims that Tibet had always been a part of China. The Mongols were supportive of Tibetan Buddhism, as they were of most religions; some Tibetans occupied key administrative posts in the new government.[6] The relationship lapsed when the Ming dynasty took charge, but the government of China did not abandon its claim to Tibet. Only after the arrival of the Qing dynasty in 1644, however, did the government of China move to assert control over Tibet. The Qing government intervened in the recurring disputes between the Dalai and Panchen Lamas (the two leading figures in the Tibetan religious establishment), thereby strengthening its grip on the region. Curiously, the priest-patron relationship was reforged: the Qianlong emperor was, among other incarnations, a practicing Tibetan Buddhist who took the Dalai Lama as his spiritual guide.[7] But even though the Chinese government had representatives in Lhasa, Tibet continued to feel like a world apart from the established state—a cluster of valleys, each going its own way, not unified by state authorities.

The gradual decay of Qing power only underlined the statelessness. When British troops led by Francis Younghusband stormed into Tibet in 1903–4 to get a trade agreement, what was surprising was how many different people they had to work with to conclude it. The British-Chinese convention of 1906 did confirm the 1904 treaty, but it was more because the British did not wish to offend Beijing than in recognition of its actual control over the Himalayan trade marts.[8] With the fall of the Qing in 1911, whatever was left of China's authority over Tibet came to an end. There were cultural and religious connections between the Tibetan plateau and China proper, but in terms of governance, Tibet was separate, going its own way.[9] The Tibetan plateau was more a part of the fourth world: a mélange of indigenous peoples and tribes that existed without a state. This is not to argue that Tibet had always been part of China, though the Chinese state had often sought to exercise control over the region; rather, being a place where the state's grip was often infirm or absent, Tibet had ways of life defined by statelessness. "Zomia" is a term social scientists have recently popularized to describe a nonstate zone.[10] Tibet was such a place.

The new Chinese state did not abandon its claims to the Tibetan plateau. Sun Yat-sen, who had spearheaded the republican cause against the Qing, claimed that the different ethnicities of China formed part of a larger Chinese family. His successor, Chiang Kai-shek, who headed the Nationalist Party in China, maintained the same line. The Tibetans were one of "five peoples designated in China," he argued; they were part of the "whole Chinese nation."[11] Chiang did manage to defend China's claim to Tibet at an international level; the United States and Britain did not recognize an independent state of Tibet, though the Tibetan Kashag—a council of ministers that conducted Tibet's secular affairs—reached out to U.S. President Franklin D. Roosevelt in an attempt to get such recognition. For practical purposes, however, Chiang's authority over the Tibetan plateau was nonexistent.[12]

For much of his tenure, Chiang was engaged in a bitter civil war against the Chinese Communists. It was the civil war that provided the Communists with their first experience of Tibet. In 1934, almost entirely beaten by the Nationalists, the Chinese Communists began the famous Long March from Jiangxi to Yanan. Weary, defeated, they trudged a route that took them along the eastern rim of the Tibetan plateau, where Khambas and local Muslims alternately fed and attacked them. The experience would stay with a young Mao Zedong—who rose to power on the Long March—as a lesson in how deeply ethnic tension ran through the Tibetan borderlands.[13] For the time being, at least, he could do nothing about it. A contest was under way for mastery of China, but none of the contestants had any real authority over Tibet.

The Nationalists and the Communists did suspend hostilities during World War II to fight the Japanese army that had invaded China. But in 1945, with the Japanese threat gone, the two parties resumed battle. The Chinese civil war was not decided easily; only in 1949 did it become clear that the Communists would win.[14] The emergence of the Cold War in the late forties meant that those ideological and geopolitical rivals, the United States and the USSR, had an interest in the struggle for mastery of China—a point not lost on Tibetans in Lhasa. In July 1949, the Kashag decided to expel a number of Chinese living in Tibet; they were to be escorted by a Tibetan bodyguard to the border crossing with India, from where they could make their way to Kalimpong.[15] What was most interesting about the decision was the language the Kashag used in explaining its decision to Indian authorities:

> There is fighting between the Chinese Kuomintang and the Communist. It seems that wherever there is Chinese Government officers and forces there rises Communism and trouble. Therefore we cannot risk the trouble that might rise to the Chinese representative in Lhasa. Moreover there are many talks saying that there are suspicious Chinese and barbas who are the people from western China staying in Tibet Lhasa etc. It is difficult to pick them out from amongst others. All the people of Tibet are very worried that such bad system communism [may] come into being in Tibet where there is the religion of Lord Buddha which is the source of happiness of all beings. For the benefit of both the Chinese and the Tibetan govt and in order to have a long reign of Budhism we must send away all the suspicious men of being Communist secret servicemen. . . . We have ordered the Chinese representative in Lhasa and his staff, the wireless officer, the school teacher, the hospital worker and the suspicious Chinese and barbas to leave for their respective places soon.[16]

The emphasis on the evils of communism, the defense that the expulsion was an anticommunist move—the phrasing showed that the Kashag was aware of developments in the larger international system, and that it would take advantage of the Cold War to further its own agenda. The Kashag had no proof that any of the Chinese being expelled were communists. Many of them seem to have been nothing more than local traders who happened to have run afoul of local authorities; in later years, after the Kashag had fallen from power, the expulsion of the Han would be cited as a move designed to destroy unity among peoples.[17] But communism was a good pretext to rid Tibet of any Chinese influence. The Kashag knew that old British civil servants had remained in India to help the new government; it knew too that in the Cold War, the British were, broadly speaking, on the side of the anticommunists. Fear of the "Koumintang [sic] party falling under Communist control" was the justification the Kashag offered for asking for British intelligence on the progress of the Chinese civil war. Anticommunist the Kashag might have been, but the other concerns it raised with the British—the progress of the Muslim warlord Ma Bufang, the direction fleeing Guomindang forces would take, the status of the Sino-Tibetan frontier[18]—suggest that it might well have been pondering what a unified China would mean for its own authority. It was one thing to maintain power in Lhasa when China itself was in chaos; it was quite another when China was united under a war-hardened leadership. There was reason to be wary. The Chinese Communists—though still locked in battle with the Guomindang—found time to make a public response to the expulsion of the Chinese from Lhasa. The expulsion, according to the official Xinhua news agency, had been planned by British and American imperialists and carried out by reactionaries in Tibet. "Tibet," it went on to say, "is China's territory, and we will never allow it to be invaded by foreign forces; the Tibetan people are an integral part of the Chinese, and we will never allow them to be separated from the Chinese nation."[19] Tibet had become a theater in the Chinese civil war and the Cold War.

The CCP's statement marked a change in its views on the borderlands. In 1934, reporting on CCP minority policy, Mao Zedong had made an impassioned defense of minorities' rights to self-determination. In the past, ethnic minorities like the Tibetans and the Hui, the Mongols and the Miao, had suffered oppression, not least in the Guomindang's model of a "five peoples' republic." The Chinese Soviet republic, by contrast, recognized ethnic minorities' rights to "national self-determination," even to the point of "separating from China, establishing their own independent, free countries." There was an answer, Mao thundered, to "imperialism the world over (including the Chinese Guomindang)."[20] It was a fascinating vision; it held forth an idea of China as something undefined, changeable, a place that had yet to be built and that could define itself in ways which excluded peoples who did not wish to be part of it. Perhaps the statement was merely tactical, a means of getting support from ethnic minorities as the CCP struggled for survival. But these were the days when the communists were young and revolutionary and idealistic: it seems quite conceivable that Mao genuinely meant what he said, that as a good anti-imperialist, he was sincere in championing the Tibetans' right to determine their own destiny.

Just why that vision changed with victory remains unknown. But as the Chinese Communists gained strength in China proper, their policy toward the borderlands changed too. By September 1949, as the Communists appeared poised for victory in the civil war, Zhou Enlai was already explaining that while no one doubted the minorities' rights to self-determination, imperialists were trying to split "our Tibet, Taiwan, even Xinjiang." Given this situation, he hoped that the minorities would not listen to imperialist provocation. And therefore, he continued, the country would be called the "People's Republic of China, and not be called 'federation.' "[21] It was a telling speech. Zhou had still held out self-determination as an option—but he had also pointed out that Tibet, Taiwan, and Xinjiang were "ours," that there were attempts to "split" them under way. It was a very different view of China from the one Mao had proclaimed in 1932; China in the new formulation had a powerful claim to certain territories, which were being split from it by imperialist conspiracies. There was a defined, cohesive China, which included Tibet, in this view, rather than a still evolving entity that Tibet might or might not opt to join.

In October, 1949, after the Chinese Communists had finally defeated the Nationalists, Mao Zedong proclaimed the People's Republic of China. The CCP now had to decide what Chinese policy toward Tibet should be, and several elements shaped that policy. There was an ideological component: Tibet was a land of serfdom and the serfs had to be liberated. But the official mind was also contemplating national security. The mainland's failure to take the island of Taiwan meant that the Guomindang had established a rival Chinese regime. This rival regime was fueling unrest in a region that was geostrategically important (control of the Tibetan plateau, as

Mao realized, meant that China's southwestern frontier was secure from a possible Indian invasion; though the Indians had expressed goodwill, this was easier to count on with a safe buffer zone between the two countries), and there were signs that it was doing so with American support. The PRC was aware that there were Guomindang agents active in the region; it was also aware that British civil servants who remained in India were keeping a watchful eye on Chinese conduct in Tibet.[22] All this challenged the CCP's right to be recognized as the lawful, legitimate government of China—something Beijing could not tolerate. Sending the People's Liberation Army (PLA) into Tibet was an act of defense; it protected Beijing's claim to legitimate sovereignty.

But the significance of foreign opposition to Chinese rule in Tibet went deeper. Since the PRC was convinced that it was an anti-imperial force, the forces ranged against it—especially the Guomindang—were, by definition, imperial forces. If Tibetans were exposed to Guomindang, British, and American influence, or worse, collaborated with those hostile agents, that would be an act of imperialism against the Tibetans and against the new China which had fought so hard against imperialism. To keep Tibet free from empire, therefore, the PRC had to liberate it. In acquiring Tibet (and other remote territories), Mao Zedong took China to its largest territorial limits since the halcyon days of the Qing; he recreated, with a few parts missing, the Qing empire. New China was an imperial formation. But in Tibet, at least, a messianic anti-imperialism had helped to push the PRC into imperial behavior. Chinese rule over Tibet was that of an empire of anti-imperialism.[23]

To be fair, the official mind of the PRC did not see matters that way. The PRC did indeed see itself as creating a multination state and liberating nations while it did so. But in the process of creating a multination state, the PRC became an empire—*even though it did not realize as much*. The Chinese Communists genuinely believed that they were an anti-imperial force and that anti-imperialism (an ideology based on liberation) demanded forging a multination PRC. But multination states can, broadly speaking, come into being in two ways. The first is by immigration: people from different nations flock to a single state. The second involves a state taking over territory and asserting sovereignty over it. A multination state forged in this manner is very much an empire. In claiming Tibet as part of a multination state, the CCP was expanding into territory that had been united under an empire: the Qing. The methods it would use in doing so—reliance on local collaboration, the use of force when necessary, the training of cadres in language and cultural norms— would have been familiar to the Qing, the British, or the Ottoman Empires. Forging the particular multination state the PRC did meant becoming an empire. The PRC was both a multination state and an empire. It recognized itself as one, but not as the other.

This particular mix of ideology, national security calculus, and anti-imperialism shaped the way China sought to conquer and govern Tibet. In January 1950, while still visiting Moscow, Mao had asked one of his ablest generals, Peng Dehuai, to move into Tibet from the north; though Tibet's population was not large, the chairman explained, its international position was of utmost importance. But the harsh terrain and the absence of reliable roads made an invasion from Xinjiang or Qinghai much too difficult.[24] A small contingent of PLA troops—comprising Han, Uighur, Tibetan, and Kazakh soldiers among others—did make its way from Xinjiang to the northern reaches of Tibet in 1951, crossing formidable terrain to reach Ali.[25] Ali was a strategically important point: it lay at the crossroads between Xinjiang and Tibet and on the still vague borders with South Asia. But it was a long way from other parts of Tibet. And so it was that the main responsibility for going into Tibet fell to the CCP's Southwest Bureau.[26]

The Southwest Bureau would need both force and diplomacy for the task. (The Tibet Work Committee it formed had an ethnic Tibetan on it—an early sign both of the CCP's eagerness to find local collaborators and of the fact that such collaborators did indeed exist).[27] It planned to move into Chamdo by May 1950, but the absence of reliable roads and military operations against Guomindang remnants in southern China meant that the liberation of Tibet would have to be delayed. And while building roads that would allow for troop movement at a suitable time, the PRC sought to negotiate with Tibetans. It would be much easier, after all, if Tibet accepted its place in the new Chinese state willingly. It was a harbinger of what was

Map 1. Ethnolinguistic groups in China. This map provides a clear picture of the PRC's security concerns by showing both the neighbors it had to deal with and the diversity of ethnolinguistic groups it was trying to govern.

Notice especially how far beyond the locality of Tibet (it was not called the Tibet Autonomous Region until 1965) Tibetans and their language extend.

to come: empire-lite would work through collaboration, discussion, with force used only if and when necessary. Sino-Tibetan negotiations proceeded through multiple channels. There was a diplomatic mission sent by the Kashag, which insisted that Tibet would maintain its independence (and therefore foundered; the PRC could not and would not agree to independence). There was a Tibetan monk from Kham who sought to act as a messenger to Lhasa, only to die mysteriously. There was a plan to use the Dalai Lama's brother, who was married to a Chinese woman, to convince Tibetans of the beneficence of Chinese rule; the Dalai Lama's brother himself, however, was not convinced. In short, all the attempts at negotiation fizzled out.

The PRC did, however, find one durable ally as it reached out to Tibetans: the Panchen Lama, a figure of considerable importance in the Tibetan religion. In one of those perpetual conflicts within the Tibetan laity, the ninth Panchen Lama had fallen out with the Dalai Lama's supporters and fled to Qinghai, along with his followers. When he died, his followers identified the tenth Panchen Lama reincarnated—only to have the Dalai Lama's officials refuse to recognize the new Panchen Lama until he had competed against other candidates in Lhasa. The Panchen Lama's officials refused and declared their own candidate the Panchen Lama.[28] It was a reflection of just how fragmented Tibet was—and now, as the PRC searched for allies in Tibet, that fragmentation would come in handy. Even as the Kashag was sending missions abroad for help in protecting Tibetan independence, the tenth Panchen Lama was maintaining that Tibet was part of China. A fourth world zone, unlike a state, can conduct several different foreign policies at the same time. One set of Tibetan chieftains worked against the PLA; a powerful lama offered his support to Chinese liberation. And these fissures within the fourth world made it easier for the Chinese to claim Tibet.

All this took place with the PLA still preparing to march to Tibet. The point was not to destroy Tibet: sending troops to Chamdo in the eastern part of Tibet could, so Mao hoped, encourage the Tibetans to reach a peaceful resolution to the problem.[29] By October 6, the PLA was ready to invade Chamdo. The actual military operations in Tibet, under the command of Zhang Guohua, proved easier than one might have expected. On October 24, Ngabo Ngawang Jigme, Tibet's highest-ranking military and political official in Chamdo, surrendered to the PRC. Ngabo would go on to encourage the Dalai Lama to negotiate with the Communists, arguing that it was the best means of preserving autonomy.[30] This would later be cited as evidence that there were Tibetans who wished to be liberated; it was certainly evidence that different groups in Tibet decided where their own political and military allegiances would lie, without reference to the Kashag or any other authority. It is true, as scholars have pointed out, that lacking a strong army or significant international support, the Tibetans had little choice but to come to terms with the Chinese.[31] But that difficulty should not obscure the fact that quite a few Tibetans felt that collaboration with the CCP had value. Ngabo, with the consent of the Dalai Lama and the Kashag, began negotiations with the CCP in the spring of 1951. Both the CCP and Tibetan officials signed the resulting Accord on the Peaceful Liberation of Tibet.[32]

The accord was significant because its provisions reflected the balance Chinese rule was trying to strike: recover sovereignty while preserving local autonomy. The accord's first provision called on the Tibetans to unite to expel (British and American) imperialism; another stated that Tibetan forces would become part of the Chinese army. The Central People's Government would be in charge of all foreign affairs. These provisions recovered aspects of lost sovereignty: they sought to create a monopoly on the use of force and a single front when it came to diplomacy. But the conquest of Tibet had relied heavily on local collaboration; so too would the region's actual governance. Collaboration would best be obtained by interfering as little as possible with the existing rhythm of life. Accordingly, there were several provisions to safeguard Tibetan culture and religion. The rights and privileges of the Dalai and Panchen Lamas would be preserved. (The CCP made a point of insisting on the Panchen Lama returning to his position in Tibet, overriding the Kashag's objections; he had, they maintained, done no harm to the state and should occupy his rightful place. Since the Panchen Lama had to be recognized by the Dalai Lama to be confirmed, the Dalai Lama had to cable his acceptance to the gathered diplomats.[33] This was important: it meant that there would be factions within Tibet and that if things went awry, the PRC could play those factions off against one another in the future.) The Tibetan language would form a part of the educational curriculum. Social reform would be conducted in consultation with Tibetan leaders, not imposed unilaterally from Beijing. And if there were Tibetans who had collaborated with the Guomindang and foreign powers in the past, they would receive an amnesty, as long as they forswore such connections in the future. In short, the accord left significant freedoms to Tibet while reasserting Beijing's right to determine what happened in military and diplomatic affairs. In leaving room for autonomy while insisting on sovereignty, it bore the fingerprints of Deng Xiaoping; later, as Yang Gongsu would note, Deng would devise a similar accord to deal with Hong Kong.[34] The phrase "one country, two systems," which CCP leaders would use to describe their governance of Hong Kong, was just as appropriate a label for PRC rule over Tibet.

Reading history backwards, it is easy to dismiss CCP promises to respect Tibetan culture and religion as hollow. At the time, however, Communist leaders were genuinely interested in protecting "ethnic minorities"; the new state had a stake in winning the goodwill of its non-Han population.[35] Besides, a happy population is easier to rule than an unhappy one; there were sound practical reasons for respecting local norms. Mao Zedong, on his frontier marches, had acquired firsthand experience of how keenly Tibetans might resent the Han; he was constantly warning Chinese cadres far from home to avoid "Han chauvinism." Well aware of the importance of the personal touch, he had himself written to the Dalai Lama in May 1951, emphasizing that the accord was conducive to the interests of the Tibetans.[36] Looking at the early years of CCP rule in Tibet, one is struck by how much success the accord enjoyed. The Dalai and Panchen Lamas accepted their place in the new political structure— the former even went so far as to express an interest in joining the Communist Party (Mao, perhaps thinking that this would exacerbate unrest, told him that this was unnecessary).[37] Chinese cadres like Yang received extensive training in Tibetan language and were schooled to respect local customs.[38] "They would sometimes share food with us or teach us Chinese. You see, they could be kind too," recalled a Tibetan who would later flee into exile.[39] Mao was certainly prepared to deal harshly with rebellions if they broke out and talked of a future when reform could be implemented in Tibet. But he also saw the need to maintain a role for the Dalai Lama and to preserve Tibetan mores for the time being; he wanted, in that useful phrase, to win hearts and minds. He really did believe that history was on his side, that in the long run the Tibetans themselves would wish for reform—if the CCP treated them with respect, if it did not try to rush into the future. Regardless of what Mao's long-term intentions were, Tibet retained many of the socioeconomic features that distinguished it from China proper until 1959.[40] The PRC was ruling with a light touch.

Perhaps the clearest example of Beijing's commitment to governing through collaboration came in 1956. The Tibet Work Committee had reported that the time was ripe for reform; in the summer of 1956, Communist cadres started streaming into Tibet to implement it. The backlash was swift: demonstrations broke out across the plateau. Mao was quick to call the reforms off; "the time now," he wrote to the Dalai Lama, "is not ripe for carrying out reform in Tibet."[41] It was a rare admission of error, a realization that the PRC had moved too fast, too soon. With the reforms halted, there was a chance for tranquility. But the trouble had barely died down when in November the Dalai Lama was invited to India—a place where he would be exposed to his brothers, who were intractably opposed to Chinese rule, and worse, to Americans, who had been funding Tibetan rebel groups in Kham. Rumors abounded that he was unhappy with the status quo in Tibet. But the crown prince of Sikkim had invited him to mark the 2500th anniversary of the Buddha's birth—and the PRC permitted him to go. To refuse him permission would have risked further rioting and created the perception abroad that the PRC was oppressing Tibet. Letting him go meant risking that he would never come back. Mao put a brave face on this possibility, arguing that the Dalai Lama's departure would provide the PRC with room to start reform in Tibet again.[42] But despite this bold stance, he did something prudent, something that he would have done only if the PRC wanted the Dalai Lama back. He sent Zhou Enlai to talk to the Dalai Lama in India.

Zhou Enlai was the PRC's most capable diplomat. He was shrewd, intelligent; though he would later be blamed for standing by and letting Mao wreak havoc on China, he was, especially in the early years of the PRC, one of the key players defending Beijing's interests in the global arena.[43] He could be sharp and unyielding, as he was in cutting through several layers of Tibetan bureaucracy for a talk with the Dalai Lama.[44] But he could also be gentle, soothing, as he was when he sat down to talk with the Dalai Lama. There was no need to threaten or push—the young man was impressed with the meeting, eager to please and be pleased. He was, he said, basically satisfied with the work being done in Tibet. There were, of course, some problems: tensions between the Han and Tibetan cadres. Zhou conveyed a message from Mao: if there were such problems, the responsibility rested with the Han, for it was the Han who needed to respect the Tibetan cadres. He, Zhou, would convey as much to the Tibet Work Committee. The Dalai Lama pointed out that land reform, conducted improperly, had caused trouble in the ethnically Tibetan province of Xikang (Kham). Many people had fled Kham for Tibet proper or abroad—and ripple effects from the unrest were felt in the locality of Tibet. Zhou was reassuring. He promised that reforms in Chamdo and Tibet proper would be carried out based on what the Tibetan leadership—the Dalai and Panchen Lamas— desired.[45] There was a subtle reminder here: the Dalai Lama's continued *political* authority over people in the farther reaches of Tibet depended on the Chinese state.

Perhaps the Dalai Lama took the cue; perhaps he simply wished to be conversable. He turned the talk to the many Tibetans who had lived abroad for a long time and were not clear on the situation at home—many of them wished to talk to him. Two of these were his brothers, and Zhou asked him, gently, if they needed money. If the Dalai Lama found it difficult to supply their wants, Zhou would instruct the Chinese embassy to give him some foreign exchange; he could give this to his brothers, without telling them that it came from the embassy.[46]

The Dalai Lama was willing, eager even, to share the information on India that he had picked up during his stay. When Indians discussed global problems, the Dalai Lama said, they said that the world was divided into two camps. There were many contradictions within the imperialist camp, but the socialist camp had made errors too, its unity fraying—a point the Indians would illustrate by alluding to Hungary.[47] It was a fascinating moment: a Tibetan leader, having talked to Indians uneasy about China's role in Tibet, was passing information on to a premier from Beijing—in effect functioning as an intelligence agent for the PRC. And Zhou, shrewd politician, sensing perhaps that the Dalai Lama would appreciate encouragement, and aware that any information could be useful, responded in kind: "India is still basically friendly toward China. The Dalai Lama's coming to visit India this time is very good; it is in the interests of unity between the two countries of China and India. We should persevere in Sino-Indian friendship, strengthen Sino-Indian unity. . . . India declares that Tibet is China's sovereign territory. This is all very good."[48]

It was perfectly done. The response held out an optimistic view of the future, and it gave the Dalai Lama a sense that he had helped shape that future. The two men closed amicably, with Zhou asking if the Dalai Lama would be willing to travel with him to Nepal the following year and inviting him to Beijing to visit Mao. Zhou was careful to communicate the results of his conversation to the Panchen Lama, for at this stage, a harmonious relationship between the two lamas was conducive to the idea that Chinese rule over Tibet was a force for good. With mutual respect between the Panchen and Dalai Lamas and their respective staffs, one could attain that lovely goal: unity. Zhou thus concluded, despite the potential risks, that the Dalai and Panchen Lamas' trips abroad had been beneficial.[49]

For all the ethnic tension on the ground, then, the PRC was attempting to collaborate with Tibetans. The PRC was weaving Tibet into empire-lite: it involved working with local power structures rather than against them. Zhou's attempt to enlist the Dalai Lama on Chinese diplomatic missions showed just how far that policy could go: if a citizen of the PRC was willing, and had the requisite religious and cultural importance abroad, he could be used to pursue diplomatic goals. Recovering the borderlands was necessary; if they were recovered with some degree of goodwill among the local populace, they could also provide opportunities in the realm of statecraft.

For much of the fifties, the Tibetan borderlands were an important source of Chinese foreign policy, crucial to shaping the Cold War in the third world.

The Five Principles

In acquiring Tibet, the PRC was taking on a host of questions relating to foreign affairs. Tibet bordered the subcontinent: people from India, Nepal, Sikkim, and Bhutan had relationships with the region that went back centuries. Pilgrims came from across the Himalayas to sacred mountains like Kailash, along passes that governments in Beijing and New Delhi would never even have heard of. Border trade continued almost completely unregulated, with merchants swapping wool and salt for grain. There were children whose parents hailed from different countries, for whom reality involved a cluster of homes on a mountain, rather than participation in a nation-state. Tibet was not the isolated mountain fastness of popular imagination; it was a cosmopolitan, bustling, thriving borderland. This cosmopolitanism resulted largely from its being part of the fourth world, rather than of the third—precisely because it was a zone of statelessness, largely untouched by national governments, people from many different countries could mingle on the Tibetan plateau. Now, Beijing was seeking to build state strength in that zone. And it would start by seeking to regulate foreign relations. Taking over "diplomatic rights," after all, was one of the few marks of sovereignty in the empire-lite that the PRC was creating.[50]

This was not the easiest task, for China's South Asian neighbors were wary of the new government in Beijing. India, which had become independent in 1947, was a large, ambitious state, eager to tell the world how the new international system should work. In 1950, for example, the Indians had told the PRC that Chinese conduct in Tibet would damage Beijing's moral standing in its quest for UN membership—something the Chinese angrily took as interference in China's "internal affairs."[51] There had been extensive debate within the Indian government about how to respond to the PRC's occupation of Tibet. Some argued that it compromised Indian security; Prime Minister Jawaharlal Nehru, however, sought security through friendly relations with Beijing.[52] So the unpleasantness over the 1950 negotiations was smoothed over, and in 1954, Asia's two largest countries set about deciding how their relationship would look on the Tibetan frontier.

The negotiations started out as an attempt to designate areas in Tibet where trade could continue legally. No one quite knew just how many trade markets there were on the Tibetan plateau or where they were located or which side of the disputed border they lay on, but these were minor issues; the PRC was far more interested in discussing the principles on which the relationship should be forged. Zhang Hanfu, a Chinese diplomat, laid those principles out in a talk with India's ambassador to the PRC, Nedyam Raghavan: "When meeting the Indian representative group on December 31, 1953, Prime Minister Zhou Enlai said clearly that the principles of the relations between the two countries of China and India should be to seek peaceful coexistence under the principles of mutual respect for sovereign territorial rights, mutual non-invasion, mutual non-interference in internal affairs, equality and mutual benefit. . . . These are the principles for negotiation suggested by the Chinese side. . . . What is the perspective of the Indian delegation on these principles put forth by our side?" Prime Minister Nehru, Raghavan responded, had a similar opinion, "though he hasn't listed them one by one like that."[53]

Thus were the famous "five principles of peaceful coexistence" born: Chinese precepts for negotiating how to trade in the Tibetan borderlands.[54] As principles go, these were rather platitudinous, but they did what they were supposed to. The parties reached a trade agreement and the merchants who had gone back and forth for centuries continued to do so, with their governments claiming credit for the relationship. Capitalism flourished in communist China's southwestern borderlands, and the Tibet Work Committee, sensible of the fact that free enterprise made governing easier, allowed it do so. Years later, when Deng Xiaoping allowed market-oriented reforms to proceed in Sichuan, he might well have been drawing almost exactly on his Tibetan experience.[55]

In the hands of less ambitious leaders, this might have concluded the story. But Mao and Nehru were confident men, fully convinced that they knew what was best not just for their own countries but for the larger world. There were important differences between them—where Nehru's idealism had a touch of naivety, Mao's was tempered by a certain hard-won peasant wisdom—but both maintained that the five principles could prove the key to peace in the third world and beyond. They held forth a vision of Asia united at peace, with powers such as the United States leaving the continent to its own devices; the five principles would underpin that peace. At the Geneva conference and a year later at Bandung—an Asian-African gathering to celebrate third world independence and solidarity—the five principles would form the keystone of China's policy toward the third world. In trying to convince Pakistan to abandon American-led anticommunist military pacts such as SEATO (South East Asia Treaty Organization) and CENTO (Central Treaty Organization), Zhou would ask Pakistani officials to sign on to the five principles.[56] When negotiating borders and relations with Nepal and Burma, Chinese diplomats would invoke the five principles. In assuring other countries of China's goodwill, Beijing would point to its observance of the five principles. In discussing the Polish and Hungarian crises with the Soviet Union in 1956, Chinese diplomats would state that the principles provided a template for the way in which socialist countries should relate to one another.[57] Years later, when Sino-Indian relations had gone sour (and when Mao had castigated Nikita Khrushchev for suggesting that "peaceful coexistence" with the capitalist bloc was possible), Beijing would continue to celebrate the principles as the definitive Chinese contribution to the cause of peace, though the lines along which they were now interpreted looked rather different. What had originated in the negotiation of a trade agreement had become, with the transition almost entirely unnoticed, a paradigm for inter-Asian relations in the aftermath of western imperialism. It was a paradigm born of the Sino-Indian entente that had been forged over a shared border; it would outlast not only that entente, but the Cold War itself. The Tibetan frontier had become a key source of PRC conduct toward the world at large.

Beyond principles of relationship, Tibet raised one more concern for the PRC: contested international borders. The lines between China and its Himalayan neighbors were far from clear. The Simla

Convention had established the McMahon Line between British India and Tibet in 1914; this boundary, however, was one the PRC refused to accept at face value, claiming it had been imposed by an imperialist regime. (Interestingly, the Republic of China, also claiming to be a legitimate Chinese government, refused to accept the McMahon Line as well.) Nepal posed a problem of a different sort—it had not been part of the British Empire, and no one knew the names of all the mountains in the area, let alone where the boundary lay. If the PRC was going to claim sovereignty over Tibet, it would have to decide how far Tibet extended.

The five principles provided the spirit with which border delineation was to be approached, but there was, understandably, some nervousness west of the Himalayas. Even in the cordial days of 1954, Nehru summed up the problem: Why did Chinese maps claim territory that was rightfully Indian? Zhou's answer was that these were old maps, made by a government no longer in power. New China had not yet had the time to investigate these cartographic discrepancies; when it had looked into the matter and consulted with neighbors like India, it would issue new, satisfactory maps.[58] It is easy to dismiss Zhou's explanation as a play for time, stalling Nehru until the PRC was ready to take all it wanted by force.[59] But how was the PRC to know just where its borders lay? Its leaders were newcomers to power, with little knowledge of China's boundaries. Some of them had been to France; Mao himself had been to Moscow; but they had not experienced—they had had no time to experience—the process of demarcating the country they now governed. So in 1958, almost entirely ignored by historians of China's frontiers, a group of government departments including the Foreign Ministry set about the hard task of trying to research where China's boundaries and boundary disputes lay.[60] The boundary commission divided China's border issues into two categories: boundaries with socialist countries and ones with capitalist countries. China's boundaries with the latter ran some 7,235 kilometers, of which about half were undecided—notably, about 1,400 kilometers between China and India. (The commission made note of another 1,000 kilometers unmarked between China and Kashmir; India and Pakistan were still sparring over which country Kashmir belonged to.) The boundary commission understood the dangers involved: if historically unde-cided border issues were left unresolved, it would jeopardize the revolution and cause neighbors to doubt China; such issues could also be exploited by the imperialist bloc to create friction in China's relations with other countries. At the same time, the tasks proved complicated; one could not approach them casually or unpre-pared. Negotiations with Burma, where the dispute was relatively clear-cut, could proceed; the Sino-Indian frontier demanded fur-ther, more intense research.[61]

The boundary commission was a serious attempt to make the new empire formal, a quest to move from empire-lite to something a little heavier, less porous in construction. In 1958, however, it was nothing more than an attempt. As the commission noted, many points remained unclear.[62] A place the size of Tibet had a multitude of small enclaves, each its own district, which would have had to conduct an investigation of where their particular patch of terri-tory gave way to India's (or Nepal's). At the time, nothing indicated that the process would be anything but peaceful. The commission had been formed, after all, as a confession of ignorance; if one got enough information, one could negotiate a border peacefully, espe-cially with as friendly a country as India. There was little reason, in 1958, for Chinese planners to assume that resolving border differ-ences with Nepal or India would require the use of force—unless they believed that the Tibetan borderlands would soon be plunged into violence.

But Tibet was not trouble-free. Even as the Chinese pondered their new Himalayan frontiers, low-intensity conflicts had persisted in the borderlands. In and of themselves, a few local uprisings might have been manageable. But the unrest spread and deepened—until it knocked out one of the keystones of China's imperial structure.

Flight from Lhasa

The trouble began with maps. Tibetan cartography had never been a strong point for the PRC; the eastern rim of the Tibetan plateau, known as Kham, was not included in the locality of Tibet, but fell across the provinces of Qinghai, Yunnan, Sichuan, and Xikang. While some of the Khambas here had collaborated with the PRC—to the point of marching into Lhasa with the PLA—others fiercely opposed outside interference. So even while Tibet proper remained relatively stable, a low-intensity conflict was under way in Kham.[63] Part of this had to do with the Khambas' lack of respect for outside authority: it was one thing to accept the Dalai Lama as a divine being, but quite another to accept that he, the Kashag, or anyone else could interfere with how they worked, plundered, and generally comported themselves in worldly affairs. But had Beijing pursued a policy of empire-lite in Kham, had it extended the same autonomy and privileges to local chieftains in ethnic Tibet that it gave to the Dalai and Panchen Lamas, Khamba resistance might have waned. The PRC, however, applied gradualism only to the locality of Tibet; reforms proceeded at a furious pace in the ethnic Tibetan areas of Sichuan, Xikang, Yunnan, and Qinghai.[64] And reform in ethnically Tibetan areas, as local officials recognized, came with its own set of problems. Tibetans in Xikang, an official report from there noted, feared Han domination. Religious sensitivities remained, and the upper classes of Tibetan society feared the impact of social and land reform. A group of Khambas had formed an association demanding autonomy in Xikang as early as 1954.[65] These problems were exacerbated by the very force Mao had warned against: Han chauvinism. Mao was adamant that there was no place for sentiments of ethnic superiority in new China; Han chauvinism was "Guomindang thought" and dangerous.[66] But it was one thing to decree the rejection of ethnic superiority from Beijing; it was quite another to enforce the idea in Xikang or Qinghai. Acknowledging errors committed, a report from Xikang noted that there were some cadres who felt it was too early to train minority cadres. Of the minority citizens who had completed training and become cadres, not many had advanced to the status of party officials.[67] There was in such attitudes a clear message to Tibetans living in these areas, one which went contrary to all that Mao had promised: you are part of new China where all are equal, but by virtue of being non-Han, you are considered ethnically incapable of participating fully in new China's governance.

Local officials did see the risks posed by the failure to secure Tibetan participation in government. There was the risk of contagion:

Map 2. The Tibetan plateau and Chinese cartography. This map shows the overlap between Tibetan and Chinese conceptions of space. Though the Seventeen-Point Agreement only applied to the locality of Tibet, Tibetan populations ranged through Amdo and Kham, in provinces the Chinese categorized as Qinghai, Sichuan, Xikang, Yunnan, and Gansu. Note also how far beyond the locality of Tibet the Tibetan plateau extended geographically.

good work on minorities in Xikang, one report observed presciently, was intimately connected to Tibet, Qinghai, and Sichuan.[68] One could picture ethnic dissatisfaction in Xikang spreading all the way to China's western frontiers, where enemies could exploit Tibetan resentment against the PRC.[69] This vision would soon be realized. By 1956, a full-fledged Khamba rebellion was under way, spreading across the Tibetan plateau. By 1958, the Goloks—a Tibetan group in Qinghai—were up in arms too.[70] The Great Leap Forward, which

was launched in 1958 and created serious food shortages, pacified none of the malcontents. Ethnic tension and hunger formed a
deadly cocktail.[71]

The Khamba rebels did have some foreign support. As early as
1951, the United States had been interested in offering covert, if limited, support to Tibetan guerrilla fighters.[72] By 1954, Zhou was com-
plaining to Nehru of American planes flying over Qinghai to drop
weaponry and communications equipment to waiting rebels.[73] As
the rebellion intensified, CIA support for the Khambas grew. A training base was established in the United States; rebels would be sent
from Nepal or East Pakistan to Tibet to wage guerrilla war. The rebels
had some spectacular successes: air-dropping propaganda materials into Tibet and capturing secret CCP documents.[74] For the PRC,
the threat went much deeper than the capture of state secrets. The
United States had refused to recognize its legitimacy as the Chinese
government and was supporting insurgents within China's sovereign realm. At stake was nothing less than the CCP's right to be
recognized as the legitimate government of Tibet and the provinces
where Kham lay. The response was a harsh counterinsurgency.

As the battles in Kham grew bloodier, disquieting rumors made
their way to Lhasa. They were carried by monks, who told of government desecration of monasteries and indescribable evil done to the
innocent in Kham.[75] On the outskirts of Lhasa, refugee settlements
sprung up as people sought to escape the bombings and violence.
Food prices rose. And in Lhasa itself people began asking the inevitable questions: Why was the Dalai Lama standing by as the Khambas were massacred? Would land reform be conducted with such a
vengeance in Tibet proper? Mao had promised that there would be
no reform for six years, and that it would be postponed if conditions
were not suitable then, but who could really trust such a man?[76] Was
the Dalai Lama being somehow coerced or deceived or both? The
PRC provincial classification had thus far ignored the cultural and
religious connections linking Kham to the rest of Tibet; now, the
PRC was discovering that events in Sichuan or Qinghai could have
ramifications for Lhasa, Shigatse, or Dingri. Roadblocks and strikes,
demonstrations and protests—Lhasa and the rest of the plateau saw
them all.

The official mind of the PRC followed these events with a certain flexibility. The government preferred peaceful reform, but a full-scale rebellion was not the worst thing in the world: it would provide the PRC with solid grounds for doing away with the reactionary elements once and for all, for the greater good of the Tibetan people. So the policy was one of watchful restraint.[77]

The Dalai Lama, meanwhile, had been studying hard. He passed the exams that would lead to the degree of *geshe* (doctor of Buddhist studies), and on March 5, 1959, marched from the Jokhang, where he had been staying, to his summer residence, the Norbulingka, that golden and white palace surrounded by gardens and marsh. And it was around the Norbulingka's gardens that the crowds gathered when rumor broke out that the Dalai Lama was to be abducted.

We may never know just how and why this particular rumor emerged; it probably started as nothing more than gossip over yak butter tea. We only know that it was extremely powerful. The Dalai Lama had agreed to attend a cultural performance at the Chinese military headquarters on March 10; when news of the date fanned, so too did the idea that the CCP would take this chance to do away with him. And so it was that on the morning of March 9, 1959, people began streaming to the Norbulingka.

They came from all directions. All day long, the numbers grew. Some stationed themselves in clusters at the entrances to the Norbulingka's gardens; others began patrolling around the palace, carrying banners that demanded an end to Chinese rule. They had come, they shouted, to protect their god from the Chinese, and they would do whatever necessary. Their anger was not confined to the Han; they were hostile to the many Tibetans who had collaborated with the PRC. One Tibetan official was stoned; in days to come, another would be killed. And they had specific demands. The Dalai Lama, they said, must not go to the Chinese headquarters—not now for the show, not ever. The Dalai Lama sent an official to inform them that he would not do so. But the crowds still did not thin significantly. They were angry, they were bitter, and they were going to stay.

Mao Zedong was in Wuhan at the time, but he and the CCP leaders in Beijing consulted closely on how to deal with the Tibetan crisis. They reached several crucial decisions. One was that while attempts should be made to retain the Dalai Lama's support, he and his entourage should be allowed to leave if they tried to do so. Second, while PLA troops should remain alert and prepared for defensive measures, they should not under any circumstances initiate hostilities. The Dalai Lama's departure and a full-scale rebellion might provide ideal excuses for dealing with reactionaries, but the PRC had to retain the moral high ground and not provoke those developments.

It was one more symptom of the weakness of the Chinese state that Beijing could not implement the second decision: to avoid firing the first shot. It was all very well for bureaucrats far removed from the scene to insist on restraint, but they were not there with the soldiers charged with carrying out Beijing's policy. It was a hard policy to maintain, for how long could Chinese soldiers, far from home, be expected to hold their fire? You were young, in a strange place where the food, the scents, the air were all different; you were not used to these mountains and skies. Around the Norbulingka, crowds eyed you balefully and growled in tongues you could not understand. You feared they were armed; you had been told that this was the place where the enemies of the revolution hid. Yet you were under orders to hold your fire. You were tired, frightened, and lonely; your nerves were stretched taut—until finally they snapped. And this was probably why a young PLA soldier fired two rounds, in sharp violation of Beijing's orders.[78] For all the fineness of Mao's decision-making, for all his brilliant ideas about the political initiative, he had no power to determine what a soldier did in Lhasa. The denouement of the Norbulingka drama was shaped not by grand strategists in Beijing, but by a moment of weakness and unauthorized shots.

Locked inside the Norbulingka, the Dalai Lama was seeking, once again, the counsel of an oracle on whether he should stay or go. The oracle had initially advised him against leaving, but this time,

To my astonishment, he shouted, "Go! Go! Tonight!" The medium, still in his trance, then staggered forward and, snatching up some paper and a pen, wrote down, quite clearly and explicitly, the route that I should take out of the Norbulingka, down to the last Tibetan town on the Indian border. His directions were not what might have been expected. That done, the medium, a young monk named Lobsang Jigme, collapsed in a faint, signifying that Dorje Drakden had left his body. Just then, as if to reinforce the oracle's instructions, two mortar shells exploded in the marsh outside the northern gate of the Jewel Park.[79]

He had the oracle; he had heard the firing. So on March 17, 1959, the Dalai Lama slipped past the crowd unnoticed, with a small train of advisors, and made his way to the Indian border. Bands of Tibetan horsemen rode out in groups of four and five for different passes; the idea, one of them would later explain, was to leave Chinese pursuers uncertain as to which route the Dalai Lama was actually taking.[80] Whether it was because Mao had decided that he should be allowed to leave or whether no one on the ground actually realized that the Dalai Lama had gone until it was too late, the Dalai Lama reached the border and crossed into India unharmed. Along the way, he paused to reject the Seventeen Point Agreement formally and declare that he was forming his own government, the sole legitimate authority in Tibet.

The Dalai Lama's departure marked the beginning of the end of the empire-lite policy. The fury and violence of the protests deepened; the PRC launched a massive counteroffensive, with more troops dispatched to Lhasa. For a while, Chinese authorities held out hope that the Dalai Lama would come back, as he had in 1956; many Tibetans marched through the Barkhor, holding up banners that demanded his return.[81]

But this time there was no coming back. This time the violence escalated dramatically: more Chinese troops came pouring into Tibet, bombing Lhasa, and engaging Tibetan forces across the plateau. Riots broke out in distant towns bordering India and Nepal. An ever-swelling stream of refugees began to make its way abroad.[82] The Tibetan crisis was massive—and the PLA's efforts to deal with the damage it caused would last well into 1961. During those years, the imperial structure would harden as Beijing attempted to strengthen state authority over the wild, unruly fourth world it claimed.

The empire's transformation was anything but painless or easy; it would reveal the gulfs between Beijing and Tibet, and between one Tibetan city and another, in all their wideness. *Tian gao huangdi yuan,* goes a Chinese proverb—the sky is high and the emperor far away. The PRC was a weak state; in 1959, the center lacked the capacity to enforce its will in the borderlands. And because Tibet was such a cosmopolitan frontier, the PRC's attempts to bolster the state's strength would have dramatic ramifications for China's foreign policy. The consequences of the transition from empire-lite to a harder, less open imperial structure were not confined to the Tibetan borderlands. They would change both the nature of modern China and the Cold War in the third world.

Imperial Crises, Imperial Diplomacy

The Quest of Gyalo Thondup

In the fall of 1959, Gyalo Thondup wrote a letter to Oland Tsang. Gyalo had a long history of opposition to the Chinese Communist Party: while his brother, the Dalai Lama, had collaborated with the CCP in the fifties, Gyalo had made his way to India, where he organized (with assistance from the CIA) some of the Tibetan resistance groups fighting against the PRC.[1] Tsang was Hong Kong's joint secretary to the United Nations Association in Geneva. Though his loyalties belonged to Hong Kong, Tsang appears to have had strong ideas about China and its role in the world; it was, he believed, the task of the Republic of China, not of India, to present Tibet's case to the United Nations.[2] Accordingly, he forwarded Gyalo's letter to Taipei.

After thanking Tsang for expressing sympathy for Gyalo's Tibetan compatriots, Gyalo summarized the situation in Tibet since the "Chinese communist troops invaded and occupied" the region: "From 1950 to 1959, the entire Tibetan people has adopted non-cooperative activities, struggling against the Chinese Communists through completely peaceful means, such as petitioning, marching demonstrations, strikes, non-service to commanders, etc. But all the demands and hopes of the Tibetan people have been one and all obliterated and ignored by the Chinese Communists."[3] Gyalo went on to explain that the people of eastern Tibet (Kham) had taken up arms against the CCP, and that the CCP had increased pressure on the Tibetans by attacking in force. His descriptions of CCP violence were graphic: he wrote of villages and monasteries being bombed, of the use of planes to release poison gas. (The details might have been added with a view to making a compelling case for genocide in the future.)

It was this completely inhumane suppression of the people, Gyalo explained, that had caused the rebellion to spread from Kham to other parts of the Tibetan plateau. The situation thus described, Gyalo made his plea: "At present, the situation is extremely harsh . . . because Tibet is in an isolated position, with no help or support from the outside world. . . . In our hopeless condition today, we are in a struggle. You have a very deep understanding of the international situation; we hope to get more and more of your instructions on this aspect."[4]

The nuances of the letter—the choice of words like "invaded" and "occupied," the reference to the "Tibetan people," the implicit suggestion that Tibet had a "position" with respect to the outside world, the hint that it wanted to understand and shape the "international situation"—showed Gyalo's intentions. He was aiming for an independent Tibetan state. For much of the twentieth century, as we have seen, Tibet did not act like a nation-state; it lacked the cohesion that the term implies.[5] The multitude of competing foreign policies Tibetans pursued at this time underlines the point. That the Khambas, believers in the divinity of the Dalai Lama, would rebel against China's assertion of control over Tibet while the Dalai Lama himself sought membership of the Communist Party; that decisions in Lhasa had little impact in Kham or along the western reaches of the plateau; that there was not a "monopoly on the use of force"; that foreign relations could be conducted by local Khamba groups, the Dalai Lama, the Panchen Lama, or Gyalo Thondup with almost no overarching coordination or commonalty of purpose—herein lay the clearest evidence that Tibet was not a state like France or even India. Even with the coming of the PRC in the early fifties, the statelessness had ebbed only slightly. Decisions made in Beijing took time being implemented in Lhasa, and authorities in Lhasa had little idea of what was happening in remote outposts like Dingri or Ali.

Now, Gyalo and others like him were trying to get statehood for Tibet. It was a moment of opportunity. The Dalai Lama had fled to India and was giving voice to the plight of Tibetan refugees. Across the globe, people were drawing parallels between events in Tibet and those in Eastern Europe in 1956. These were years when new states were being born all the time; they rose, almost every year, from former imperial holdings. Some of them were cobbled together hastily, looking a bit rickety as they set about trying to create a government; others swaggered onto the world stage as if they had always belonged there. In either event, statehood was something people could realistically dream of. The third world was becoming sovereign—and there were Tibetans who wanted to join in.[6]

The Dalai Lama's departure and the resulting flurry of rebellions across Tibet revealed the weakness of the Chinese state in the region. The PRC's main goal was to strengthen state control of the Tibetan plateau—and a significant part of this task was making sure that the notion of an independent Tibetan state did not gain international legitimacy, whether through a resolution at the United Nations or through Tibetans forming diplomatic ties with other countries (which could, of course, then lead to a resolution at the UN). And this was an area where the Chinese state was woefully handicapped. Excluded as it was from the UN, it was not as well positioned to defend its claims in the global arena as it would have wished.[7] From a twenty-first-century perspective, it is difficult to understand why the PRC would care about the UN, but at the time states took the organization seriously. The UN paying attention to Tibet could have practical consequences: attention could become concern, concern condemnation, and if matters went far enough for the Security Council to pass a resolution, troops could appear to remedy what the outside world called a wrong. It was the UN, after all, that had intervened in Korea; the soldiers poised on China's northeastern frontier wore blue helmets. (Castigating the Pakistanis, once, for bringing up the Kashmir dispute at the UN, Zhou told them not even to mention the UN to China; it was depressing. The words were uncharacteristically harsh, emotional; they showed just how deep Chinese fear of the UN ran.)[8] The PRC could not run the risk of letting things get to the point where the UN passed a resolution authorizing intervention to prevent genocide in Tibet. (There was, of course, the symbolic aspect of the matter too: belonging to the UN meant a country belonged to the international system, on par, at least in theory, with the big powers.

Condemnation from an entity that should include the PRC but did not was bound to sting.)

This chapter explores the PRC's attempts to win international public opinion in the face of the challenge emanating from its borderlands. The stories here are farther removed from the Tibetan borderlands than the ones told in succeeding chapters, but no less important for that. Winning international neutrality, if not support, allowed the PRC to deal with the Tibetan question without having to combat a large-scale global intervention. There were hopes that the UN would intervene; Tibetans and people who sympathized with them lobbied hard for a resolution that would allow action against the PRC. Had they been successful and the UN Security Council decided to endorse a resolution creating an independent Tibetan state, the problem confronting Beijing would have taken on an entirely different complexion, more like that of Korea in 1950. State-building attempts in the borderlands would have taken place under the shadow of a multinational invasion; relations with neighbors and policies within the borderland would have looked completely different. The story of why Tibet did not become another Korea is crucial to understanding why events in the Tibetan borderlands unfolded the way they did.

In undertaking certain diplomatic maneuvers to prevent international intervention in Tibet, the PRC changed. There was a shift in tone as it discussed Tibet with other countries; in that shift, one sees the transition from empire-lite to a harder, less flexible imperial structure. This transition certainly helped the country to strengthen its control of the borderlands—it put other countries on notice that what they did and said would affect their relations with the PRC, that Tibet was something Beijing took seriously—but so too did the fact that it was operating in an environment where empires were still intact. Support, both deliberate and unwitting, came for the PRC from states that had imperial interests and a seat at the UN. Historians describe this as a time of decolonization, when the UN and third world nationalism ushered empire out of the international system.[9] This chapter argues that the opposite was true: empire was perpetuated between 1959 and 1962, with the UN, third world civil society, and first world empires all working toward that perpetuation. Like a lantern flaring suddenly in a cave, the Tibetan question revealed the imperial formations still clinging to the wall.

The Panchen Lama in Beijing

It was when the Dalai Lama fled to India that the PRC had a crisis on its hands. Until then, the unrest could be dismissed as the work of bandits funded by the Guomindang and the CIA. The PRC's control of the Tibetan borderlands had rested on collaboration: the Dalai Lama, the young man who was god of the land, was working with the Chinese. This had gone some way toward creating legitimacy for PRC rule of Tibet, both on the plateau and in the wider world. But with the Dalai Lama gone, the PRC had to find new sources of legitimacy for its rule in Tibet. The cascading violence in the plateau was enough to keep the PRC occupied; to make matters worse, there were protests and muttering in the world beyond the Himalayas too. Kalmyks, citizens of the Soviet Union who practiced Tibetan Buddhism, were marching through New York demanding that the UN take action against the PRC. In India and Sri Lanka, Buddhists asked why Tibetans were being persecuted (it galled the Chinese; they kept explaining that they were not trying to destroy Tibet's Buddhist religion and heritage, merely trying to assert their sovereignty in the region against enemies threatening their state). Groups of concerned citizens, such as the Tibet Society in Britain and the American Emergency Committee for Tibet, sprung up to lobby their governments to support the Tibetans.[10] The Dalai Lama's flight had made Tibet an issue of global significance.

Faced with a problem of this scale, the PRC turned to tradition for help. In the past, the imperial state had relied on tensions within the fourth world to exert authority over it: China could exploit the struggle for power between the Dalai and Panchen Lamas to exercise some measure of control on the Tibetan plateau. Local officials were aware of the deep "contradictions" within Tibet that had come down through the ages;[11] with the Dalai Lama's intentions inscrutable, the state decided to enlist the Panchen Lama's support.

The Panchen Lama owed much to new China. It was the state that had intervened in his dispute with the Tibetan laity, securing his passage back to Tibet. Since returning to Tibet, he had, Mao acknowledged in 1953, done much to foster unity between Han and Tibetans, as well as between Tibetans themselves.[12] When chaos erupted in Tibet, he had struck the right chords, condemning the rebels as treasonous to the country and the people, and encouraging his associates to cooperate with the PLA.[13] Accordingly, central authorities asked the Shigatse Work Committee to investigate the political attitude of the Panchen Lama and his clique.[14]

Three cadres sat down to talk with the Panchen Lama and some of his associates. The results proved favorable. Though the Dalai Lama's statements to central authorities had been pleasant, his instructions behind the scenes had differed, hinted the Panchen Lama: "By Tibetan custom, if he were not bad, no one at the lower levels would dare to be bad." Having received a telegram from Lhasa explaining the situation, he, the Panchen Lama, condemned the rebellion in no uncertain terms. It was a betrayal of the country, the party, the people; it had been surreptitious at first, but had now burst out into the open and become much larger, more serious than in the past—and the Kanting (the Panchen Lama's own little government in the heap of different factions in Tibet) was willing to work with the Tibet Work Committee to help in any way it could.[15] Two of the Panchen Lama's associates even offered to take some thirty people out as cavalry to patrol the farther territories and give the people support—an offer the work committee politely declined.[16]

The Panchen Lama's clique, it was concluded, saw the futility of attempting to drive the CCP out of Tibet; indeed, the CCP's departure from Tibet went against their interests, leaving them without an ally in the struggle against rival Tibetan powers. It had expressed its patriotism and faith in the central authorities clearly. It would not join forces with the rebellion.[17] With such goodwill and with his high standing in the Tibetan religious establishment, the Panchen Lama was a good man for the PRC to have on its side in this time of crisis—which made it all the more interesting that he had expressed an interest in visiting Beijing. Such a trip had advantages: it would have a good impact on both domestic and international

opinion; it would further his own education (especially important if he was set on becoming a keystone in the regional power
structure).[18] It ran the risk, of course, of provoking a split within
the Kanting—but this was just the cost of doing business.[19] If the
Panchen Lama remained willing, having him in Beijing was worth
thinking about.

This was a classic move in dealing with an indigenous insurgency: if one chieftain turned against the state, the state would enlist
the support of his rival. A third world imperial state was seeking
to strengthen its hand by cooperating with elements in the fourth
world. And if the immediate impact on the ground was less dramatic
than the CCP might have hoped, the Panchen Lama's visit to Beijing
did help with international public relations. Historians have listed
Tibet as one of the causes of the Sino-Soviet split, but in those uncertain days of 1959, the Tibetan crisis forced Beijing and Moscow
closer together.[20] Beijing might not trust Moscow, but it needed
Soviet support for its policies on Tibet. That support, as the PRC was
well aware, could not be taken for granted. As early as March, the
Soviets had not quite approved of the way the Chinese were han-
dling Tibet; it would be unwise, officials in Moscow had hinted, to
let the Dalai Lama and the rebels flee the border, since this would
only create more trouble in the long run.[21] Later, those wonderful
intelligence agents, foreign students, would report that though the
majority of the Soviet masses were supportive, some of them did not
really understand what was happening in Tibet. They were asking
strange questions. Why had rebellion broken out so long after the
entire country was liberated? Why had the rebels been allowed to
flee across the border so easily? Were all ethnicities in China really
equal?[22] These remarks were not official Soviet policy, but they suggested some unease—unease that could be allayed, to some extent,
with the Panchen Lama's cooperation.

So the Panchen Lama came to Beijing for the May Day celebra-
tions. There he found the chance to talk to diplomats from the Soviet
Union and from Eastern Europe. He made, his minders reported, a
good impression. The Soviet and Czechoslovakian diplomats com-
plimented him, invited him to Moscow and Prague; the Panchen
Lama, good patriot, good citizen, replied:

Thank you for your invitations. But work is very busy right now. Although the rebellion has already been basically suppressed [this was not true, but it would remain the official party line], this is only the start of our work in Tibet. We still need to conduct social and democratic reform, still need to build a booming, prosperous . . . Tibet. Once all the work has reached completion, I too hope to go to the Soviet Union and other fraternal countries.

. . . We share a goal with the Soviet Union and other fraternal countries: we too want to conduct construction according to the intentions of Marxism-Leninism. . . . I also hope that, hereafter, when diplomatic envoys from the fraternal countries visit our country's interior, they can come to see Tibet.[23]

The language was a bit stilted and formulaic—it is one of the very few conversations in the Beijing archives that feels somehow forced, unnatural, even scripted—but the Panchen Lama was making a vital point on behalf of the PRC. Chinese communist conduct in Tibet was good for Tibetans and ideologically correct. A key figure of the Tibetan religious establishment was glorifying Chinese policy in Tibet, on grounds that any good Soviet official would find unexceptionable. (The ideological rhetoric helped in another way too: at a time of intense ideological debates,[24] it emphasized that the PRC was clinging to real, true socialism, whatever the Soviet Union thought.) The advantage of the fourth world's multifaceted nature was that parts of it would testify to the good conduct of a third world country. Here was proof that the Chinese were working for the Tibetan people, not against them.

The Soviets might still have had some lingering discomfort about Tibet, but they tried to help Beijing with the diplomatic problems Tibet raised. Moscow, at the time, was caught between its ostensible loyalties to Beijing and its increasingly cordial relations with New Delhi.[25] With Beijing angered—though not yet intractably—by what it perceived as Indian support for the Tibetan cause, the USSR found it difficult to maintain friendly ties with India and the PRC at the same time. Like a parent trying desperately to keep peace between two quarrelling children, Moscow shuttled messages back and forth between China and India, hoping that they would somehow see one another's point of view. Of course Soviet diplomats in India had explained that Tibet was part of China and that outside interference in the matter was intolerable, but China should try to understand the difficulties of the Indian position. No one wanted to see a deterioration of Sino-Indian relations—except, of course, the American imperialists who would seek to exploit a rift. That was what the Soviet ambassador tried to explain to vice minister Chen Yi one evening in Zhongnanhai.[26] It was not an easy task. Nehru's demand that the Dalai Lama, India, and China all sit down for a conference was unacceptable (naturally, since it implied that India had a right to discuss what happened in Tibet), said Chen; Nehru himself had created the difficult position he was in. Reality showed, Chen argued, "the correctness of Leninism's principle: only after passing through criticism and dispute, can unity then be attained. At the end of April, the Indian consulate in Lhasa issued some hundred certificates, wanted Tibetans to get Indian citizenship. This too is Nehru's difficulty: he is incapable of control. *We* did not protest; moreover, we did not publish the information in the newspapers."[27]

This was not quite as uncompromising a line as it seemed. Chen did hint at an eventual unity, and by emphasizing China's restraint in not publicizing the Indian consulate's activities—activities that would prove far more destructive to the Sino-Indian entente than a casual listener hearing Chen might have suspected—showed that Beijing was willing to be reasonable. Well into 1961, as we will see, China continued to attempt to resolve its differences with India. But allowing India to assume that it had a right to participate in decision-making on Tibet was unthinkable—and Moscow, as Beijing saw it, would just have to accept that.

The Soviets did seek to reassure Beijing that they would not side with India against the PRC on the Tibet issue. At a meeting in Moscow on May 8, 1959, for example, a Soviet defense official explained that though New Delhi was trying to gain Moscow's sympathy for its stand on Tibet, thereby winning Soviet support against the PRC, this would never happen; Moscow would stand by Beijing.[28] But perhaps the most important proof of Moscow's good intentions was its support for Beijing at the UN. On September 28, 1959, Malaya and Ireland moved to discuss Tibet at the fourteenth session of the General Assembly. They offered blunt grounds: "Prima facie evidence of an attempt to destroy the traditional way of life of the Tibetan people and the religious and cultural autonomy long recognized as belonging to them, as well as a systematic disregard for the human rights and fundamental freedom set out in the Universal Declaration of Human Rights."[29] Such a move had support. Gyalo, in cooperation with his CIA comrade in arms, John Kenneth Knaus, and the lawyer the CIA had hired, Ernest Gross, was working furiously for Tibetan independence. "Backstairs diplomacy," Knaus would later call it, as he described the meetings between the three on the stairs at the backs of hotels in New York, he and Gross trying to convince Gyalo that they could not get a resolution supporting Tibetan independence, that it was important to move step by step, to take what they could get.[30] As it turned out, they got very little, because the Soviet Union—and much of the eastern bloc—stood firmly behind the absent PRC. Tellingly, the Soviets cited the Panchen Lama's statements as proof that Tibet's heritage was being respected. And they echoed the PRC line: Tibet was an integral part of China, meaning that a resolution on the subject would violate Article 2, Chapter 7, of the UN Charter, which precluded interference in a state's internal affairs.[31] The General Assembly did manage to pass a resolution "calling for respect for the fundamental human rights of the Tibetan people and for their distinctive cultural and religious life,"[32] but in the absence of Soviet support, UN military action against the PRC was out of the question. Other countries cited Article 2, Chapter 7, too, but the Soviet vote was crucial, for the Soviets had a reliable veto in the Security Council and thus the power to block collective security action against the PRC.

This process would repeat itself in the coming years. On August 19, 1960, Malaya and Thailand tried to inscribe Tibet on the General Assembly's agenda, pointing to the continuing violations of human rights there; again, the Soviets supported the PRC, making the passage of a resolution through the Security Council impossible (and, for practical purposes, rendering the debate in the General Assembly irrelevant).[33] Now and then, the question of Tibet would get entangled with the question of whether the PRC should be represented at the UN. The Soviet Union—and even India—would argue that it should take its place in the comity of nations. The ROC and the United States would cite possible genocide in Tibet as just one of many reasons why the idea of the PRC at the UN was unthinkable. Then the Soviets would repeat that the CCP was doing a wonderful job in China—and the debate would drag on unresolved. For all the sound and fury, the UN was paralyzed when it came to the Tibetan question; Gyalo Thondup's quest was proving fruitless. And the longer UN intervention did not happen, the more time the PRC had to pacify Tibet.

Not that the PRC was content to sit complacently and rely on the Soviets to continue parrying resolutions concerning Tibet. To the official mind of the PRC, the crisis in Tibet was a weapon being wielded by a hostile United States and the Guomindang; China's enemies were seeking to capitalize on its weakness and to do it harm.[34] Other countries would have to know that the stand they took on Tibet was a barometer of their friendship to the PRC. Beijing would consider any support of the Tibetan cause, whether at the UN or elsewhere, an act of aggression. Thus, when Norbu, the Dalai Lama's eldest brother who was seeking support for the Tibetan cause, visited northern Europe, the PRC kept a watchful eye on his movements. Norbu was trying to bring Tibet's plight to global attention, and he did so in moving terms: "The Chinese people have killed approximately six hundred thousand Tibetans and banished many. Six million Chinese colonizers have moved in, making the Tibetans a minority in their own country." Such were his remarks in Copenhagen, as he traveled across Europe. Norbu's journey, the PRC embassy in Sweden explained, was an American-directed political offensive. It targeted China on the eve of the General Assembly's opening session; the goals were to neutralize the warm atmosphere created by Soviet-American state visits, to conceal American conspiracies in Cuba, and to create contradictions between China and neutral or semineutral countries such as Austria, Sweden, and Denmark.[35] The PRC took up these concerns with the Danes and the Swedes. When Denmark replied that it had a friendly relationship with the PRC and really did not see why a citizen visiting privately should pose a problem, the PRC's response was telling: "Letting Norbu into the country to conduct activities slandering the PRC and destroying Sino-Danish relations violates the Danish government's fine wishes." And could Copenhagen do something about those television stations whose language about China was so unfriendly? To the Danes, it was just the nature of free debate; to China, it was an insult that had the potential of becoming dangerous. Though the Chinese diplomats concluded—quite rightly—that Denmark was basically friendly, the watchfulness, the sensitivity, and the vehemence of the language showed just how seriously Beijing took Tibetan diplomatic efforts.[36] Similarly, when Pakistan—which had gone some distance to assure the PRC of its goodwill, despite its participation in SEATO and CENTO[37]—voted in support of the resolution on Tibet in the General Assembly, the Pakistani ambassador in Beijing was summoned for a scolding from vice minister Geng. China wanted to preserve good relations, Geng said, but Pakistan's behavior at the UN was extremely unfriendly. Pakistan had followed the American government in interfering in China's internal operations and it had supported America in opposing the PRC's recovery of its lawful position in the UN. Tibet was a part of China; pacifying the rebellion and conducting democratic reform there was China's internal affair, and no international organization had the right to interfere.[38]

With the benefit of hindsight, it is easy to dismiss the PRC's concerns as overblown. At the time, however, much of the world had yet to recognize the Beijing government. In the United States and the ROC, it had a set of enemies it would not underestimate. And above all, it had firsthand experience in Korea of what UN intervention could look like. The risk of having troops with blue helmets appear on the Tibetan frontier was a genuine security concern that Beijing's leaders could not have ignored—not least because that frontier was still far from pacified, and rumors of foreign intervention could exacerbate unrest. Perception is colored by experience; having seen how much force a UN resolution could unleash in Korea, Beijing could not take discussions at that forum lightly. Tibetans appealing to countries for support at the UN were a threat. And in countering that threat, the PRC's diplomacy changed. It sought to cooperate with the Soviet Union despite ideological and political differences. It made sure that countries supporting resolutions on Tibet at the UN understood that they were supporting an American-sponsored effort to attack the PRC. And it made sure that everyone knew that

Tibet was a part of China, even though violent conflict in the borderlands continued.

These changes would not have been necessary if Tibet had not erupted in chaos. Beijing would not have had to be so consistently vociferous in its protests that Tibet was part of China if it had had solid control of the region. Until 1959, it had not been compelled to conduct the sort of diplomacy it now found itself forced into. A crisis in the fourth world had forced a third world state to alter its statecraft. Empires, when their borderlands pose a challenge, often move from empire-lite to harder, heavier imperial structures.[39] To the world beyond the borderlands, that transition is clearest in a change of diplomatic tone, such as that which the PRC undertook in 1959.

Empire Strikes Back

Beijing's new diplomacy, then, made it clear to other governments that if they wished to remain on cordial terms with the PRC, they would have to deny that the UN (or anyone other than the PRC) had the right to interfere in Tibet. PRC diplomats did this quite effectively. But they worried about one source of power they could not control: civil society initiatives. At first glance, the Afro-Asian Council's conference in 1960 would not seem to be of much importance to PRC concerns. The conference comprised some three score intellectuals from third world countries. These delegates did not speak for their governments; what they said or did was in no way binding and had no official weight. What the convention did have, however, was the power to lobby world leaders. The convention's president, Jayprakash Narayan, was well connected, and he put considerable energy behind Tibet's cause at the UN. Politicians around the world could be convinced to make Tibet an election issue. In India, for example, the opposition had seized the opportunity to put pressure on Nehru; in Britain, the government tried to balance its own perception of strategic interests with the demands of parliament and the Tibet Society.[40] Historians of later decades would describe transnational movements: individuals around the globe banding together to push their governments for a cause, a principle.[41] The

Afro-Asian Convention on Tibet was part of such a movement. As with all such movements at the time, it bore the marks of the Cold War—but it also showed how actors could break free of Cold War concerns to pursue their own agenda.

This was reason enough for the PRC to pay close attention to the conference in New Delhi, but there were additional considerations. The list of participants read like a catalog of the CCP's enemies. There were participants from Hong Kong who had close connections with the Chiang Kai-shek regime.[42] Norbu and Gyalo were present, as was a Khamba representing the Han-Tibetan Alliance against Communism. The East Turkestan independence movement, which called for a sovereign Xinjiang, came to participate. And the United States–Taiwan nexus (as the PRC saw it) was providing money, to say nothing of flying in agents from Hong Kong. Volunteers from right-wing Indian parties came—and for all the talk of the unofficial nature of the conference, Chinese diplomats believed that Nehru was giving it too much help, seeking to use it to apply pressure to the PRC. The conference was timed deliberately, as the embassy saw it, just ahead of scheduled Sino-Indian discussions on disputed borders—it was meant to provoke.[43] The PRC had every reason to see the conference as a propaganda offensive in the stop-start war America and the ROC were waging against it. The PRC embassy in India, therefore, kept a watchful eye on the convention's proceedings.

According to the embassy, the main objective of the conference was to "oppose China, oppose communism"; second, there was some notion of criticizing "colonialism." The PRC was denounced for a "new style of colonialism" and compared to the Soviet Muslim republics. Chinese expansionism, directed toward India and other countries, came in for criticism too. Finally, Chang Kuo-sin, a Hong Kong journalist who sent detailed reports on the convention to Taipei, claimed that the PRC wanted to establish direct links with the Indian Communist Party and create a civil war in India.[44]

Such declarations mattered. If the convention's efforts were effective in bringing the matter to UN attention, and if Soviet support at the UN somehow vanished (Khrushchev was not the most reliable ally in the world), a small group of people could have threatened PRC national security. The ifs mattered: PRC policy planners had to consider them and prepare for the worst contingencies. More immediately, statements made in New Delhi could reach Tibet, whether by word of mouth or through radio broadcasts, thereby undermining the PRC's state-building attempts in the region. They could make it difficult for New Delhi to engage in meaningful talks about the border; by appropriating the term "Afro-Asia," they undermined Chinese efforts to foster third world cooperation. The Afro-Asian convention was a source of potential danger.

The PRC did seek to counter the threat by redoubling its own propaganda efforts, circulating information on all the good done in Tibet since the rebellion had been pacified.[45] But one blow never came. For all its rhetoric about colonialism, the convention did not repudiate China's claim to sovereignty over Tibet. And this resulted from an unlikely convergence of policy. On the ground, as the subsequent chapters will show, ROC-Tibetan collaboration was a concern for Beijing. But on the overarching concept of what China was, the two rival Chinese governments agreed: Taipei was as implacable as Beijing in its insistence that Tibet was an integral part of China. The disagreement was simply about who the legitimate government of China was.

The main story of the Afro-Asian Convention on Tibet therefore went like this. Some of the Indian delegates at the conference believed that Tibet was an independent country, with no connection to China. As evidence, they cited treaties concluded between Britain and Tibet, and later, between India and Tibet. If Tibet could sign a treaty with a foreign government, it had been a sovereign state—and, presumably, was one now. The Chinese delegates at the conference found this view unacceptable. The treaties in question had been signed at a strange, troubled time in Chinese history. When a country went through great internal turmoil, the ROC delegate Chou Jingwen explained, many districts would strenuously proclaim their independence. When China had been semicolonized, many warlords had sprung up to call themselves independent—an independence that would later "vanish like smoke and disperse like clouds." The Japanese had occupied China's northeast and invented the "so-called Manchukuo"; with the Japanese gone, however, no one was going to question that the northeast was part of China.

Anybody could sign a treaty: Zhang Zuolin, a notorious warlord of the northeast, had done so. Just because Tibet had signed treaties at a time when its true sovereign was weak did not make Tibet an independent country.[46]

Not that the Communists had sovereign rights to Tibet or anywhere else. Communist China did not represent the Chinese people or even the Han, continued Chou; it was a tool of Moscow.[47] This was why the ROC delegation found charges of neocolonialism acceptable: they were directed at the Communists, not the Chinese. Sovereign rights to Tibet remained vested in the rightful Chinese government: the Guomindang.

The Hong Kong–Guomindang perspective on Tibet prevailed. The convention's final report did not treat Tibet as a sovereign country; indeed, the Hong Kong delegates were careful to make sure that the words "aggression" or "invasion" were not used in the resolutions to describe Chinese Communist actions in Tibet—for those words could imply that Tibet was an independent state. (The word "aggression" did make it into a report on committee deliberations, but a footnote catalogued Nationalist China's objections to the term.) The Chinese suggested generously that at some point in the future Tibet might be allowed "self-determination."[48] Given the tenacity with which the Guomindang delegates had insisted on China's sovereignty over Tibet, the Tibetan delegation's skepticism about this promise was understandable. The convention was, reported Chang Kuo-sin,

a great diplomatic victory. We are afraid the Convention might come out in full support of the view that Tibet has never been part of China and that Tibet should be given complete independence immediately. This is what the Tibetan delegation wanted and the atmosphere was in their favor. All the important Indians, including Mr. Narayan, supported the view that Tibet had been independent since 1913. If the Convention were to endorse Tibetan's demands, we would be put in a very embarrassing position. What we want to do is maintain that Tibet is and will remain an integral part of China but we would grant them self-determination, as President Chiang had announced. After many debates and discussions, we succeeded in getting the Indians to support us though they still believe in their hearts that Tibet has been independent of China since 1913 and the result was that our view was accepted.[49]

Gyalo Thondup, who had campaigned so hard for Tibetan independence, was less than pleased. Later he would complain to Chang that Hong Kong's was the only delegation that had opposed Tibetan independence, and point out the many ways in which "free China" was making it harder for the Tibetans to get what they wanted. Chang pointed out that the idea of independence was insupportable and that self-determination was a great concession indeed.[50]

In successfully defending China's claims to Tibet at a transnational level, Chang had perhaps won a diplomatic triumph. There was, however, one curious thing about it—the PRC was not exactly displeased with the results of a convention at which so many foes were ranged against it and about which it had had so much reason to feel nervous. No agreement had been reached endorsing Tibetan independence; on that one point, it was almost as if Taipei had colluded with Beijing. The Pakistani delegate had only wanted to discuss Indian imperialism in Kashmir. The Kenyan delegates had come to the PRC embassy in India after the conference to say that they had had no idea what the conference was about and that while they certainly opposed imperialism, they had no complaints against the PRC or what it did in Tibet.[51] Afro-Asian civil society was not quite as united in its condemnation of the PRC as the PRC's enemies had made out. What could have become a vehicle for forcing the UN to take action against Beijing had turned into little more than a curiosity for a historian to ponder.

Chang had a simple explanation for his "great diplomatic victory." "All or most of these Indian delegates are my friends," he wrote happily, "so they co-operated well."[52] Personal bonhomie might well have played a role, but there is a darker, more disturbing reason: the very human inability to believe that victims of injustice or oppression can be unjust or oppressive themselves. The Chinese delegates had been swift to remind the gathering that their country had been a *victim* of imperialism. They invoked the era of treaty ports and warlords, as well as Japanese imperialism in China. And one cannot help suspecting that once reminded of China's status as a former victim of imperialism, the delegates could not fathom that it would become an empire itself. If China had suffered imperial rule, surely it would be incapable of practicing it.

Logically, of course, there was no reason that a former imperial holding could not become an empire. But we are unaccustomed to the idea of victims as perpetrators, and this was why the Indians were willing to fall in line with the ROC. China had been occupied by other countries; China, therefore, had been somehow morally immunized against the evil desire to occupy other countries. The Afro-Asian convention's refusal to call China's actions an invasion of Tibet stemmed from the belief that Afro-Asian states, as former colonies themselves, could not and would not behave imperially.[53]

This is not to condemn the delegates. Later historians, who wrote of decolonization in the third world at this time, would start from the same premise.[54] Our twentieth-century impressions of imperialism and decolonization are cast, inevitably, in the mold of the nation-state. We tend to assume that imperialism involved one state conquering or controlling another; conversely, decolonization involved one state getting rid of a state that had conquered or controlled it. Wearing this statist lens, we interpret the emergence of third world nation-states as decolonization. This is, of course, partly true. But newly decolonized nation-states often mapped themselves onto territory formerly held together in an imperial structure. The act of state-building could be imperial, because the absorption of stateless, fourth world peoples by a third world nation-state is a form of imperialism.[55]

First world imperial states understood this—and their sensitivity to the Tibetan question and their reluctance to challenge the PRC's line spoke volumes about the true nature of the international system. The Soviet Union was not the only UN member to deny the organization's right to weigh in on the Tibetan issue. Looking at the PRC, officials in London and Paris recognized an imperial cousin. In 1959, Britain and France would number among those who argued that passing a resolution on Tibet amounted to an intervention in internal affairs and thus violated Article 2, Chapter 7.[56] This was partly because they were trying to improve relations with Beijing at the time.[57] But it was also because both Britain and France remained imperial states, with an interest in continuing to hold territories abroad. To discuss China's conduct in Tibet would cast an uncomfortable spotlight on the empires London and Paris wished to maintain. (The United States was an empire too, but with one important difference: it was an informal empire. It did not hold colonies the way Britain and France did; the very informality of its imperialism allowed it to be—like China—an empire in denial. The kinship Britain and France perceived between their own empires and the PRC would be lost on the United States.) Nothing clarified the stakes as sharply as a meeting between the Americans, the British, and the French in New York on September 18, 1959. Christian Herter, the American secretary of state, expressed his desire to see an item on Tibet inscribed on the General Assembly's agenda. The British secretary of state admitted that it would be difficult not to support raising the Tibetan issue at the General Assembly, but pointed out that a trail of embarrassment lay that way: "We should be acting contrary to the line we had always taken on Article 2 (7) and the precedent which the inscription of such an item would create would be very dangerous. It would open the way to the discussion in the United Nations of the subjects like Oman, Nyasaland, Ulster, and perhaps even segregation in the United States." Couve de Murville, the French representative, wanted nothing to do with Tibet because of the parallels it would raise with French authority over Algeria. And there were always countries like Belgium, the Netherlands, and Portugal, which, as the three diplomats realized, "would have serious doubts because of the effect this precedent might have on their own overseas territories."[58]

The reasoning was simple: first world countries had their own problems that were disquietingly similar to the PRC's in Tibet. The existing international order was one of states, but also one of empires. Britain exercised, and wanted to continue to exercise, authority over Oman and Nyasaland. France exercised, and until Charles de Gaulle decided to cut his losses, wished to continue to exercise, authority over Algeria. Far from being an age of decolonization, as it appears in retrospect, this was also a time when empires struck back, remaining intact in certain parts of the world for far longer than one might have thought possible. The debate about Tibet showed that. To discuss Tibet at the UN would open one's own colonial holdings to condemnation—and therein lay danger. London's archives are brimming with reminders of how closely Britain's policy on Tibet was tied to the fact that it was still an empire. In 1960, it voted to inscribe Tibet on the agenda, but then abstained from the resolution, citing Article 2 (7). As 1961 came, with the need to decide once more on how to deal with the Tibetan question at the UN, British citizens lobbied their government to condemn Chinese "colonialism" in Tibet.[59] In a delightfully candid note, Michael Stewart, the British chargé d'affaires in Beijing, summed up the pros and cons of this approach:

> I agree that at first sight this is a tempting line of attack. But there may be some clue to the likely Chinese retort to this in the line which the members of the Russian mission here take when we tax them with Hungary and Tibet in answer to their assertions that the USSR and the Communist powers are the champions of the colonial peoples. They remark that we bring up these subjects only because of sensitivity to attacks on our own colonial record. There is of course some plausibility in this argument, particularly if we take a stronger line on Tibet than India, who is more closely concerned. It becomes slightly more plausible if in the session in which our own colonial policy has been under violent attack, we strengthen our position on the Tibet vote; and the Chinese are likely to make this point.[60]

It was a fair appraisal. If you were an empire, you would find it difficult to fault another country for being one too. Any resolution on Tibet would draw attention to Oman or Rhodesia,[61] but using the word "colonialism" would only make things worse.

Such were the calculations underpinning Britain's championship of Article 2 (7) (though by 1961, the country had found its way toward supporting a General Assembly resolution calling for the "cessation of practices which deprive the Tibetan people of their fundamental human rights and freedoms, including their right to self-determination").[62] The preference for maintaining an imperial world order did not go unremarked. Narayan, comfortably ignoring the Afro-Asian Convention's own equivocation on Tibet, sent a scathing letter to the British:

It is disheartening to note the line of argument propounded by certain delegates that the Assembly should not consider the Question of Tibet because the People's Republic of China was not represented there and this was contrary to Article 2, Paragraph 7, of the Charter of the United Nations and that since Tibet was and is an integral part of China, what happens in Tibet is the domestic concern of China. There might be a certain logic in the claim, but it is a logic resting on premises which would debar the Assembly from discussing many other items such as South Africa, Algeria, and the Portuguese colonies. It is a line of argument all of us who have lived under colonial rule have rejected in relation to ourselves, a line of argument that would have kept half the nations who have taken their rightful place in the comity of nations in eternal servitude.[63]

The rhetoric was overblown, but the words posed a crucial problem: How did one draw the line between fourth world people and a third world nation-state? What conferred the rights and privileges of sovereignty on a people? Who had a "rightful place in the comity of nations"—and, by extension, who did not? Tibet raised these questions, and it showed that there were no clear answers to them. They were resolved piecemeal, inconsistently. The outcome of a quest for statehood depended on an empire's tenacity in the face of a serious challenge (and on how strong that challenge was), on the ability of the "strong [to] do what they can and the weak [to] suffer what they must."[64] Algeria got a state because the French, weary of the burdens of empire, decided to give it up; the PRC was not so easily dissuaded, and Tibet remained an "integral part of China." Empires died in some places at this time, but in others they found a second wind, and won international legitimacy.

The Diplomacy of Imperialism

Merely observing that China was an imperial formation at the time is not very interesting. What is interesting is that it was an empire changing in response to weakness; its use of "the diplomacy of imperialism" was part of that change.[65] An empire unthreatened by a crisis can afford to be relaxed in its diplomacy. It has no need for shrillness or creativity to defend a frontier, because the frontier is not in jeopardy. Once a crisis erupts in an imperial borderland, however, the empire must strengthen its grip on that borderland—and this often means having to change one's diplomacy. Perhaps this was even truer in the twentieth century, when international legitimacy mattered. An empire seeking to secure a frontier had to get some form of public acquiescence.

The PRC was no exception. The Tibetan crisis revealed state weakness; one aspect of that weakness was the PRC's absence from the UN, an absence which meant that it was not fully equipped to defend its claims in the global arena. Addressing that weakness required diplomatic dexterity. Beijing needed to reach out to the Soviet Union for support, to cooperate despite deepening suspicion. It raised an unpleasant subject with countries it took as friends, with unflagging insistence. This helped, but so too did good fortune. Beijing profited from the fact that Taipei shared its imperial ambitions, and from the fact that first world empires could understand and empathize with Chinese imperialism. Statecraft and serendipity allowed the Chinese state to gain acceptance of its claims to Tibet.

To someone living in the Tibetan borderlands at the time, debates at the UN or diplomatic fencing in Copenhagen might have seemed a world away. News from the outside did make its way to Tibet frequently, but it often arrived distorted, and if you were trying to survive a raging war and food shortages, the language of high politics might have seemed out of touch with reality. In one respect, though, diplomacy and world opinion made a crucial, negative difference—one that shaped the course of events in Tibet dramatically. Despite Gyalo Thondup's best efforts, despite the concerted push from many individuals around the world, large-scale global intervention did not happen—and this was significant. The absence of such intervention gave the PRC more breathing room than it would otherwise have had as it struggled to secure the Tibetan borderlands. And it meant that other shifts from empire-lite to empire-heavy could proceed, albeit with greater difficulty than the one the PRC had enacted on the global stage.

CHAPTER**THREE**

Border Crossers

The Sino-Nepali Frontier

Three Men from Dingri

As spies go, the men of Dingri were not terribly subtle. On August 23, 1960, Pubu Ciren, Asuo, and Chenbo were chosen by Dingri's masses (this is the official government term) to cross the border into Nepal and convince the Tibetans who had taken refuge there to return. They set out with pamphlets on the Three Antis, Two Reductions campaign (the PRC's concept of the revolution was summed up as antirebellion, antifeudal structure, and antislavery, along with the re-duction of rent and of interest). They were apprehended almost im-mediately by the Nepali police. Good collaborators sent to persuade their less loyal compatriots to return to the PRC could not be left to languish abroad, so a team was dispatched to look for the missing agents. Ciren Seda, who headed the new team, ran into a lama who told him that he had heard that the three spies had been arrested. The lama counseled Ciren Seda to return; the team was traveling without goods or livestock, an absence bound to draw attention from Nepali troops. Traders and nomads crossed the border all the time, after all, but what kind of men would make the passage empty-handed? But Ciren Seda was a stubborn man and a good revolutionary; he would not stop for what the lama said. He pushed onward into Nepal, where he encountered a Tibetan family from Dingri. "Have you three seen Pubu Ciren, Asuo, and Chenbo of Dingri come here or not?" he asked. It was an unfortunate beginning. The family was one of those that had fled to Nepal and not well disposed to conductors of com-munist propaganda. Ciren Seda explained hastily that they had not come to convince people to return, but the damage was done. Fearing arrest, he retreated to Tibet and told his story.[1]

Nobody was very happy about this. The Tibet Work Committee pointed out that with Sino-Nepali negotiations under way, everyone should stop such initiatives: if cadres encouraged such behavior, it was very wrong indeed. The General Staff Department noted that it had already asked all districts to stop propaganda activities. Shigatse, the prefecture to which Dingri belonged, warned that Dingri's conduct violated directives from the central authorities, work commission, military commission, and military region.[2] Whatever the three men had been up to, the bureaucracy sought to make clear, it was not the official policy of the People's Republic of China.

In Dingri, meanwhile, emotions ran high. Dingri was not a town so much as a few dwellings scattered among the mountains, a community of herders living in the shadow of Everest. Here you were closer to Nepal than to Lhasa or Shigatse. The big cities did not notice you often; central directives arrived late, if at all, and had little to do with the rhythms and concerns of life. Now, the local citizenry was furious and demanded that Nepal release the men immediately. Their wives longed for them. "After we heard the information, we have been unable to sleep every evening . . . after today how are we to attend to livelihood, to production?" They demanded that the government provide them with support (which it apparently did; the extra cost of this arrangement, borne by the community, might explain some of the outrage). It was not, however, a substitute for the men who had gone away.[3] With so much simmering resentment, there was always the chance that friends in Dingri might try to get the three out themselves—just the sort of move that would create an international incident.

It was a messy, complicated, and potentially dangerous situation—typical of China's experience on the Tibetan frontier at the time. Scholarly accounts relying chiefly on records of high-level negotiations portray the PRC as cool, controlled, and disciplined in its dealings with Kathmandu; the border agreement between the two countries and the suppression of Tibetan rebels are cast as almost inevitable.[4] The view from the Tibetan plateau, however, differs starkly. Officials stationed in remote outposts were constantly writing to their superiors with tales of border crossers and the dangers they posed: criminals fleeing retribution through hidden passes, spies linked to Taiwan and the United States, troops appearing where they were not supposed to be.[5] Nothing was certain for the officials or the people they reported on—and as a result, nothing was certain for Beijing.

Telling the stories of some of the border crossers, as this chapter does, is invaluable, for it shows something of what it was like to live in the Tibetan borderlands and recovers something of the confusion confronting people at the time. But these stories do something else. By highlighting the gap between center and periphery, they show the PRC seeking to address something it has not generally been accused of: state weakness. And by exploring the means the PRC used to deal with the complications Tibet created for Sino-Nepali relations, these stories show how events in the Tibetan borderlands redefined Chinese policy during the Cold War—and indeed, China itself. For it was during these uncertain times on its Himalayan frontier that the PRC made the transition from empire-lite to a harder, more heavy-handed imperial structure.

Foreigners or Not?

Tibet in 1959 was in a state of war. The People's Liberation Army (PLA) had been engaged in a low-intensity conflict with Khambas on the eastern rim of the plateau since the early fifties, but Lhasa had remained relatively peaceful. In March 1959, when the Dalai Lama made his way to exile in India, violence came home to the spiritual heart of the region. It was not a centralized violence, a considered, martial response to the PLA's deeds. Instead, it came from multiple, conflicting Tibetan groups that had little in common with one another.[6] There was the resistance based in India led by the Dalai Lama's brother, Gyalo Thondup. There were rival Khamba groups in India, also claiming to represent Tibet. And there were sporadic uprisings all over the plateau—groups of people, in remote towns and villages, suddenly deciding to take up arms against the PRC. If the fragmented

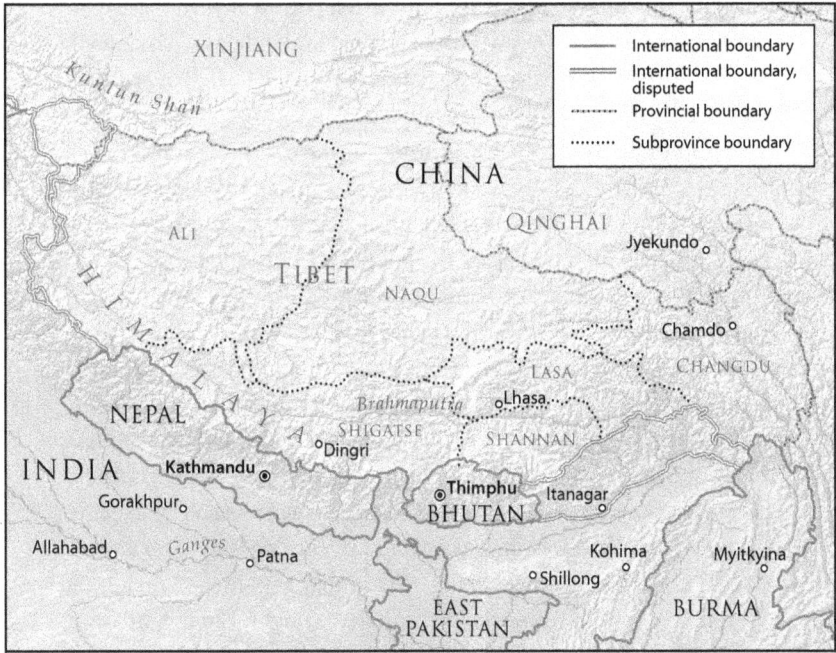

Map 3. Regional divisions of the Tibetan plateau. Shown here are the various administrative divisions located in Tibet. Notice how large the region is and how far places like Dingri were not only from Lhasa but also from the capitals of the prefectures they belonged to.

nature of the Tibetan resistance meant that it would not prevail over the long run, the immediate effect was to make it a much harder problem for the PRC to deal with. The state authorities were not fighting any single foe, but many—and foes who were hard to identify.

As in all such wars, the fighting was not confined to military operations or insurgency. There was looting and robbery, rape and coercion, with no discrimination between combatants and civilians.[7] And as in all such wars, foreigners were caught in the flood of violence. For the Nepalis, Indians, Bhutanese, and Sikkimese who traded, worshipped in, and visited Tibet, 1959 brought hard choices about whether to stay or leave. The diplomats charged with protecting their citizens were not immune to the danger. On March 20, 1959, the Nepali consul general, A. B. Basnyat, awoke to the sound of fighting; minutes later he found slugs, glass, and spent metal in his room. He tried to call the Chinese authorities, but the telephone lines had stopped working. There was no way of getting help and little way of knowing who was attacking or why. Basnyat was convinced he had been in the way of PLA troops firing at Tibetans; the Chinese assured him that it could only have been rebels who attacked the consulate, not Chinese soldiers. Basnyat did not press the point—he knew that his country needed a friendly PRC—but he made it clear that he wished to be assured of safety for himself and the people he represented.[8]

But if Nepali diplomats would bear with the chaos in the name of practical politics, the citizens they represented were a different matter. If you were a foreigner in Tibet at the time, you were vulnerable to demands for your money, your support against the communists, or both. In Lhasa, you could find yourself confronted by Tibetans demanding that you join the rebellion; in Kyirong, a wild outpost near the border, where you had gone only so as to be able to provide for your family, you might be cornered by the "people of Xikang"— Khambas from the province that once bore that name—threatening you with dire consequences if you failed to fight. (Your hard-won earnings, presumably, would prove of great help too.) And you had no legal recourse. Until such time as control was restored, the regional authorities could not offer much more than advice that the foreigners respect the laws of the country and not be led astray by bad people.[9] The Foreign Ministry added helpfully that for the present, it would be best to avoid going outside.[10]

These were serious failings: they amounted to nothing less than a breakdown in political order. The Chinese state could no longer guarantee the safety of foreigners within its boundaries. It had invited, even encouraged these foreigners to come to China's Tibet; now, it could no longer enforce the measures needed to keep those foreigners secure. The problem was not simply crime—crime happens all the time. The problem was violent crime without means of governmental redress or protection. There existed a zone now where the state was claiming sovereignty, but where its writ did not reach. And if China could not guarantee Nepali safety, it was perfectly possible that the Nepalis would turn to those who could: the Tibetan rebels. In areas where the PLA was absent or ineffectual, agreeing to help those in charge could seem the safest option.

Local authorities were well aware of this risk. Though there were some foreigners who expressed support for the PLA's activities, the Tibet Foreign Affairs Office warned that others had colluded or had commercial ties with the rebels and reactionary feudals.[11] As PRC authorities tried to restore order, foreigners got caught up in the flood of arrests—and they were difficult to keep track of. By 1960, Nepal and India between them had reported 139 nationals in Chinese prisons: 104 Nepalis and 35 Indians. These numbers were by no means exact. The Tibet Foreign Affairs Office grumbled that the Nepali list was full of repetitions and the PRC, unlike India, did not believe that people from Ladakh, Sikkim, and Kashmir were Indian nationals. But whatever the numbers, everyone acknowledged that there were foreigners in the mix of prisoners. Some people simply disappeared into the system, with the officials reporting that because their location had changed, they could not investigate their situations promptly.[12] But some were located, and their tales can be found in the archives—fascinating glimpses both of Tibet's cosmopolitanism and the problems that cosmopolitanism created for the PRC:

Qiangba Luozhuo, male, 33, was a Nepali hunxue'er [Chinese for mixed blood, meaning, in this case, the child of a Nepali-Tibetan marriage] born in Lhasa; has already chosen Nepali citizenship; became a lama in Sela Monastery. . . . Principal crimes are: On February 4 and 9, 1959, participated twice in the Kham Hamlet Rebellion Conference; sent lamas to the rebel commander to receive guns . . . curses our party.

A Wang Jinba, male, 24, of Sikkim, came to Ke Monastery in Yadong in 1941 to become a senior monk; came to Lhasa in 1942 to become a senior monk at Sela Monastery. Principal crimes are: during the rebellion, he spread great rumors, schemed intensely to help the rebellion. As a "senior monk" gave the bandits 600 protective icons and encouraged them saying, "Opposing the Communist Party is an important matter; to sacrifice is to be honored" etcetera etcetera. . . .

Jianceng, male, Nepali, came to Tibet in 1954, works in Gyantse in an Indian trader's company Ajunda. Principal crime: stole a bicycle rented out by an Indian trader Babu.[13]

We will return to some of the other prisoners later. But these cases show how Tibet's extensive connections to the outside world made it impossible to treat the chaos as a purely internal affair (no matter how much the authorities wanted to do so). A Sikkimese lama—and a man, his captors acknowledged, of high standing in his community—was giving support to Tibetans considered subjects of China; for religious and political purposes he was Tibetan. Qiangba Luozhuo's very blood showed the difficulty. He was of both Nepal and Tibet. In 1956, Nepali and Chinese officials had agreed that the hunxue'ers could choose nationality when they came of age,[14] but no one bothered to implement this agreement, not least because no one knew where to start. Until 1959, when the crisis suddenly brought Qiangba Luozhuo to the attention of authorities, he would never have been told to choose who he was one way or another. Citizenship had not been something lived in this part of the world; one moved as easily between identities as one did through the mountain passes. The coming of the CCP in the early fifties had done little to change that.[15] When trade, pilgrimage, and travel were going smoothly, there was no rush to ask questions about national identity.

As violence came and people sought to leave Tibet, however, those questions became inevitable. Just who was leaving and why? Not all the foreigners were as foreign as they seemed. A resident could register as a Tibetan with Chinese authorities, thereby claiming Chinese citizenship and all the benefits that went with it—a work permit and schooling for children, for example. But that same citizen could then apply to the Nepali consulate for a passport, demanding the right to return home—and the protection due to a Nepali citizen.[16] Even if one's credentials as a Nepali pure and true could be established beyond doubt, there remained the question of what prompted departure. Some foreigners, authorities admitted, genuinely wanted to return home; others, however, had committed "unlawful activities" and were now seeking to escape retribution.[17]

It is impossible to know just how many people were forced to choose between being foreign and Chinese. The officials themselves were unsure, and this uncertainty was part of what disturbed them. But regardless of the numbers, one thing was certain: the state was going to intrude on people's lives in the most fundamental way. It was going to force people to choose who they were. What that meant was that it was no longer possible to be both Nepali and Tibetan, or to be a citizen of both Sikkim and China. Now was the time to stand up and be counted by a state, to declare your loyalty and the jurisdiction you fell under. When an empire goes heavy, it ceases to be tolerant of those who fall across its frontiers, illegible and undefined.[18] It wants peoples to be categorized and accounted for. And by trying to fit the hunxue'ers into boxes, the PRC was changing what life in the borderlands had meant. People would now have to be part of a state, one state and no more. The imperial structure was no longer one in which you were allowed to contain multiple worlds; you had to be sifted, parsed, and allotted to your proper sphere. Whatever the number of people affected (based on the cable traffic, a few thousand official cases, with many more going undetected, seems a reasonable estimate), policy on the hunxue'ers represented a change in the PRC's preferences on what its borderlands should look like. The rim would no longer be open, messy, and cosmopolitan. A line was being drawn.

If there was a need to divide peoples, there was also a need to agree on a boundary line, to demarcate territories within which Chinese and foreign jurisdictions would apply. It was the need for such agreement that took Zhou Enlai to Nepal, and his trip brings us to the story of one of the most fascinating border crossers of all: Ma Tengbiao, a Tibetan turned Guomindang spy.

Spies in Kathmandu

Much was riding on Zhou's visit to Kathmandu in 1960. In addition to reassuring the Nepalis that all would be well in Tibet (important to keep them from joining Tibetan forces and important to keeping face), Zhou wanted a border agreement with his neighbor. The border dispute was not a particularly tangled one. Both sides claimed Everest and there were a few disputed sectors, but by and large, there was an easily recognized customary dividing line to serve as boundary. Neither side would lose much by compromising. At stake, however, were domestic politics. The Nepali prime minister,

B. P. Koirala, had visited Beijing earlier in the year and had agreed on the general outlines of a solution: set up a boundary commission to decide on the sectors and claim sovereignty over different slopes of Everest (China would get the northern slope and Nepal the southern one). But a final agreement had yet to be signed. Koirala, so he claimed, needed a little time to carry domestic opinion with him.[19]

Zhou had two main goals for his visit: a pact to govern relations while a solution to the border question was pending (which he got) and a formal agreement on the Everest proposal (which he did not).[20] Border issues aside, there was a larger objective. China needed to send the world a message: it was still committed to the five principles of peaceful coexistence. A successful visit to Nepal—especially given the festering dispute with India and the criticism of Chinese conduct in Tibet—would show China as a peaceful and responsible third world country.[21]

Nepal was not the easiest country to woo at the time. Many Nepalis felt a genuine concern for the Tibetan plight; some politicians talked of an alliance with India to counter a potential Chinese threat.[22] Wedged as it was between two enormous Asian powers, however, Kathmandu had good reason to pacify Beijing. Shrewd balance-of-power politics demanded playing China and India off against one another.[23] It would be helpful to have the border issue resolved, especially since Beijing seemed willing to compromise. Besides, there was money to be had. Koirala was not a man easily embarrassed; he brought up the subject of aid in his talks with Zhou in Beijing and detailed how much he was expecting from the United States, the USSR, and India. Zhou returned that while China would help insofar as it could, it was not going to try to exceed what Koirala's other benefactors had to offer.

"Why not exceed India?" Koirala said.

"You understand," said Zhou, "we're not competing with them."

"It should," declared Koirala, "be the same as the Indian amount."[24] He could make such demands of all the players in the Cold War—for his was a country that was very small, very poor, and, all of a sudden, very important.

But perhaps the most fascinating economic interest inclining Nepal toward cooperation with China was its eagerness to learn from the PRC's commune system. It is difficult to fathom this in hindsight, when Mao's economic planning is ridiculed widely, but during the fifties and sixties, many in the third world saw China's as the way of the future. Communes, adapted to the needs of their own countries, would lift their populations out of poverty. States as different as Cuba and India sent representatives to Beijing for guidance on how the new system worked. Nepal shared this admiration. The Nepali consul general in Lhasa, expressing his goodwill toward the Chinese, explained that the communes had made a deep impression on him and that he believed the system suitable for Asian countries.[25] Learning how to adapt the communes to Nepali conditions merited improving relations with Beijing.

Zhou's visit, then, offered an opportunity for China and Nepal to set their relations on a better footing. For those not particularly fond of the PRC, the visit also offered an opportunity—as a target for disruption or worse. It was the Chinese embassy in India that first warned Beijing of danger. An embassy is a government outpost that can spy with diplomatic immunity. Admittedly, much of its spying—and this is true of that dark craft in general[26]—is rather straightforward. Many of the Chinese embassy's reports from New Delhi, for example, concerned Indian calls for closer ties with the Soviet Union, debates within the parliament, and the strange workings of the Indian economy. These were certainly important issues, but collecting intelligence about them proved a mundane task; for the most part, it involved little more than a careful reading of Indian newspapers.

Occasionally, however, an embassy can bring off a real intelligence coup: the discovery of truly vital information that could not be obtained but for extraordinary luck and well-connected sources. Such was the case in 1960, when a source within the Nepali Communist Party informed the Chinese embassy in New Delhi that a Tibetan named Ma Tengbiao was cooperating with Taiwan.[27] At the time, the Communist Party in Nepal was beginning to split into opposing factions, some favoring the Soviet Union and others China[28]—so it must have been gratifying to Beijing to know that it could count on some support in times of need. (Later, as Sino-Indian tensions rose, Chinese officials would fear Indian attempts to use a faction within the Nepali Communist Party to damage Sino-Nepali relations.)[29] The source identified Ma Tengbiao as "one of the chieftains of the Guomindang in Nepal." Like many people in this part of the world, Ma was a man who went by many names: he was Lokchung Tinglai to the Nepalis and Kaku to his family. He came from Qinghai, that wild, rebellious province where China rises into the Tibetan plateau and agriculture gives way to the nomadic life of Tibetans, Kazakhs, and Mongols.[30] The place meant—and still means—danger for China; it was in Qinghai that America had dropped weapons and supplies for Tibetan rebels, and it was Qinghai that had provided many Tibetan recruits for the CIA.[31] Ma attended the Beijing Nationalities University, an experience that might have gone some way in awakening a sense of ethnic identity distinct from China. This might also have been fostered by one of his brothers, who was a monk,[32] for it was through the monasteries that word of Chinese evil traveled.

In Nepal, Ma's activities were many and varied. He got funding from Khambas in India to support Tibetan fighters along the Sino-Nepali border. He had ties with Damodar Prasad, a Nepali politician who helped organize relief funds for Tibetan refugees; some believed he was cooperating with Lokchung Elei, a member of the Mimang Tibetan party, one of the many Tibetan groups fighting communism. Ma was also connected to Wang Shengfu, another man of Qinghai origin (with his name, it seems likely that he was ethnically Hui or Han). Wang had gone to Nepal from India; there he had helped with the work of a Tibetan relief association.[33] These were people whom the official mind of the PRC viewed with deep suspicion, not least because men like Prasad were trying to bring the Dalai Lama, the rebellious Khambas, and the Guomindang together.[34] They represented an attempt at consolidating forces ranged against China.

In Nepal, Ma also met a Muslim from China named Ismail. Ismail's origins are uncertain. One report identifies him as being from Xinjiang;[35] another dispatch claims he was from Gansu;[36] he might well have hailed from either of those two provinces or from Qinghai, which has a large Muslim population. (He could also have been a Tibetan Muslim.) Ismail had been on China's officially approved Hajj list, heading for Mecca in 1958. He decamped and disappeared into India, before appearing in Nepal, where he and Ma decided to work for the "Guomindang in Tibet" with "propaganda opposed to the PRC."[37]

The links between the Guomindang and Tibetan rebels remain almost completely unstudied by historians; for a long time, there was doubt about whether or not those links existed, though official Chinese histories are adamant about them.[38] The intelligence reports from Beijing, coupled with sources from Taiwan, show that the Guomindang-Tibetan relationship was real, even if the partners often found themselves at cross-purposes. In Taiwan, the defeated Nationalist leader Chiang Kai-shek had been dreaming of taking back the mainland. The Tibetan uprisings, as Chiang saw them, were the first steps toward the fulfillment of that dream. The Communists now faced armed opposition on the mainland; he, Chiang, would support it as best he could, delivering statements and possibly weapons.[39] The Americans were unwilling to help with the weapon delivery plans Taiwan formulated[40]—an unwillingness that caused Chiang considerable annoyance; much of his diary is taken up with complaints about how unreasonable Americans refuse to help with good anticommunist activities.[41] But even in the absence of American help, Chiang remained hopeful about the prospects of Tibetan unrest. When the Communists took control of Lhasa, he pondered the rumors of surviving resistance on the eastern rim of the Tibetan plateau: despite the Dalai Lama fleeing to India, he concluded there was hope while rebellion lasted in Qinghai and Xikang.[42] As late as November 1960, Chiang saw Tibet as a beachhead for an anticommunist revolution. His grand plan seems to have involved developing resistance in the Kham areas, coupling it with Guomindang special forces in Southeast Asian regions bordering China, and eventually bringing the mainland back under Guomindang control.[43]

There was a difference here, of course, between what various Tibetans were fighting for and what Chiang was supporting. The uprising had a multitude of causes—money, ethnic tension, religion—but Tibetans, by and large, appear to have wanted some version of freedom from China. Chiang, by contrast, though giving lip service to self-determination, wanted all of China—including Tibet—back under his control. It was ROC delegates, as the previous chapter showed, who defeated calls for resolutions supporting Tibetan independence both at the UN and at the Afro-Asian Convention on Tibet. Chiang himself was careful to emphasize that the Tibetan uprising was against communism, not China. As he saw it, different Chinese ethnicities should help one another out:[44] hence his support for the Tibetan struggle. Once Tibet had helped defeat the Communists, he promised, Tibet would be granted "self-determination"—a promise Tibetans had heard before. The operating assumption Chiang's diaries reveal about the Tibetans is that the Guomindang would return to rule them—benevolent, noncommunist rule to be sure, but rule nonetheless. More than most leaders, Chiang Kai-shek knew how to remain ambitious in defeat.

If American intransigence scuppered the plans to get weapons to Tibetan fighters, other schemes were more successful. Chiang appealed to Chinese in Taiwan and abroad to support their Tibetan compatriots; *huaqiao* (overseas Chinese) who could provide relief funds were identified and money channeled—with very haphazard accounting—to Tibetans in India. Such relationships could provide valuable intelligence: Chinese living in India could report on the needs and dispositions of Tibetans in exile. One such list came from a Chinese compatriot in Kalimpong, identifying the main staff of the Tibetan resistance in Nepal. Among others named was Wang Shengfu, Ma Tengbiao's friend affiliated with the Tibetan relief efforts.[45] (The PRC, let it be acknowledged, was not bad at gathering intelligence; its spies had connected Wang with Ma.)

Chiang placed enormous emphasis on the propaganda effort. His writings were to be distributed among the Tibetans[46]—and it was here that Ma and Ismail were most useful. The two distributed Taiwanese pamphlets against land reform among Tibetans in Nepal, translated, curiously, into Nepali.[47] The pamphlets had blunt titles: "People's life under the communes," "Face to face with the communes," "What are people's communes?" They shared a general preface that began with a quotation ascribed to Lenin: "To control a person, you must control that person's stomach." The communes, the preface went on to argue, were a way of controlling people by controlling their stomachs—not quite how the Communists pitched the idea—which had brought unprecedented calamity on China and would have a "disadvantageous influence" on humanity at large. Some of the writing was devoted to philosophical assaults on the problems and contradictions (communists did not have a monopoly on the word even then) of the commune system, but perhaps the most powerful pieces are dispatches and letters from those who had experienced communes firsthand or had relatives living on them: "Since . . . the communes were established, the situation has become increasingly pinched. Fish, meat, dim sum—people have money, but cannot buy it. Even a grain of food, a little pastry cannot be seen—but the production is so much greater than before. Where has it all been taken? No one knows. . . . My spirits are vexed; my tale cannot be told in one go."[48]

Such tales from the communes were important assaults in the struggle against the mainland. It was not just that they discredited China's efforts at agrarian reform when the rest of the world was watching (though the loss of face was bad enough, especially at a time when the PRC was trying to establish ideological credibility in the face of the Sino-Soviet split). The deeper danger was more practical. Ideas traveled easily across the mountains; tales going around Kathmandu could make their way to Dingri or Lhasa. And in Tibet, land reform was seen as the key to pacification. One of the main problems in Tibet, as PRC officials on the ground saw it, was feudalism and land mismanagement; by June, 1959, they were taking steps toward land reform in Tibet. Many Tibetans, alienated by the poverty imposed on them, the officials believed, could be won over. Eventual land reform was therefore crucial to putting down the rebellion.[49] Such reform would go more smoothly if the Tibetans were convinced it was in their own best interests. But how could that be done when Ma Tengbiao and his like were circulating horror stories about land communes? The more credence such stories gained, the harder it would be for the PRC to establish full control over Tibet.

The pamphlets would have deepened the PRC's impression of an arc of insecurity stretching from its east to west. The pamphlets were printed in Taiwan; the stories told in them were gathered from media outlets in Hong Kong (where the mainland also complained of harassment from Guomindang special forces); now, they were making their way to the Himalayan borderlands. Ideas and their circulation linked China's enemies in a perimeter that seemed to surround the mainland. The perception of such a perimeter would almost certainly have led the PRC to suspect a connection between Ma and the Guomindang agent known as Chou Shu.

We do not know for sure if Ma and Ismail ever met Chou Shu, but it seems likely. All of them had spent time in Calcutta, where, as the PRC later scolded India, Chinese sympathetic to the "Jiang clique" gathered[50]—just the sort of place where a Taiwanese special agent might recruit a dispossessed Tibetan. We know even less of Chou than we do of Ma: only that she was married to a Guomindang special agent in Calcutta; that she was originally from Jiangsu and aged forty-four in 1960; that she was suspected of involvement with "American-Jiang special forces," and that she had extensive ties to the Tibetan resistance movements. Just before Zhou was due to fly to Kathmandu, Chou Shu arrived there herself in the company of an American named Backman. Backman is a mysterious character who does not appear in any archival record; he might have been one of the CIA handlers who sometimes accompanied agents of Chinese descent to Tibetan resistance strongholds.[51]

The precise nature of the threat that PRC intelligence apprehended from all this was left unclear. But Zhou had already survived one suspicious accident; his was one of the few lives that no one in China was taking any chances with. Given past experience, given how many Tibetans were making their way to Kathmandu, and given how dangerous they could be, extreme caution was necessary. The following note, therefore, was dispatched to the Nepali foreign secretary on April 23:

> The Chinese government has the pleasure to learn that the Government of the Kingdom of Nepal and Prime Minister Koirala show grave concern at the safety of Premier Chou En-lai and his party who are coming to pay another visit to Nepal, and are making arrangements in advance. The Chinese government is deeply grateful for all these.
>
> According to reliable informations received by the Chinese government from Taiwan, the Taiwan special agent organ, on

learning the news of Premier Chou En-lai's visit to Burma, India, and Nepal, immediately plots in all quarters for scheming activities to inflict harm on Premier Chou En-lai and his entourage. Since the close friendship between China and Nepal is further developed after Prime Minister Koirala's visit to China, Taiwan special agent organ is all the more anxious to collude with other hostile elements and to exploit every opportunity for carrying on sabotage. The Chinese government is confident that the Government of the Kingdom of Nepal has the same eager desire as we do to smash the disruptive scheme of Taiwan special agents. In order to facilitate the government of the Kingdom of Nepal to take suitable measures, the Chinese Government wishes to intimate His Excellency the Prime Minister the following relevant informations obtained:-

The Taiwan special agent organ has decided to carry on vigorously scheming activities during Premier Chou En-lai's visit to Nepal in case their conspiracy of inflicting harm on Chinese Premier and his entourage fails in Burma and India. For this purpose, Taiwan quarters have recently given secret orders to Lokchung Tinglai (alias Ma Teng-piao, a Tibetan from Tsinghai, China), the special-agent-in-charge, who is now at Kathmandu to organize and buy off a number of Tibetan rebels who fled into Nepal and other hostile elements to carry on activities of inflicting harm. It is learn that following the acceptance of the above mentioned mission, Lokchung Tinglai has made contacts with Ismail (alias Min Wen-liang, a Hui national from Kansu, China), another Taiwan special agent at Kathmandu, and Tibetan rebels, such as, Anima, Lokchiungggeli, etc., and have gone respectively to the monasteries at Syambhu, Boukh, Bhodaheti, etc., where Tibetan rebels concentrate at to actively engineer disruptive activities. At the same time, the Taiwan special agent organ adopts a "detour" tactics by sending a number of special agents from Calcutta, Kalimpong and Darjeeling in India to Kathmandu under the name of touring, visiting, lecturing, surveying or calling on families and relatives etc. to arrange disruptive activities. Among them, there is one woman special agent of Taiwan, named Chou Shu, who, by order, flew from Calcutta to Kathmandu in company with an American, named A. H. Backman, in early April. Because she has a very close relation with Tibetan rebels such as Gyalop Tenchu and others, and has years of experience in the work of special agent, Taiwan special agent organ asks her to play an important role in these disruptive activities.

The Chinese Government request the Government of the Kingdom of Nepal to keep the above informations furnished by the Chinese Government highly confidential while taking measures so as not to make the special agents aware. The Chinese Government shall be grateful for the friendly assistance rendered by the Government of the Kingdom of Nepal.[52]

Perhaps the most interesting thing about this message is that it was written at all. Beijing was relying on Kathmandu to keep the information confidential—a gamble, given where the Sino-Nepali relationship stood at the time, but one worth taking. Of all the relations that exist between governments, intelligence sharing is one of the most intimate. Beijing had obtained information from a faction in the Nepali body politic; it had pieced that information together with other signals and was now sharing the full picture with the Nepali government. It was not quite a border agreement, but it was a step toward something approaching trust.

At this point, Ma's trail goes cold and the historian is brought to a frustrating halt. None of the available sources in Beijing or Taiwan tell us what became of him, Ismail, or Chou Shu. Perhaps there never was a threat to Zhou Enlai, and PRC officials were simply taking precautions. Perhaps the agents examined the security arrangements in place for Zhou's visit and decided their plans were too risky. Or perhaps Nepali officials dealt with the threat as Beijing had hoped they would—quietly, effectively, leaving no trace. We simply do not know. And before accusing the Chinese intelligence and diplomacy apparatus of paranoia, we should remember that they did not know either. After the fact, the threat might seem exaggerated or immaterial. But before the visit, the PRC had no way of knowing just how serious the risk was. They based their measures on an assumption of the worst. Given what they knew before Zhou left Nepal safely, this was prudent. Sound intelligence collection and analysis had informed diplomacy.[53]

And what of Zhou's visit? As these things go, it went reasonably well. He was feted; he was lauded; he had done much better, the Chinese were told, than Jawaharlal Nehru had on his trip to Nepal.[54] Later, Nepali officials informed their Chinese counterparts that there had indeed been a Tibetan threat—that there were people who had planned to insult Zhou by raising a black flag when he came; that more than a hundred Khambas had planned to storm the airport; that Tibetan bandits had mysterious links with the American embassy—that all these plans had been foiled only by the quick thinking and commitment of Nepali security (even when it involved being diplomatically impolite enough to station an observation vehicle equipped with bright lights in front of the American embassy).[55] In protecting Zhou Enlai from harm, Nepali officialdom had been second to none.

The talks with Koirala had been slightly more complicated. Koirala had given Zhou a long lecture on how Everest was clearly Nepali based on its name; at one point, Zhou, interrupted in his response, was compelled to point out that he had not finished speaking. Eventually, Koirala returned to the position he had taken in Beijing. He was willing to agree to a solution based on Chinese sovereignty over the northern slope and Nepali sovereignty over the south, with the boundary line running across the peak. But he needed time to carry public opinion with him. Given the picture he sketched of Nepali opposition parties (one the Chinese concurred in) who would accuse him of being a false democrat and a false patriot, Zhou was more than willing to be patient.[56]

What Zhou did get was an agreement to negotiate the border amicably. One of the provisions of this agreement was that both countries' troops would maintain a distance of twenty kilometers from the disputed boundary.[57] It was a marvelous agreement, reached despite Indian pressure on the Nepalis to avoid it, one which stood as a symbol of China's peaceful intentions. It was one that Zhou would soon regret.

Somewhere along the Line

Somewhere in the Tibetan borderlands at some point in June 1960, PLA troops opened fire on a group of men. One died; the others were seized and their property confiscated. It was an excellent

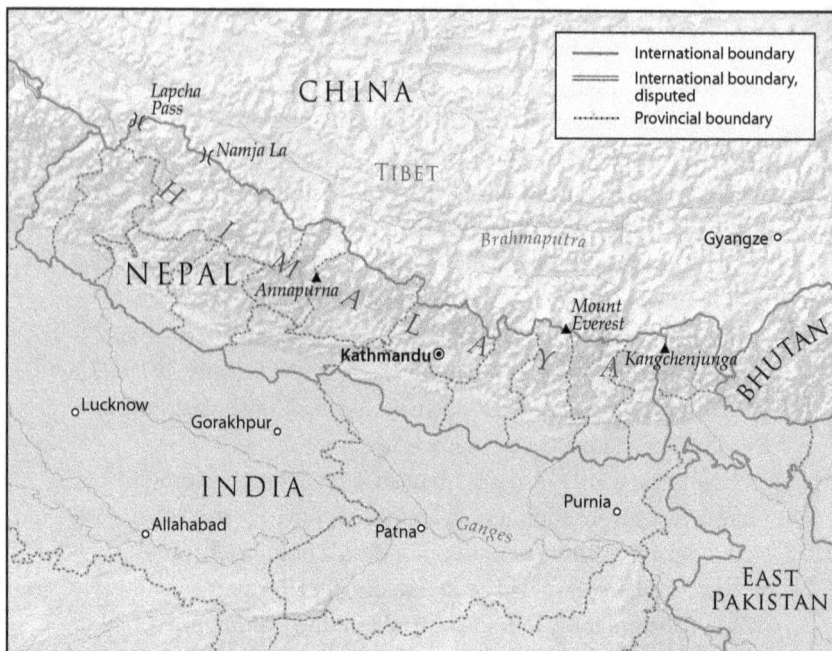

Map 4. The Sino-Nepali border. Note that the boundary follows the Himalayas, with Everest's slopes divided between the two countries as Zhou proposed. The map does not—and could not—show all the passes that people would have used to travel, and the terrain was harder to police than any map could truly indicate. Drawing a line was the easy part; recognizing it when one approached it was much harder.

counterinsurgency operation, except for one thing: those attacked were Nepalis. And in encountering them, the PLA might have crossed into Nepali territory.

We do not know just when or how Zhou found out about the incident, but he made a point of acting on it before the Nepalis came to protest.[58] On June 30, 1960, the Foreign Ministry in Beijing sent a message for Nepal to its embassy in India and the Tibet Foreign Affairs Office. The Chinese government had received information that PLA troops had encountered and killed Nepalis on the Sino-Nepali border. The Chinese government was paying exceptionally close attention to the situation and would investigate the truth on the ground. Once it knew what had happened, it would let Nepal know. Ambassador Pan when delivering the message impressed on the Nepali ambassador that the Chinese had been paying all due attention to the incident *before* the Nepalis lodged a complaint.[59] Such attentiveness was meant to prove that China took the matter seriously. It would show all the goodwill it could.

The first problem was ascertaining just where the blood had been shed. On June 29, Koirala sent a letter to Zhou through Pan (the letter was delivered at seven in the evening and would not be read until the next day; hence the claim on June 30 that the Chinese had started addressing the matter before Nepal protested). Chinese troops, according to Koirala, had crossed into the Nepali territory of Mustang, where they had killed some Nepalis, captured others, and taken the goods and horses of private citizens. Koirala's letter had all the heat and indignation such behavior should occasion; he observed that the border pact had been violated and demanded compensation, the release of Nepali prisoners, and the return of their property.[60] Pan, however, refused to believe that Chinese troops would cross the border. Perhaps Tibetan bandits had done this and called themselves Chinese troops, he suggested to the Nepali ambassador. How could the Nepalis be *sure* that Chinese troops were responsible?[61] It was a neat position of defense, for how could anyone be sure of anything that happened in the Himalayas? State weakness could be useful after all.

Zhou then wrote to Koirala with the results of the Chinese investigation. Based on the report sent in by Ali's defense troops, Zhou maintained that the incident had taken place in Chinese territory. PLA troops that had gone to deal with Tibetan rebels had discovered people approaching them, about one kilometer north of Keli Mountain. Mistaking them for the enemy, the PLA troops opened fire, killing one person and imprisoning ten others (one of whom had been wounded). Only afterward was it discovered that the attacked were Nepalis, not Tibetans. The incident, Zhou was careful to point out, had taken place north of Keli Mountain, north of the customary line between Nepal and China—and therefore not in Mustang, and certainly not in Nepali territory. The Chinese authorities responsible had been ordered to return the prisoners, the corpse, and the seized property, but the incident had taken place on Chinese soil.

Nevertheless, China was willing to consider Nepal's demands for compensation.[62]

It is difficult, if not impossible, to be sure which location is correct, but the Nepali ambassador to India asked a good question: Why would Nepal, knowing it was a small, vulnerable country, march onto Chinese turf?[63] The Nepali soldiers could, of course, have made an honest mistake, but it seems strange that they would not have attempted to identify themselves when they saw PLA units. It is much more likely that PLA troops in pursuit of Tibetan enemies blundered across the border without realizing it, then opened fire on the first group of armed men they saw. For threats did lurk in Nepali territory. As early as 1959, Tibetans who had fled to Nepal could cross back and forth, armed with guns, menacing CCP control of towns like Nyalamu. Such crossings inevitably meant a buildup of troops and concomitant border tensions: when the CCP increased the number of soldiers stationed in Nyalamu, Nepal increased the number of troops it had stationed across the line.[64] This was perfectly understandable: given the border dispute and the warnings of Chinese expansionism, Nepal had no way of knowing where and when PLA troops would stop. But Tibetans had triggered this particular escalation; non-state actors were shaping the defense policies of two states.

China continued to perceive a threat from Tibetans in Nepal, both before and after the attack on Nepalis in unknown territory. (It is worth remembering that Ma Tengbiao, Ismail, and Chou Shu had been working well within Nepali territory; their distance from Chinese territory did not make them less worthy of attention.) There is now a small shelf of literature on Tibetan guerrillas in Mustang affiliated with the CIA; the opening of Chinese archives shows something of the intelligence system that kept Beijing aware of the threat. With the appointment of a Chinese ambassador to Nepal, the PRC could gather intelligence on Tibetan activities in that country directly—which it did principally through a careful reading of the press, but also with the occasional tip from the Nepali communists. The reports came streaming in: the Dalai Lama was helping the Khambas; a thousand armed Tibetans in Zhuankala, calling themselves refugees; six thousand on the border altogether, with four thousand of those in Mustang, aided by Indians (this last bit of information was forwarded to military commanders in Xinjiang and Tibet by Chinese intelligence).[65] Military commanders fighting Tibetans in the borderlands added to the intelligence stream. South of the Namuzha mountain pass in Nepali territory were a hundred armed men, joined by "bandits" from India and Sikkim. Some of the rebels launching attacks from Mustang were arrested when a mission into Chinese territory went awry. These people had escaped to Nepal but were now penetrating China's perimeter, armed and angry. Interrogating them, PRC officials learned of at least six hundred armed men in Mustang, with another two hundred from Kalimpong in India. Such information kept trickling in from captured Tibetans and, every so often, from a report from the nomads.[66]

Whether it was exaggerated or not, this news was bound to make the soldiers nervous.[67] In war on the frontier, you did not take chances. It was a hard life; you did not know the place, the passes, and you could wind up dead any moment. It was all very well for Beijing's bureaucrats to send messages about peaceful negotiations and respect for Nepal's border; they were not here, waiting for the next armed group to fall on them, knowing that the Tibetans found the border meaningless—wherever the border might be, for no one knew that either. You had to pursue those forces or else they might kill you—and this was most probably what led the PLA troops into their meeting with the Nepali column.

Wherever the soldiers had been (Zhou and Koirala politely agreed to disagree on this), they had come within twenty kilometers of the border, thereby violating the agreement Zhou had championed in Kathmandu. Zhou pointed out that the PLA had had to advance to this zone to deal with the Tibetans and claimed that the Nepalis had been warned of this approach on June 26. Once the security issues were resolved, the PLA would withdraw. Conciliatory as ever, the Chinese premier called for direct communications and an early start to the working of the joint boundary commission.[68] Koirala was not exactly thrilled with this response—but he did not cut off communication altogether. He contented himself with demanding that he receive notification when PLA troops had to fight Tibetans within the twenty-kilometer zone and suggested that the border commission meet in Kathmandu during the first week of August. Zhou closed the exchanges by noting that PLA troops had now withdrawn.[69]

For all the displays of anger in the correspondence, both sides had worked hard to defuse the situation almost immediately. Zhou's proposal of compensation aimed to calm tempers. The Nepalis, for their part, told Pan that they did not mind the Chinese approaching the border; they understood that the Tibetans were a threat. All they asked was advance notification; they might even be able to help. Nepal, the diplomats explained, did not want to give people an excuse to say that China was violating its agreements.[70] Part of this was realpolitik—one did not want to alienate Beijing regardless of how one felt about the Tibetans—but part of it was also that Nepal too saw the Tibetans as a security problem. In 1961, for example, the Nepali defense secretary would notify the Chinese ambassador that Nepali troops would be in the border area—to deal with Khambas linked to the Indians.[71]

This was a surprising turn of events: Tibetans, by endangering Sino-Nepali friendship, had triggered diplomacy that would bring the two countries closer to one another. It could all have turned out very differently. The border incident could have undone the entire accord and reversed the gains made by Zhou's visit. China could have pursued a much more aggressive policy in eliminating Tibetans, thereby alienating Kathmandu. Another leader—Jawaharlal Nehru comes to mind—could have been less willing to pursue a boundary settlement and might thus have signaled a different set of intentions to Beijing.[72] Under any of these circumstances, the Sino-Nepali relationship would have taken a far less amiable turn than the one it did. The border crossers forced distant governments to deal with the problems they created, but they did not cause the response to be set in stone.

It is unlikely that Koirala would have done much to alter the course of Sino-Nepali relations. Despite his fiery rhetoric on Everest, he appears to have been intent on sealing the border agreement, and it was presumably on his orders that his ambassador told Pan that Nepal might help China against Tibetan fighters. As it was, he did not get the chance to do much either to facilitate or impede a border agreement. In one of those sudden twists characteristic of

Nepali politics, the Nepali king dismissed Koirala's government in December 1960. The king, however, was well disposed toward the PRC; even though he had heard of the border incident while traveling abroad, he had been, so he said, sympathetic to the Chinese explanation.[73] The border commission's work went smoothly and the boundary was demarcated, with a treaty finally signed in 1961. Koirala, after imprisonment, disappeared into exile, accused, darkly, of being an Indian spy.

Line of Empire

The fourth world, then, that mélange of non-state actors, had a powerful impact on the foreign policy of the PRC. The movements of the border crossers exposed state weakness, not least by triggering unpredictable responses from local authorities distant from the capital. Beijing had been unable to stop Dingri from sending propaganda agents even though this undermined official Chinese policy. It had been unable to stop its soldiers from attacking Nepalis (though it could make belated compensation). It had been unable to tell who its citizens were, and it had been unable to protect foreigners on legal pass. It had been unable to stop enemies of the state finding safe haven across the border and making common cause with a rival government. The fourth world showed that even as large a third world country as China had a way to go before it became fully sovereign. In the Tibetan borderlands, the PRC found itself a weak state indeed—at least until 1961, when it began to cement its control over Tibet.

The PRC responded to the problem with state-building. A troop surge was part of this, as was a rapidly developed intelligence system. But equally important was a policy of exclusion.[74] Beijing made the decision to exclude certain peoples and certain territory from its jurisdiction. Foreign prisoners, provided they had done nothing too heinous and had acknowledged how well they were treated by the Chinese, could count on eventually being escorted to the border, shoved into their own countries, and being asked not to return unless on legal pass for trade or pilgrimage. The hunxue'ers who lived in the Tibetan borderlands had to give up part of who they were, so that the state could decide whether it was responsible for them or not. The demarcation of the border meant that there was a realm within which the PRC would exercise its growing strength—and conversely, that there was a realm in which it would not.

Related to this was a policy of delegation. Certain moves would be left to Nepal. South of the line it would fall to Nepal to deal with the Tibetans however it saw fit. Barring the strange events of June 1960, there would be no PRC incursions into Nepali territory (or if there were, both sides worked very hard to keep them quiet). Nepal would pay due attention to the activities of the Tibetans and make sure they did not use their newfound refuge as a base for attacking the PRC. This worked astonishingly well. In 1963, the Nepalis would try to interest the PRC in joint operations against Tibetans who had gone from Nepal to India, then returned and killed Nepali soldiers. The Tibetans were suspected of acting at the behest of the Indian army. The PRC would turn the Nepali request down politely,[75] but that the idea was raised at all showed how far Sino-Nepali relations had come since 1959. The end of empire-lite was bound to alter China's relations with its neighbors, but, as the Sino-Nepali relationship shows, the change could be for the better.

Improved relations with Nepal opened up broader possibilities for Chinese diplomacy. With Kathmandu on its side, Beijing could still claim to stand for the five principles and champion the cause of the third world, even as its relations with India turned sour. New Delhi had been less pliable, less open to negotiation on the issues state weakness raised. And as New Delhi threatened to cut off trade to Tibet, the official mind turned to a road from Lhasa to Kathmandu. The economy of the Tibetan borderlands would no longer be vulnerable to threats of an Indian embargo.[76]

In 1961, the three men from Dingri were released. Two of them made their way back home.[77] But the place they returned to was different from the one they had left behind. What does it mean to live in an empire that is hardening? The question is not one that historians of imperialism often ask. This is a pity, for it is the changing lives and experiences of people that constitute the changes in the larger polity to which they belong. In the Tibetan borderlands, the range of identities one person could encompass was narrowing. The ease with which one moved across national boundaries was lost; police and troops on both sides made the passage harder. All this spoke of a changing China. The PRC was drawing a thicker, darker line of definition around itself.

But though the border crossings diminished, they never ceased altogether—and as the PRC sought to exploit the gains of its new relationship with Nepal, more people would move. To the desperate and the determined, no boundary is impermeable.

Muslim, Trader, Nomad, Spy

The Sino-Indian Frontier

The Market in the Mountains

As quietly and as suddenly as wild mushrooms do by night, a market had emerged at Wure. First there was nothing; then it had been there for a year, with merchants from India and Tibet flocking in to do business. They traded what people always had along Himalayan frontiers: the Indians brought in grain and brown sugar, while the Tibetans supplied them with wool (the finest cashmere in the world comes from the Tibetan plateau). When Suonan Daji, an official of the Ali Prefecture's branch of the Chinese People's Political Consultative Conference, visited the market in 1962, there were some forty-four Indian trading houses and sixty Tibetan ones.[1] Wure lay in disputed territory: though the Chinese claimed it, it fell beyond their actual line of control and was under Indian administration at the time. But the arguments over sovereignty had done little commercial harm. Business was flourishing and the border peoples were satisfied. There had been just one hint of trouble.

That hint had come when Indian officials started hindering the trade. The masses governed by Suonan Daji were displeased by this, so he went to Wure to negotiate. To the Indian officials who had "invaded" Wure—this was the term the Tibet Foreign Affairs Office used—Suonan Daji gave a gift: wool from four sheep. Then, on behalf of the masses whom he governed, he expressed the wish that the Indian traders would start coming earlier (like most Himalayan markets, this one was seasonal, with people starting business only after the first melting of snow had made traffic permissible) and bring more goods when they came. The Indian officials bade him that they would tell the government. If bilateral relations between Beijing and New Delhi were good, their message went, there would be no problem in doing business.

"The masses can come themselves," said Suonan Daji. In his calculations, there was neither Beijing nor New Delhi, neither border dispute nor high politics, only the needs of the people he governed. His mind was racing ahead: he saw an entrepôt where the border peoples could participate in a thriving economy, all growing richer and happier. "There is no means of controlling them."

"You had best write a written report," said the Indians. ("Write a written report" is redundant, but in the world of officialdom, that was a virtue.)

So Suonan Daji wrote a report addressed to "Nehru and Indian officials." It was not good, he said, to impede the traders the way the Indians had this year—especially those engaged in the traditional exchange of wool for food. "To not let grain be transported to our side," he wrote, "is even worse." He closed with the hope that next year, there would be no hindrance to trade among the border peoples. If the trade did the Indians any harm next year, they should let him and his fellow officials know.[2]

When Suonan Daji informed his superiors of what he had done, they were incensed. India, as the Tibet Foreign Affairs Office read it, was exploiting the masses' need for grain to make Wure a market and thus legalize their occupation of it. Suonan Daji and his fellow officials were told that they must write no more reports; meanwhile, the masses must be educated that they could no longer go to Wure. Another solution would have to be found to their need for grain.[3] Any notion that India had the right to decide what happened in Wure had to be quashed. Indian officials were already acting as though they owned the place, asking Tibetans what brought them there, as if they had the right to determine who came and went. To request permission or assistance of the Indians in Wure implied that they held legitimate authority there—and thus compromised China's claim to sovereignty.

The spontaneity with which the border peoples had created a market in the mountains was typical of the Tibetan borderlands at the time—and so too was the confused alarm which that spontaneity triggered at all levels of the PRC government. As was the case in its conduct on the Sino-Nepali frontier, China's response to the problem marked a transition from empire-lite to empire-heavy. But where Nepal had been a willing if difficult partner, India was altogether different: its refusal to compromise on the border dispute, its perceived assistance to the Tibetans, and its attempts to exploit ethnic tension within Tibet all marked it as a hostile power in the eyes of the PRC. Historians focusing on the negotiations between top-level Chinese and Indian diplomats miss how fundamental the frontier and its peoples were to PRC grand strategy. On the ground in Tibet, PRC officials confronted a flood of non-state actors: nomads moving between alpine grasslands, traders of Indian citizenship integral to the Tibetan economy, hunxue'ers who claimed both Chinese and Indian descent. The Tibetan rebellions had made these actors potentially dangerous, and the rise of Sino-Indian tension meant that the PRC began to see non-state actors as agents of a hostile state. In the past, traders and pilgrims coming from India had been relatively harmless people; indeed, by keeping the local economies functional they had helped governance. But from 1959 onward, PRC officials became ever more convinced that the border crossers were a source of danger. Blundering into disputed areas, they undermined Beijing's territorial claims. They could spy for an increasingly hostile New Delhi, run weapons to Tibetan fighters, or spread rumors among an already discontented and fractious populace that life abroad had more to offer. They could, in short, test state power at its weakest points. In the context of the crises confronting the PRC on its Tibetan frontier, non-state actors moving freely between China and India were a national security problem. Fourth world movements, once unremarked, were now seen through the lens of counterinsurgency and a state-to-state dispute—and thus had a decisive impact on PRC policy.[4]

This chapter tells the stories of some of the people who traveled between China and India, and of the officials who had to decide on how to deal with them. The stories end in hunger—for the non-state actors, by exposing state weakness, caused the PRC to terminate the cross-border trade, thereby cutting off food supplies to the Tibetan plateau. The famine that hit Tibet in 1962 remains deeply misunderstood; it is either conflated with the agricultural policies of the Great Leap Forward or politicized in accounts of Sino-Tibetan relations.[5] Neither view goes far enough in comprehending its causes. The Tibetan famine was not the inevitable result of the PRC's occupation of Tibet (as Tibetan opposition groups maintain), and though disastrous agricultural policies pursued despite warnings of the consequences played a role, there was one more crucial factor which ensured that Tibet went hungry. This was the deliberate decision, in 1962, to terminate the Sino-Indian trade agreement, even though local officials warned that the consequences could be mass starvation and political unrest. Central authorities ignored these reports. That gap between center and periphery, and the decision to let hunger take its course in Tibet, tell us much about the nature of Chinese grand strategy.

But foreign policy starts with intelligence, with the assessment of threats and challenges. Our story begins, therefore, over the disputed border, in the Indian town of Kalimpong.

The Living Buddha and Other Spies

In and of itself, a border dispute is not insurmountable. Reasonable people can disagree over where to draw the line between them; if they sit down to talk it out, willing to compromise and exchange, they can usually solve the problem. Even if the dispute proves intractable, there is no need for it to sour relations: as long as there is sufficient goodwill, one can agree to disagree and leave a final resolution to the future. Such at least was the PRC's view on the matter[6]—and the historical record would seem to bear it out. Give-and-take worked in border negotiations with Burma and Nepal; it would prove fruitful with Pakistan. Even with India, there was little reason, at first, to assume that the dispute could not be settled or that it would flare into violence. The two countries had agreed to shelve the border question since 1954. There were several contested points, but two held particular importance: the western sector of Aksai Chin, which gave the Chinese access from Xinjiang to Tibet, and the eastern sector that now forms the Indian province of Arunachal Pradesh. Even after armed clashes broke out in 1959, there seemed to be hope that the dispute could be resolved peacefully—hope that took Zhou Enlai to New Delhi in 1960. When Zhou suggested a territorial swap in his meeting with Nehru in 1960—Indian recognition of China's right to the western sector in exchange for China relinquishing claims to the eastern sector—Nehru declined.[7] This did not cause the Chinese to abandon the idea of a settlement. Zhou, at a press conference in New Delhi following the failed talks, said that the friendship between the people of China and India was permanent, whereas the border dispute was temporary; the talks, he said, had increased the two sides' understanding of one another. This was not mere rhetoric: Zhou still hoped to reach an amicable settlement with Nehru.[8] As late as 1961, the PRC sought a modus vivendi with India, discussing the border issue at length with R. K. Nehru, India's foreign minister, when he visited Beijing. If only the two sides were willing to keep talking, they could conceivably learn to live with their differences.

A border dispute takes on a very different aspect, however, if it is seen as part of a general pattern of hostility. China's problem with India was not that India was claiming a few hundred square miles intransigently; the problem was that it was doing so while condemning Chinese conduct in Tibet and supporting rebellious Tibetans. This made it "unfriendly" to China, and evidence of that unfriendliness could be found all over India. Some of the evidence was there for all to see, in the newspaper editorials condemning China, or in Indians pasting a picture of Mao on a wall in Bombay and then conducting "wanton insult by throwing tomatoes and rotten eggs at it."[9] But some of it came from human intelligence ("humint," to use the abbreviation of tradecraft), such as the Living Buddha who sought out the Chinese trade office in Kalimpong.

Her name was Sangzheng Duojie Pamu, she was twenty-two years old, and her family was from Gyantse. She was a Living Buddha—a reincarnation of a being who had achieved enlightenment—and one of those Tibetans who felt there was much to be gained by collaboration with the PRC. It was her brother-in-law who first came to the trade office to tell her tale. The story was simple: she had been abducted by Khambas in early 1959, dragged to India through Bhutan against her will, and then—still against

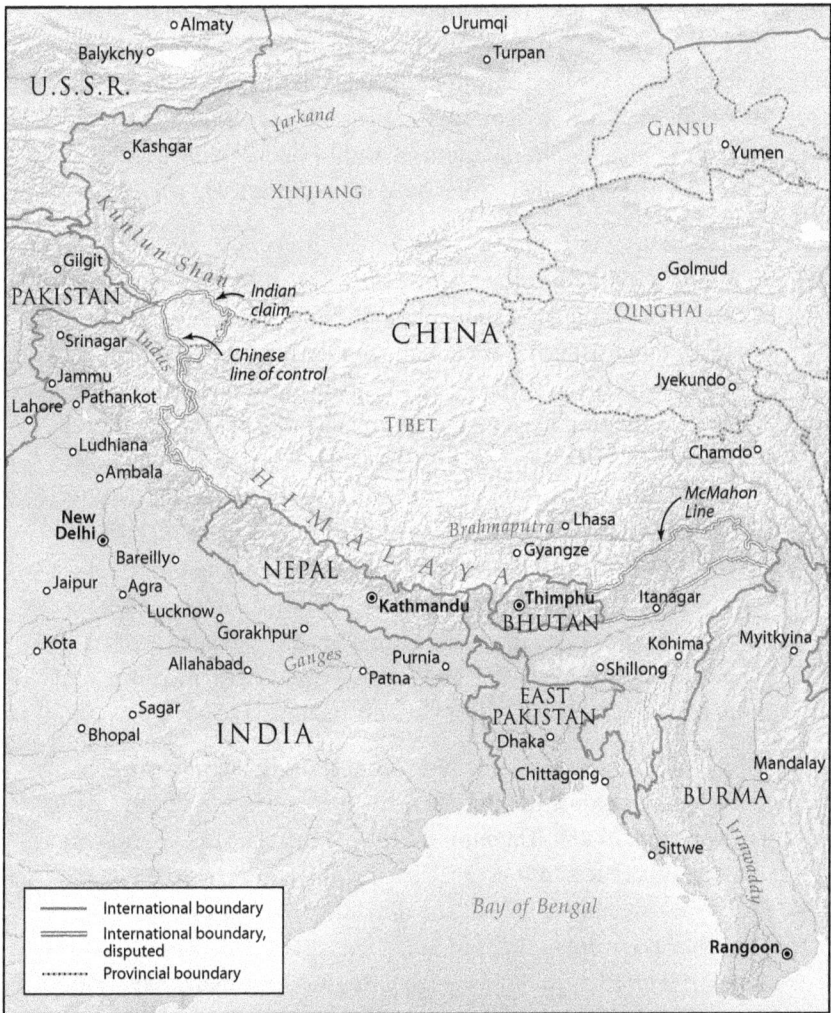

Map 5. The Sino-Indian boundary dispute. The two main contested areas were the western and eastern sectors, though several points in the central sector were disputed as well.

her will—sent to a refugee camp named Buxa. She wanted, so her brother-in-law said, the trade office's help to get back home.[10] Later, Pamu told Chinese officials in India her own story. It is impossible to know how accurate she was—at certain points, one suspects, she was telling her interlocutors what she believed they wanted to hear—but the fear and the loneliness of being forced to leave home ring true:

> In the middle of the second month (by the Tibetan calendar), Khamba reactionaries suddenly burst into my nunnery.... [They] said, you already live in enough comfort, now we should enjoy material happiness. The Khambas made my nunnery a fortification for their war.... [Later] a letter came from one Khamba, said I must leave immediately; the PLA was coming ... and the Dalai Lama had gone to India. I didn't want to go, but under the threats, coercion of the Khamba forces, I did not dare to not go.... We took small, snowy mountain roads over sheer cliffs ... there were times when we encountered narrow roads, narrow channels, which we crossed only by hanging onto the draught animals' tails and passing under their heads and abdomens. My elder sister was already pregnant at the time ... [she] lost the child.[11]

There was a touch of irony in the nun enlisting the support of a communist state against the impoverished Khambas, but the PRC records did not note it. The nun was too interesting. She reported on the Khambas she had seen once she left the border; she had heard there were five hundred, but she did not encounter that many, although there were enough to make her afraid. This was valuable intelligence, but even more valuable was what she had to say about Tibetans in India:

> After we got to Kalimpong, we rented a room to live in. Often, Indians and Khambas or Tibetans come to my residence. The Indian officials say to me: "Your coming to our India is very right; we welcome you greatly. The Communist Party is terribly bad; our Indian government can help you. The Communist Party will soon flee Tibet. . . ." The Khambas say: "The Communist Party is too bad, oppresses us, we just want to drive them out. Tibet

wants independence, wants to establish an independent country of Tibet. We have the help of the Indian government; America also wants to help us; Britain also wants to help us; furthermore, there is the World Country (meaning the UN) which also wants to help us. The Communist Party just has the one Soviet Union able to help them." [They] also said: "We still want to wage war; Taiwan's Chiang Kai-shek has bombs, America has planes and the atom bomb. We will definitely win. The Communist Party will definitely lose; decidedly, it cannot win." But I did not believe these speeches. . . . [12]

This was information that confirmed the PRC's worst fears: that non-state actors were finding support from states hostile to the PRC. Officially, the Indians were continuing to deny that they were aiding the Tibetan rebels, but here was intelligence, obtained from a well-placed source, that showed Indian officials seeking to undermine Chinese rule over the Tibetan plateau. It is worth emphasizing, since so little is known of PRC intelligence gathering and analysis, that the Chinese authorities in Beijing and Kalimpong did not simply accept Pamu's story; a message was sent to Tibet to see if there were more details on her affiliations and loyalties. The reply was reassuring. She was generally sympathetic to the PRC, had participated in state-organized commissions on Buddhism in Beijing, and had wanted to remain in Beijing to study. When Tibet plunged into chaos in 1959, she had sent emissaries to Lhasa with reports on the situation in her nunnery; apart from making amulets for the rebels (possibly under threat), she had done no harm to the state. [13] The Living Buddha was a source capable of exaggeration, as most sources were, but in essence, the intelligence she was providing could be judged sound: India was providing Tibetan rebels with succor and encouragement in their war against the PRC. As a reward, Pamu was spirited home. Afraid that local Indian authorities might harm or hinder her, Chinese officials made arrangements to bring her to New Delhi and took up the matter of her departure with Indian officials in the capital. She stayed at the embassy before boarding a flight for Afghanistan. [14] From there, she made her way to the Soviet Union, where she stopped off for talks with Soviet leaders, before coming home. There she was welcomed by Mao and Zhou; the premier, she would later recall, congratulated her on returning to "the bosom of the motherland."[15] It was a fancy arrangement for one nun, but good intelligence was hard to come by, and the propaganda value of having a Tibetan return to China was high indeed. In Kalimpong, according to the embassy in India, rumors abounded about how she had made her return. Some said she had gone to Lhasa via Yadong and then followed the Panchen Lama to Beijing; others thought she had gone to China through Pakistan. Her return had caused consternation among both the Tibetan bandits and the Indian government; both Tibetans and Indians were now tightening their control over the Tibetan refugees.[16] The Indian government's attitude confirmed what the PRC had suspected all along: India, like the Tibetan rebels it hosted, was not pleased to see Tibetans working in harmony with the Chinese state.

Pamu's mention of Taiwan was especially interesting, for the PRC was wary of Guomindang activities in India—all the more so because the Indian government seemed to tolerate, even encourage, such activities. The tone for Sino-Indian exchanges on the Guomindang was set in 1960, when Chiang Kai-shek was reelected as president of the Republic of China, and Chinese living in West Bengal organized a celebration. At 7 P.M. on May 20, 1960, about three hundred people gathered for dinner in a church to shout "Ten thousand years to President Chiang." The PRC was infuriated and asked Indian officials to stop the celebration, but the response had been unhelpful. It was a private function, and there was not much that the government could do about it, said an Indian official; later, his superiors explained that while they did not support two Chinas, there was a Taiwan and it had to be dealt with. There had been Chinese living in India well before the revolution that brought the communists to power; it was not for the Indian government to interfere with their thinking. Democracies could not interfere with private gatherings. These explanations carried little weight with the PRC.[17] The incident prompted irate Chinese diplomats to compile a long list (for internal use) of the "Chiang clique's" activities against the PRC in India. The extensive catalog included the "Asian-African Conference on Tibet." Not only had India allowed Chiang clique members from Hong Kong to participate in the conference, but it had also facilitated their meeting with the Dalai Lama.[18]

Links between the Guomindang and Tibetan rebels went undisturbed by Indian officialdom. Before Zhou's visit to India in 1960, PRC intelligence continued to receive information on Chiang special agents in the country who might threaten the premier as he sought to negotiate the border. Bo, a known agent, had flown to Delhi from Hong Kong to participate in a conference on Tibet; he was not to be allowed to the press conferences.[19] The Central Investigation Bureau (CIB) discovered that ROC intelligence had been sending spies to India for over a year. One of them was Huang Mou. Huang Mou had originally lived in Tainan, Taiwan; in March 1959, he had arrived in Calcutta via Hong Kong. Chen Cai, another Chiang special agent, had arrived in Calcutta after passing through Macau. He had been a colonel in Chiang's air force.[20] Finally, there came the news that nine Tibetans had left India for Taiwan, passing through Hong Kong. The CIB believed that they were some of the top rebels who had acted against the PRC.[21] All this was in addition to the usual suspicions that Tibetan rebels in India would try to disrupt the ceremonies surrounding Zhou's visit.[22] Just how much of a risk these Guomindang operations posed to Zhou is unclear, though there was something obsessive about the way in which Chiang followed Zhou the "Bandit's" travels.[23] As we have seen in previous chapters, Chiang did have agents in the subcontinent and hopes that they could combine successfully with the Tibetan rebellion to take back the mainland. Without the benefit of hindsight, PRC intelligence had to assume the worst and plan accordingly; one mistake could have left them a prime minister short. What was clear to the Chinese official mind was that India, for all its reassurances, was a place where agents opposed to the PRC could gather and collaborate with relative impunity.

But perhaps nothing exemplified the link between non-state rebels and the Indian state as neatly as a request the PRC received in July 1961. R. K. Nehru ("Little Nehru," the Chinese called him) approached Ambassador Pan as a "private person" on behalf of a Tibetan named woman named G. N. Taring. Taring, said Nehru, had followed her husband to India some two or three years ago. But she had left behind four children: Nordon, Jigme, Kunsang, and Tenzin Norbu. They were very young (the youngest was Tenzin Norbu at six, while the eldest, Nordon, was only thirteen). The children lived with their aunts, but Taring wanted them home with her. So she begged R. K. Nehru to see if there was some way of getting her children from Tibet to India and he, in turn, asked Ambassador Pan.[24] Perhaps it was simple humanity that moved Pan; whatever the reason, he forwarded the request to the Foreign Ministry.

The answer that came from the Tibet Foreign Affairs Office was uncompromising. G. N. Taring was a criminal who had fled Tibet illegally. In India, she worked for criminals. The aunts' political attitude was uniformly bad; they had been warned to keep a better eye on the children. While it might be possible for Taring to return to Tibet, on no account would the children be sent to her in India. R. K. Nehru, the Foreign Affairs Office said in closing, had no right to raise the matter. The concerned individual should have gone to the embassy directly.[25]

So G. N. Taring did not get her children back, but PRC officials got confirmation that a top-level Indian diplomat would ask a favor on behalf of a Tibetan criminal. R. K. Nehru who in July had come to China on an ostensible mission to work out the border problem, R. K. Nehru who had argued that China had no right to negotiate boundaries with Pakistan because those boundaries were India's to decide on—this same R. K. Nehru was on friendly terms with an enemy of the Chinese state.[26]

A picture was emerging from these details—and it was one that did not cast India in a favorable light. The refusal to accept the territorial swap could be seen not as a disagreement between friends, but as something more sinister, as one more way in which India was unfriendly to the Chinese. And the whispers of Chinese weakness to the very Tibetans the PRC was seeking to conquer suggested Indian aggression. Well before the outbreak of war in 1962, Chinese officials had what they could construe as solid evidence of covert, political warfare waged against them from Indian territory.[27] Non-state actors were receiving state support against the PRC. The danger was all the more pressing because it did not stop at the Indian side of the disputed border. Even as the PRC struggled to assert state authority in Tibet, its efforts were being undercut by Tibetans acting in concert with unfriendly states. Knowing this would cause the PRC to see border crossers as a danger—even though there had been border crossers well before the trouble arose.

Old Rights, New Worries

On November 27, 1961, fourteen nomadic herdsmen of Ladakhi origin entered the grasslands of Seerya. They brought with them some eight hundred cows and goats to pasture. The prefectural authorities of Ali informed them that they needed to sign in and pay a tax for grazing; the chief herdsman countered that they had customary grazing rights in Indian territory. This shocked Ali officials. The herdsmen, they explained, were on what was unquestionably Chinese land. Once this had been explained the nomads backed off, but the problem confronting the PRC on its Tibetan frontier had been defined.[28] Traditional patterns of movement had become tangled inextricably with the Sino-Indian border conflict. Once upon a time nomads crossing the border had just been people in search of pasture for their animals. Now they *could* be agents of Indian territorial expansionism, staking claim to disputed territory.

What made the problem so hard was the almost complete ignorance officials had concerning the fourth world. No one knew just how many nomads there were, only that they had been there for as long as anyone could remember. They came and went with the grass, and since grass pays no heed to the squabbles between states, most of the nomads saw little reason to do so either. Local officials were not blind to the complications. There were, they reported, customary nomads and non-customary nomads, nomads in search of pasture and nomads who had come from India only to do harm to the PRC, nomads who fell within the boundaries China claimed but outside the area it actually controlled. There were nomads who were Chinese by citizenship but who went to India and returned following their customary routes—and no one knew what sort of ideas and political attitudes they might have picked up on their sojourns abroad. One of the reasons they had left in the first place was their failure to understand PRC policy; it was fitting, therefore, to improve their understanding by being gentle with them. But you could not guarantee that they were safe to let in.[29]

It was the classic dilemma of counterinsurgency: to detect and crush real troublemakers without alienating ordinary citizens. How could you tell the traditional nomad from the hired spy, the follower of grass from a government agent subtly claiming more land? You did not want to disrupt traditional patterns of movement unnecessarily; to do so would exacerbate economic difficulty and social unrest. But those patterns posed a threat, for mixed in with nomads moving from pasture to pasture were more malevolent characters, who "clearly . . . are in the service of the Indian reactionaries to conduct an armed provocation and invade our sovereign territory."[30] You wanted to foil Indian conspiracies while winning over the Indian nomads (who might, properly placated, be useful) and preventing an international incident. You wanted your own people to feel welcome in what you told them was their homeland—and yet you were wary of letting them into the enemy's country.

It was a murky, complicated problem—and the measures you adopted reflected that murkiness. You would allow customary nomads in and out, but not tolerate new ones. You would pay careful attention to the nomads who came in, keeping an eye out for subversive tendencies. You would educate your own nomads, encourage them to graze in places deep within Chinese Tibet instead of on the border (where their movements were more likely to take them into contested areas). And you would check everyone stringently.[31] These were measures designed to gather more information—about subjects and neighbors. To someone far from the action, such measures might sound mundane, but the state was weak at the edges, and to strengthen it, you had to do the mundane things properly. These people had to be mapped, accounted for, if you were to be safe. Out here in the borderlands, national security depended not on grand strategic concepts, but on careful police work, on a distinction drawn in time between friend and foe crossing the frontier. Nomadic movements caused the state to attempt to strengthen itself at the edges.[32]

At least one could tell a nomad when one saw one. The hunxue'ers—the people whose ancestors came from both sides of the disputed border (well before there had been a border to dispute)—were even more difficult to parse accurately. As was the case with Sino-Nepali hunxue'ers, these were people with dubious citizenship. Though discussions with India on the subject did not prove quite as amicable as they had with Nepal, the PRC was willing to allow such people, if they could produce suitable proof of their parents' backgrounds, to choose their citizenship. But it was not till 1959 that the choice was thrust on them as an immediate, pressing question. Before the Tibetan uprisings, the hunxue'ers were too far from the day-to-day concerns of the state for anyone to force a choice on them. Only when they were imprisoned on charges of participating in the Tibetan rebellion did the issue of citizenship become important. The key difference between Nepal and India, as PRC officials saw it, was that the latter sought to use the hunxue'ers against the PRC, especially hunxue'ers who were part Indian. One such case was that of Hamite (pronounced Hameed), known to us from a report sent by the Tibet Foreign Affairs Office to the Foreign Ministry in 1961.[33]

Hamite was thirty at the time, a Tibetan Muslim of Kashmiri ancestry. (Tibetan Muslims were a mixed lot at the time—Tibetan by centuries of cultural exchange and intermarriage, but vulnerable to Indian suasion that their true home now lay across the mountains in Kashmir, a place the Tibetan kingdom had once governed.) Hamite had been born in Lhasa. Between 1940 and 1948, he made his way to and from India thrice. In 1948, while the Chinese civil war raged in China proper, Hamite met a former British special agent, Reginald Fox. There were men like Fox all over Asia at the time: servants of the British Empire, at loose ends now that that empire was dissolving, but still in love with the mysterious East and still burning for adventure. Fox had been in the civil service in India; when the Raj ended, he stayed in Asia and went native. He took employment with the Tibetan government and married a Tibetan woman, with whom he had several children. The British would maintain, wearily, that Fox was no longer an employee of Her Majesty's government;[34] the PRC (perhaps understandably) refused to believe this—to them he would always be the *British* special agent Fox. Fox and Hamite ran special operations together for the Tibetan government in Chamdo. From Fox, Hamite learned that important skill: how to work a telegraph machine. Between 1950 and 1953, he put that skill to use for the Tibetan government. In 1959, he took part in the rebellions against the PRC. Most damningly, he had been known on at least two occasions at this time to report to the Indian consulate in Lhasa. When Chinese authorities eventually captured him, they found, in his room, a camera used for special assignments and a copy of Fox's diary.[35]

Hamite's case showed how difficult it was to categorize people in Tibet. He was Tibetan and Kashmiri, Indian and Chinese—who could say what he was? This fluidness of identity was genetic, but it made him an invaluable spy; he could rouse a rebellion and supply information to India precisely because he spanned so many worlds. To counter the threat people like him posed, the PRC had to pin them down and decide who they were. The state could no longer tolerate multiple identities.

Hamite's faith added another layer of complication to the state's task. The literature on Tibetan Muslims is sparse, but they were a fascinating mélange, and attempts to classify them for purposes of determining sovereignty would become a major bone of contention between China and India.[36] In theory, the Muslims could be divided into two categories: the Kajis and the Hui.[37] The Kajis traced their ancestry back to Kashmir; trade and cultural exchange had brought them to Tibet, where most of them had settled in the seventeenth century. Now, India claimed that by virtue of being Kashmiri—proof of this was their Muslim faith—they were Indian citizens. The PRC could not accept this position for two reasons. First, to admit that being Kashmiri meant being Indian would be to side with India in its dispute with Pakistan over Kashmir—something that went against China's policy of neutrality on the Indo-Pakistani conflict. Second, centuries of intermarriage, China claimed, made the Kajis Tibetan and thus Chinese. Lhasa boasted about a hundred Kaji house-holds at the time; being involved in the cross-border trade, they were important to the frontier's economy.[38] The problem was never altogether solved: some Kajis were allowed to opt for foreign citizenship, others were not. At no point did the PRC admit to the general principle that all Kajis were Indian.[39] But the ambiguity posed a risk. Indian agents, as local officials in Tibet saw it, were seeking to turn Kaji nationalism against the PRC. And there were some Kajis willing to oblige. Aduani, like Hamite, had been born in Lhasa and enjoyed excellent connections with the chief Kaji entrepreneurs of Lhasa. In August 1959, he was apprehended and charged as a foreign citizen. His principal crime: he and other Kajis had schemed with the Indian consulate to mobilize the Tibetan Muslim population against the PRC. He had used the classic methods of insurgency: organizing illegal meetings, sending people to "horse around" at the Foreign Affairs Office and Public Security Bureau, and printing documents opposing the people's democratic revolution despite orders not to do so.[40] In asymmetric warfare of the kind then being waged in Tibet, such actions were crucial, and there was a multiplier effect to them. A pamphlet circulating through Lhasa could create more rebels than the PRC had put down; a single demonstration could inspire more Kajis to take arms against the Chinese government. A man like Aduani could tax the state's already stretched resources and fan discontent, making the task of strengthening governance all the more difficult.

The Kaji movement created ripples that touched the other main category of Muslims in Tibet: the Hui (or Hanhui as local officials sometimes called them, perhaps to emphasize their Chineseness). Hui Muslims, from other parts of China, had long been settled in Tibet, where many of them made significant fortunes in trade and had become part of the local government. But once the Kajis were given the right to leave, many of the Hui decided that they wished to do so too. By 1962, the Muslim population of Lhasa—and it was proving difficult to tell the Kaji from the Hanhui—was rioting en masse. They would come to the Foreign Affairs Office twice or thrice a week; they took the opportunity to embarrass China by doing so at a banquet held at the Nepali consulate in Lhasa (the Nepalis, PRC officials believed, must have let word of the banquet slip to the Indians who would have encouraged the Hui to disrupt it). They heard talk of war on the Sino-Indian frontier; they heard Chiang Kai-shek claiming he was ready to take back the mainland; and they felt that this was their opportunity to leave for India.[41]

There were, according to official estimates, some 173 Hui households in Lhasa, with about 900 people. Of these, 91 households, or about 558 individuals, had been clamoring to become foreigners and leave. After intensive work on the part of the Tibet authorities, 20 households had stopped rioting; another 15 were undecided. Of the 49 cadres who had resigned their posts in the government to riot, 11 had come back to work—and 11 more were wavering. It was becoming clearer to the masses, the Tibet Work Committee noted, that mass riots had hurt production and livelihood. Indeed, some of the Muslims who had fled abroad were now coming back. Some of them might have been sent by foreign countries, but the majority of them were definitely "good people." This was one of the positive consequences of implementing the correct policy.[42] (It might have been, or it might have been that life was not good abroad either: many Tibetans died in the heat and squalor of life in India, where they were put to hard labor in a stifling climate, with diseases that they had never encountered before.[43] The choice of places to flee to was not always a pleasant one.) The work committee was aware of the need for patience and understanding, and there were, it reported, reasons for optimism. Contradictions were developing between the Hui ringleaders and the masses. The masses needed to be given a message: that there was no problem of choosing nationality, no religious or ethnic problem, but simply a band of troublemakers who wanted to oppress the people and patriots and thereby destroy everyone's peaceful life. This, along with steps to reintegrate returning Muslims into life in Lhasa, would keep the problem from spreading. The state would exploit the rifts within society to cement its power.

But the frontier people had no shortage of reasons to leave. Tibet was a violent place, and the Hui heard the siren call, from the Indians, of a better job in a better home across the mountains with their fellow Muslims. There were people from the Indian consulate who would go among the Hui, using Kajis like Aduani, saying, "Are you not Kashmiri? Why don't you go register [to become a foreigner]?"[44] They did this without bringing the matter up with Chinese officials; one did not want to be too obvious about interfering in China's internal affairs. But India's goals, as local CCP officials read them, were hostile: the Indians were seeking to create a rift between the state and its people, and exploit China's difficulties.[45] The success of Indian propaganda directed toward Tibetan Muslims hurt the Chinese state in many ways. It undermined the state's claim to provide a good home for its citizens. It removed an important source of taxable income. And it sapped state strength directly, for many of the Muslims were cadres: they were supposed to govern Tibet, not flee it. In a very real sense, the Muslim movement was eroding the keystones of state power.

The simplest solution was to declare, unequivocally, that while the Kajis could choose to become foreign, the Hui, being Chinese through and through, could not. But the Hui too claimed mixed descent, with Kaji blood in their veins. Some of them, the officials conceded, had a case. With centuries of intermarriage, after all, some Kajis might well have married some Hui. If mixed blood was a legitimate cause to allow someone to choose foreign citizenship, then there were indeed some Hui who could claim to be foreign. But—and here the officials found themselves confronted with higher mathematics—there could not be so many of them. "Many people claiming they are of Kaji descent," read the report, "are fake. *But we have no way of checking.*"[46] *We have no way of checking*—that was the state at its most vulnerable. Who could determine the bloodlines of those claiming a right to go home? Who could tell if they had the right to go into the Indian consulate and return with travel papers and a helpful list of forebears? Who could summon up those dead ancestors, swear them to the truth, and make them bear witness for or against the Muslim claims? As you fumbled around, meanwhile, trying to figure out the ways and origins of these strange people, the Muslim movement continued apace: more people gathering in mosques, more rumors of Indian special agents, more cadres slipping slowly away. There was little you could do to prevent it. You could educate them, try to cushion the blow you admitted your taxes and business policies had dealt them, try to respect their customs—there was a reason you did not want to burst into the mosques and demand what all these people were doing—but there was no guaranteeing an end to the exodus.

The nomads, the hunxue'ers, and the Muslims exposed China's ignorance of the peoples it purported to govern; they also exposed how dangerous such ignorance could be when trying to pacify a region in turmoil. The danger of ignorance was exacerbated by Indian adeptness at taking advantage of it. In an ideal world, one would hinder traditional movements as little as possible; they were part of the fabric of life, and letting them continue would go a long way in winning hearts and minds. But the implacability of the Tibetan rebels and their alliances in India made this much too risky.

What is surprising is how far local officials went in trying to approximate the ideal world. Until 1962, at least, they made genuine efforts to distinguish customary from non-customary nomads. They sought clemency for Muslims who cooperated with the state. They emphasized the importance of trying to integrate, not shun, Muslims and nomads who returned from India; while some of the returning individuals might indeed have been recruited by intelligence agencies abroad, others could become responsible members of Tibetan society. There are two sides to any counterinsurgency: a hard side, which involves crushing implacable opposition, and a soft side, which involves giving people a reason not to oppose the state in the first place. Officials in Tibet saw the need for both. Re-education could work miracles, after all; even a man who had taken armed action against the state and received support from foreigners, could, after proper re-education, reflect on life as a PRC subject: "I am already a person of more than sixty years. In the time of my later years, I have something to rely on politically; I have guarantees for a livelihood; this could only be attained under the leadership of the magnificent Communist Party."[47] Such changes of heart, as officials in Tibet could see daily, made governance much easier. Beijing, however, perhaps less sensitive to the frontier's fabric of life, had a different tack in mind. It would continue negotiating its differences with New Delhi, but it would also seek to regulate and eventually stop the border crossings altogether.

The End of the Trade

In old times, before China was China and India India, there had been trade along Tibet's Himalayan frontiers. Grain came from the subcontinent; in return, Tibet supplied salt and cashmere. In 1903-4, when the Qing dynasty ruled China and India was part of the Raj, a group of British imperialists led by Francis Younghusband burst into Lhasa and signed a trade agreement with Tibet. And in

1954, China and India signed an agreement allowing trade in the region. Commerce burgeoned, Indian and Chinese traders alike using some of the facilities built in the days of the British Raj. Only with the chaos that raged over Tibet in 1959 did the trade tighten, and even then, it did not cease altogether. The Indians had blockaded Tibet: the transfer of food, petrol, and a few other essentials had come to a halt. Tibetans traveling to India for trade had been challenged. But by April 1960, small amounts of food had started to trickle in (though stringent restrictions remained on metals and transportation resources). In the coming year, Chinese officials planned on exporting goods worth Rs. 7 million and importing about Rs. 12.5 million worth of goods, not including the unregulated trade that Indian and Tibetan trading houses ran between themselves. To an outsider, these numbers might seem insignificant, but to Tibetans, with their small population and their almost complete economic isolation from the rest of the world, they made the difference between life and death. Twenty-four new contracts, incidentally, had been signed with Indian trading companies in Yadong—the town by which the Dalai Lama had fled to India. The trade had been largely unmanaged thus far, but it would, so officials claimed, become progressively supervised. This shows the hopes they had for trade growth; one does not wish to supervise the insignificant.[48]

But the trade was based on freedom of movement—and such movement now came with political strings attached. In 1960, three men from Ritu were stopped in Ladakh, where they had gone to trade. Indian officials accused them of being special agents and criminals. They were held for a day, on suspicion of being agents of the Communist Party. Then they were expelled.[49] It was a minor incident, one of innumerable similar cases, but it showed the difficulty of normal trade relations at a time of spiraling political tension.

Despite Chinese attempts to resolve differences in 1961—in supporting India as it recovered Goa and in extensive talks with R. K. Nehru in Beijing—the border dispute had dragged on into 1962. Perhaps it was the recognition of the importance of the trade to the PRC's frontier that gave India the idea that it was a source of leverage. In 1961, the Tibet Foreign Affairs Office reported that the Indians were denying goods that the Chinese needed, interfering with the traditional barter the border peoples had practiced, and trying to terminate Nepal's trade with China too. They were doing so while stationing troops on the border and using the Tibetan bandits to create chaos in the borderlands, including along the twenty-kilometer demilitarized zone between China and Nepal. Based on what its agents were seeing, the Foreign Affairs Office concluded that India had two objectives: to weaken China on the western sector of the contested territory and to disturb China's relationships with Nepal and Bhutan.[50] Without full access to Indian sources it is impossible to be sure, but Chinese officials had cause to believe that the Indians were linking trade rights to the boundary dispute—and, that if they saw vulnerability, they might seek to do so again. The trade agreement was due to expire—and local officials reported that Indian trading authorities were not above using the threat of expiration to try to force territorial concessions. At a merchants' meeting in Yadong on April 5, 1962, an Indian trader stood up and declared that the destruction of Sino-Indian relations was "created by the Chinese government" and that if negotiations were to take place, "China must recognize the invasion" (presumably referring to the disputed territory which China occupied).[51] In Ali, there were threats of war: with the trade agreement gone, the rumors went, war would be the only way of solving the problem, and India would definitely win. But perhaps the most damaging rumor Indian traders circulated in Tibet was that when the agreement expired there would be no food—and that the Tibetans would not be able to go to India to buy it.[52] To PRC officials, the lesson was obvious: India was trying to scare China into abandoning its legitimate territorial claims by raising the specter of a trade embargo. Such conduct was not, to borrow a PRC phrase, friendly to the Chinese people.

It is a pity that the literature on PRC reactions to trade threats is so small,[53] for sanctions can reveal a country's priorities, its inner nature. An effective embargo brings clarity: it forces a country to declare how much it is willing to sacrifice and what it is willing to sacrifice for. The gap between local and central reactions to the prospect of an end to trade was significant. Local officials wrote extensively about the dangers the end of commercial passages posed to stability on the plateau; central officials, despite being briefed on the risks, had no qualms about telling the Indians that the trading relationship must come to an end.

On the ground in Tibet, the border traders were horrified. According to the Tibet Foreign Affairs Office, Indian traders wished to stay, but their government had refused to provide them with food or to be responsible for their livelihood and well-being if they had not returned to India by June 2. The traders asked Chinese officials if they could remain in Yadong after the expiration of the agreement. Meanwhile, some Indian traders took their case to the Tibetan masses: "Now you masses can still rent rooms, sell wood, transport goods. Once the Indian merchants are gone, there will be no livelihood. You will only be able to soak in the sun."[54] These were serious threats. One of the keys to pacifying a restive population was to keep it well fed and employed. If the Tibetans got the idea that their livelihoods were in danger, PRC officials could find themselves confronted with another round of rebellions. Talks between officials and well-respected Tibetans in Yadong were not encouraging. They feared war and the havoc the Indians might wreak by blocking transport and goods.[55] In Lhasa too people harbored worries about the coming Sino-Indian conflict—mixed with hope that the war might bring the Dalai Lama back. In Gyantse, the masses did not wish to become dependent on India again, though some who had worked in the trade mission—and whose thought was still backward—asked the government to give them more land.[56] What was clear was that border peoples in both China and India depended on the trade relationship for sustenance.

The question of which side was responsible for the end of the trade has been a charged one, with the PRC claiming that India rejected invitations to renew the agreement and India lamenting that the PRC did "not show any genuine desire to maintain normal trade and intercourse between the two countries."[57] It is certainly true that India sounded an adamant note in turning down Chinese proposals to renew the trade on December 15, 1961, and again on April 11, 1962.[58] But it is also true that when the Indians changed their mind and expressed hope that a new agreement could be reached, the Chinese flatly rejected the offer. India had sought, until 1962, to exploit Tibet's dependence on the trade by threatening an embargo. As the expiration date came upon them, however, the Indians found that it was harder to dismantle the trade apparatus than they had thought; there might well have been a dawning recognition, in some Indian circles, that forcing people to find other ways of getting food was not easy, perhaps even risky. In exchanges with Chinese officials, there were hints that India wanted to extend the trade agreement. Then, on June 6, 1962, S. Sinha, the director of Chinese affairs at the Indian Ministry for External Affairs, met Ye Chengzhang, a Chinese diplomat, in New Delhi to discuss the issue of the withdrawal of the trade offices. Sinha asked for more time within which to remove the trading mission, and then he explained, almost pleadingly, that it was not that the Indians had rejected the negotiation of a new agreement, but that they wanted to find common grounds for the new agreement; they welcomed the words for it.[59] This was quite a turnaround, and yet, as Sinha spoke, one could see the logic of his position. Despite the expiration of the agreement, he pointed out, trade relations still existed. It was a way of thinking that would have come naturally to Sinha; he had first gone to China as a student in the forties (the Chinese record of the conversation identifies him by his Chinese name, Shen Shumei), studying Chinese history, among other things, in Sichuan.[60] How could you terminate relationships that had existed for centuries? How could you stop people moving through the mountain passes when their lives depended on it? The exchange had existed before the states had—could they shut it down when they found they were no longer in harmony? The Indian was asking for a renewal of the treaty—and Ye turned him down. The Indians had already rejected requests to negotiate a new agreement, Ye said, and he hoped that the Indian traders would withdraw in a timely fashion.[61] It was a response that made perfect sense—if the PRC had already decided that it was not interested in resuming trade relations.

This decision was made after one alternative had been tried and found wanting. There being no direct roads between Lhasa and Kathmandu at the time, the Sino-Nepali trade had been conducted largely by traders passing through India. As Sino-Indian relations deteriorated, fears rose that the India would block Nepali traders en route to China.[62] Plans were made for roads to connect Kathmandu to the larger cities in Tibet—Lhasa and Shigatse—directly, leaving the trade immune to New Delhi's threats and whims.[63] These plans were to proceed with due deliberation, but the larger policy was evident: closer commercial links between China and Nepal. With a bit of luck, some of the trade with India could be replaced by an increased exchange with Nepal. This was, after all, one of the benefits to the closer Sino-Nepali relationship Zhou had worked for.

But there were limits to what citizens of the PRC could get from Nepal. While discussing a food transport agreement with the Chinese ambassador in Nepal in December, 1961, a Nepali official had mentioned that there were certain food shortages in Nepal's own mountain districts: food from the east and the west of the country was being sent to Kathmandu. He did not state that this would cause his government to cut off exports to Tibet altogether, but in March, 1962, Nepal's food shortage began to make its effects felt in Tibet.[64] A Tibetan named Basang Ciren made his way, along with nine colleagues, to Nepal. The Tibetans had gone there for the traditional salt-for-grain trade—the salt dredged up from the great saline lakes of the Tibetan plateau, the grain harvested in the subcontinent's more congenial clime. After eight days, they came back via Nyalamu (the terminus of the proposed road). There they were stopped by Nepali officials: "Do not come to Nepal to carry away grain. We don't have enough grain for the Rongba to eat." Then they took away the grain.[65]

For PRC officials in Tibet, Basang Ciren's failed expedition was a source of both confusion and worry. Confusion because no one was sure whether it reflected a Nepali bureaucrat's whims, a temporary measure on a given day, or a general change in Nepal's policy. Worry because if Nepal was no longer a reliable exporter of food, there was no way of feeding Tibetans along the border. The Foreign Ministry encouraged both the Foreign Affairs Office and the Chinese ambassador in Kathmandu to make inquiries,[66] and by May 1962, the situation had become clearer. For the time being, Nepal had put an end to all food exports (presumably because of a food crisis of its own). The General Staff Department and Foreign Ministry gave clear instructions. India was trying very hard to create a tense situation on the Sino-Indian border and to destroy the Sino-Nepali relationship. Provocations on the Sino-Nepali frontier would play into New Delhi's hands. So officials in Tibet had to be sure to improve the education of their masses and make it clear to them that they were no longer supposed to go to Nepal for food.[67] The directive spoke volumes about the PRC's priorities. Food scarcity in Tibet was a local problem. The balance of Asian power, weaning Nepal away from India, mattered more—so much more that Beijing authorities did not even bother to provide any thoughts on what alternative sources of food there might be.

So there was no food coming from Nepal when Ye made sure that no food would be coming from India either. The toll of the Great Leap Forward meant that China proper could not supply Tibet with much food. (Even if agricultural productivity had been better in Sichuan and Gansu, even if food had not been shipped abroad or left to rot in silos, the absence of reliable roads meant that places like Ali, Nyalamu, and Dingri would have gone largely unfed.) There was one powerful reason to keep the trade going: the people had to eat. Against this, there were two reasons to terminate the exchange. First, (and this might well have been the highest consideration for certain Chinese officials) there was credibility: one could not let the Indians get the idea that the PRC was a country easily pushed around. This was all the more important because Indian memoranda were linking the renewal of a trade agreement to a resolution of the border dispute; they asked "the Government of China to reverse their policy of aggression and respect the boundary between the two countries. . . . Only then can the climate of friendship and goodwill be restored, negotiations for a fresh treaty on trade and intercourse undertaken and peace in Asia strengthened."[68] To the Chinese, this was an unacceptable line. Accepting it would have shown weakness, giving the Indians the idea that they could use the trade to push their territorial agenda. Second, there were the ways in which the trade was undermining Chinese national security. Since Indian traders were seeking to conduct the boundary dispute through unfriendly means, staking out claims they had no right to make, they would have to be stopped—not least since the position they took had the backing, so it seemed, of the Indian government. Since one did not know what the people who crossed for trade were doing, since one could not stop them from spreading rumors of coming trouble among an already agitated population, the simplest thing to do was to put an end to the border crossings altogether. For PRC officials in charge, the latter two considerations proved more important. So Ye's rejection of Sinha's request was final—and the people of the frontier would have to go hungry. The transition from empire-lite to empire-heavy cut off traffic—and thus food.

Hunger and Exodus

For local officials, like Suonan Daji, the decision to end the trade was a genuine blow. How could it not be? You relied on these people to help you with governance; you knew that they would be cooperative only as long as they felt that their country, their government had something to offer them. If you failed to feed them, there was no telling what they might do. You were hungry too—and perhaps you felt a twinge of conscience. These were your charges; were you not letting them down? Could you not excuse them for thinking that abandoning new China was for the best? Along with the formal trade, the Indians had stopped the customary exchange of salt and wool for grain—and that meant hunger.

The full extent of the Tibetan famine might never be known, and debates about its causes and victims remain politicized and bitter.[69] This chapter cannot provide a definitive estimate of how many died. But drawing chiefly on reports from Ali, it can say something about *why* hunger came and what it looked like. Existing accounts either blame the disastrous agricultural policies of the Great Leap Forward—and the famine caused by that was coming to an end in most areas at the time—or a policy of ethnic cleansing.[70] But much of the Tibetan plateau was not agricultural (though in some districts production certainly suffered due to the Great Leap Forward); it was fed by trade with the subcontinent. A significant part of the hunger and food inflation was caused by the decision to terminate the trade with India. Once that decision was enforced, food supplies fell short of what Tibet needed.

It was fitting that the Foreign Ministry would have reports from Ali, for it was here that the line between foreign and domestic policy blurred. Data on the famine—especially in Tibet—are difficult to come by, trickling out, as a general rule, village by village. Ali, by virtue of its location, had to report things to the Foreign Ministry, which means that we can reconstruct at least some of what happened there. More than almost any other place on the plateau, Ali crystallized all the forces at play. It lay directly in the disputed territory, linking Aksai Chin to Tibet. It was the place where intelligence on Indian activities was picked up most easily, where one heard of Indians organizing rebels and bandits to do murder in Tibet.[71] It was one of the crossroads of the nomads' ways. It is not surprising, then, that the most detailed accounting of the consequences of the elimination of trade came from here.

In Ali—from where you had once reported Indian machinations against the state—you now sat and wrote to Beijing of what was happening to your people. Your first report mentioned the people's reliance on the salt-for-grain trade, how they feared that in its absence, there would be no food, and asked the central government to solve the problem of how the masses were to eat.[72] No answer came. Hoping to strike a responsive chord, you tried again, this time citing the old proverb, *Min yi shi wei tian*: for the people, food is heaven. And the people were worried. If they could not go to get food, if the Indian merchants would not bring it either, there would be no food to eat this year, and then how would they survive? In districts slated for agriculture, like Pulan, some of the masses had become apathetic. If the food situation was not resolved, there would be great turmoil among the herdsmen. They might flee in droves. When autumn turned to winter, they might even be worried enough to slaughter all their animals—which would mean they had given up all hope of staying their hunger and would have nothing left. The Nepalis were bringing some food in, but with India refusing to supply food and interfering with Nepali supplies, prices had skyrocketed—and you had no control over it. You pointed out that this would cause a reverse in the masses' thinking, undoing the work of the revolution (this being the ideologically correct way of saying: hungry bellies create rebels, making my life harder). The total grain you consumed in a year came to 6,100,000 *jin*. You had produced 3,460,000 jin this year and there were about 700,000 jin that the masses had saved from the trade last year. You had managed to obtain some 1,100,000 jin from other districts. But you were still 840,000 jin of food short. You closed with some suggestions. Regardless of how it was done, someone should be found willing to trade wool at a stable market price so that Ali could get grain. Some grain had indeed been imported to alleviate the shortages caused by the Great Leap Forward, but with China's roads (and trains) in the condition they were, it was difficult to get this grain from the ports to China's interior, let alone to Ali at the very western tip of Tibet. You could continue to try to develop trade with Nepal, though that country's production difficulties made this problematic. Perhaps you could break the Indian blockade and import some food from there. However you did it, you made clear, it had to happen as soon as possible.[73] (This was just one area, and though experiences of the famine would have varied from place to place, it is reasonable to assume that similar shortages plagued other districts in Tibet.)

The report from Ali did nothing to reopen the trade, and with the agricultural mayhem in China proper just ending, it is difficult to see what alternative sources existed. Just how many people died remains contested, but the number would probably have been at least in the high thousands.[74] Many more would suffer from malnutrition; food inflation would make life harder in Lhasa and Shigatse.[75] The food shortage does not seem to have been a deliberate policy to kill people of Tibetan ethnicity by starvation; instead, it was the product, at least in part, of a national security policy that claimed the lives of people living on the Tibetan frontier almost as collateral damage. Part of their tragedy was that they remained uncountable, their fates never wholly beyond debate. There are no documents that certify their deaths (though there is no explanation for how they would have gotten food: we know that China proper was just emerging from a period of self-starvation, that trade with Nepal remained a trickle rather than a flood, and that trade with India did not reopen), and with census data as wildly inaccurate as it is for Tibet, there is no way of making an accurate estimate. What is certain is that this was a time of food scarcity, and that every little bit would have helped. By closing off the main supply of grain to Tibet, central authorities perpetuated hunger.

All this happened because the fourth world was caught in the quarrels of the third. Those who could, left. In Ali, there was a rise in the number of people seeking passes to go abroad;[76] others slipped off without bothering officialdom (the number of Tibetan refugees abroad grew at a steady pace until around 1963). The place they had called home had changed dramatically—a certain ease of movement, a fluidity of being was gone. The PRC had shifted its policy toward the fourth world because of crises on its frontier. The Tibetan upheavals revealed state weakness: an ignorance of who and what fell within the state's boundaries, a gulf between local and central needs, which local officials might see fit to address on their own. The dispute with India made these weaknesses especially dangerous and the fourth world a source of vulnerability. In addressing that vulnerability, the PRC continued its transition from empire-lite to a harder imperial structure, with less room for the passage of pilgrims, nomads, and merchants. With Nepal, a border had been demarcated by agreement. With India, it would have to be left unsettled after a show of force. But well before that war, decisive changes within the structure of the PRC and its foreign relations had taken place. No more could people claim to be both Chinese and Indian. No more could traditional migrations be allowed to continue unsupervised. And nothing marked the transition to empire-heavy as clearly, as lethally, and as finally as the severance of trade relations with the subcontinent. The burden of that transition was heaviest on the people who lived there, but the change in the PRC's imperial structure had ramifications that went beyond the local. It spelled an end to the order of the five principles (mutual respect for sovereign territorial rights, mutual noninvasion, mutual noninterference in internal affairs, equality and mutual benefit)—an order that had, after all, emerged in negotiating a trade agreement—and thus an end to a certain vision of what the third world should look like. The dream Mao and Nehru had celebrated in 1954, of an Asia united against imperialism, had disappeared. The final rupture between Asia's two largest countries predated the border war of 1962. With the trade agreement and its spirit of the five principles gone, the entente had come to an end.

It was Suonan Daji's misfortune to be charged with providing for Ali at a time when the empire was hardening. He had gone to Wure hoping to help the people he governed; he might well have been desperate, given the food shortages Ali faced. For his efforts, his superiors on the Tibet Work Committee reprimanded him. There was no redress from the central authorities. When the Foreign Ministry heard of his trip, it wrote back from Beijing, concurring with the views of the Foreign Affairs Office: Suonan Daji had been wrong to write to India—his doing so disadvantaged China's claim to jurisdiction over Wure. The situation required a vigilant eye. The education of the masses on this point had to be strengthened. China could not tolerate Indian's illegal occupation of "our Wure." Henceforth, central authorities ordered, such incidents must be prevented.[77]

By the time this telegram arrived in Tibet, the Sino-Indian border war of 1962 had already begun. We still do not know just how and why the PRC decided on war at this particular moment, but after all the intrigue and diplomatic fencing, the encounter was almost anticlimactic. It was short and decisive: by late November, the PRC had defeated Indian troops handily. The casualties were low; more people probably died as a result of the trade embargo than were killed during the war.[78] In a way, the war simply underlined the point made by the failure to renew the Sino-Indian agreement on trade in Tibet: that the imperial frontier, once so permeable, was being sealed.

Epilogue

Worlds Shattered, Worlds Reforged

Homecoming

There were many reasons to leave Tibet, but there were many reasons to come back too. You never knew whether you would be met with a warm welcome or bitter suspicion in Nepal; in India, with its unbearable, spirit-sapping heat, the government set you to work clearing jungle to build roads; your friends died around you of strange diseases, and you could only wonder whether you would be next.[1] Besides, you missed the old, familiar places: the mahjong tables in the back alleys of Lhasa, or the way the grasslands glistened gold beneath Everest in Dingri. The violence in Tibet seemed to have subsided, and the authorities there were promising amnesty and religious freedom. Maybe, just maybe, it was safe to go home.

So you came back to Tibet, but the place you came back to was different from the one you had left behind. The empire was hardening in the borderlands—the change was gradual, but unmistakable. With the Dalai Lama gone, the PRC saw little reason to continue delaying reform in political Tibet; indeed, it saw reform as one of the keys to pacifying the insurgency. In June 1959, gradual land reform was introduced to the agricultural areas, based on the idea that people who sowed the crops would reap the benefits. In December that year, the Tibet Work Committee was investigating ways of bringing reform to the nomadic zones too.[2] By 1965, central authorities could take some satisfaction in what had been accomplished over the course of six years. Some twenty thousand agricultural cooperatives and a few thousand nomadic ones had been established—all this on top of mobilizing the masses, pacifying the rebellion, and defeating the invading Indian forces. The next step was launching people's communes in Tibet.[3] Mao Zedong had long been convinced that communes were the way of the future;[4] they were larger, more all-encompassing than the cooperatives, and where cooperatives were mainly agricultural, the communes would draw on industrial resources too. In the days of empire-lite, the locality of Tibet had been largely untouched by the chairman's economic policy; Mao had been content to let the borderlands drift along their own socioeconomic path, their own way of living and being. He had, by and large, honored the agreement reached in 1951, which provided for different systems within the same country. But things were different now, and the administration in Tibet was to be homogenized with that in China proper. Mao had long suggested to his fellow CCP members that the day for such homogenization would come, but until 1959, he had done nothing to accelerate its arrival; indeed, he had cheerfully postponed it until some unspecified time in the future. When a crisis threatened in 1956, he promised—and kept his promise—to avoid reform in political Tibet for a while longer. And absent the crisis of 1959, there would have been little reason for the CCP not to continue this way. Only after the crisis and the response it triggered did the PRC set about transforming Tibet by imposing a system that already governed China proper. The question CCP authorities were discussing by 1965 was not if but how and how soon people's communes would come to the region.

Some of the inspiration came from ethnic Tibet. In Aba—a Tibetan-populated area in the northern reaches of Sichuan—cadres believed that they had had some success in setting up communes. Given the ethnographic similarities, officials in the Southwest Bureau saw Aba as a paradigm for political Tibet.[5] There were several ironies here—that Sichuan was one of the provinces worst hit by the famine caused by Mao's decisions; that it was the unrest in ethnic Tibet that had triggered the uprisings in political Tibet in the first place—but these were lost on the official mind of the PRC.

Not that caution had been abandoned; it was simply that caution would not interfere with working toward the goal of reform. The central committee thought it was possible to establish communes directly, without creating more cooperatives, but it was aware that Tibetan cadres, though they had matured, did not have much experience with communes. Nor, for that matter, did the Tibetan masses. So reform would proceed gradually. Cadres should strengthen the existing collectives; they should proceed with further collectivization by starting with the poorest peasants and nomads, before proceeding to the rich ones (the former had the least to lose). Propaganda about the communes was to be avoided. Propaganda was a tricky thing: one never knew when it would alarm, anger the very people it was meant to reassure. Above all, one should proceed with a firm eye on conditions; one should remain practical.[6] It was an odd directive, eloquent on the long-term goal but vague on the time table. In that strange combination of clarity and ambiguity, in the repeated emphasis on waiting for conditions to be mature, one sees the fears that haunted regional and central authorities alike. If they advised against a move to communes, Mao might blame them, which was dangerous. If they moved too fast with land reform, the borderlands might break into violence again—and there was blame to go around for that too. But one thing was clear: the era of Tibet being exempt from the economic policy that applied to the rest of the PRC was over. Looking to Aba for a model underlined the key point: what was good for China proper would henceforth be good, with some modifications, for Tibet.[7]

So land reform proceeded, and with it came hunger and suffering, as they had across China. Meanwhile, there were other changes: the mass education sessions that extolled the virtues of communism, the compulsion to choose between citizenships, the end of the easy cosmopolitanism that had come with free trade and lightly regulated borders. One Tibetan, who returned hoping to help his people, summed up what had been lost: "A lively central market. . . . the cramped booths full of wares, the voices of salesmen and customers laughing and haggling. . . . Food was rationed, and there was almost no meat or potatoes."[8]

In and of themselves, such changes to life in the borderlands were significant enough. But because those borderlands had played such a crucial role in defining the third world project and because of the particular ways in which the PRC's imperial structure hardened, the effects would extend well beyond the Tibetan plateau. The fourth world caused China to define itself as a multination state—and in doing so, it changed China's policy toward the third world, as well as the course of the Cold War.

The Rise, Fall, and Remaking of the Third World

The main source of China's third world policy lay in the agreement it reached with India on trade in Tibet. That agreement, as we have seen, had been based on the five principles of peaceful coexistence. When visiting New Delhi to finalize the agreement, Zhou had been enthusiastic about the potential the new Sino-Indian entente had to improve relations across Asia: "To create a peaceful zone in this part of Asia [Southeast Asia], we would like to see circumstances like those in place between the two countries of China and India; this is very advantageous. Regarding the principles in the preamble to the Tibet agreement, if we would extend those principles to every country in Asia, this would be advantageous."[9]

It was a pleasant dream, this vision of Asian countries relating to one another on the basis of mutual respect for sovereign territorial rights, mutual noninvasion, mutual noninterference in internal affairs, equality and mutual benefit. Those principles were everything that imperialism—that same imperialism which China, India, and countries across the third world had suffered—was not: they provided for the respect of sovereign rights and territorial integrity, for a zone free from the wars caused by one country invading another, for economic and cultural relations based on equality; they were platitudinous, perhaps, but they spelled peace. And as such they became one of the keystones of PRC foreign policy; long after the Cold War, Chinese leaders would continue to invoke them.[10]

The Chinese worldview encapsulated in the five principles was simple enough at first. Asian countries should unite as India and China had, settling their differences with mutual respect. They should repudiate western imperialism, as embodied by the United States, though if the imperialists were willing to treat third world countries as their equals, there was room for peaceful coexistence.[11] The applications of the five principles were many and diverse. They could be a rallying cry for third world cooperation and unity, as at

Bandung in 1955. They could be used to counsel a more equal relationship between the Soviet Union and other socialist countries, when crises broke out in Poland and Hungary in 1956.[12] They could be celebrated when signing a border agreement with Burma; they could be used to ask why countries like Pakistan were willing to provide military bases to the United States. They could, in short, be applied to many situations; at their core, however, they were about mutual cooperation among countries that had suffered imperial rule. But the paradigm for that cooperation had been the relationship between China and India. The crisis in the Tibetan borderlands rendered the Sino-Indian entente highly vulnerable—a vulnerability that threatened China's view of the third world.

It is worth emphasizing here that the Tibetan uprisings did not render a Sino-Indian conflict inevitable. Well into 1961, as we have seen, the PRC made efforts to reach some sort of modus vivendi with India, as it had managed to with Nepal. That the fourth world would affect the Sino-Indian relationship was natural, unavoidable—but it *could* have had a very different impact from the one it did. Nehru could have accepted Zhou's offer of a territorial swap in 1960 and reaffirmed the five principles. India could have curbed the activities of the Tibetan refugees it was hosting, or refrained from claiming that the Kajis were Indian citizens, or not threatened an embargo on the Tibetan trade; such moves would have rendered the border dispute less disturbing. Any one or more of these steps could have gone a long way in dispelling PRC suspicions of India.[13] (One wonders too what would have happened if China had taken the Indian hint that a renewal of the trade agreement would be desirable; there might well have been an opportunity for reconciliation that Beijing missed. Such a renewal would not have altered India's capacity to deal with the Tibetan refugees, however, leaving Beijing's basic objection to New Delhi's policy intact.) The affection of the fifties might well have dissipated, but the two countries could have renewed the Tibet trade agreement and avoided a war.

Instead, the PRC perceived an erstwhile friend exploiting China's domestic troubles to push an invasive territorial agenda.[14] To the official mind of the PRC, a straight line connected the Tibetan crisis to deteriorating relations with India—and Chinese diplomats drew that line clearly, both for their Indian counterparts and for the third world in general. In 1961, the Indian foreign minister, R. K. Nehru, visited Beijing; it was one of the last sustained attempts to put Sino-Indian relations back on an even keel. Nehru and the Indian ambassador to China met with many PRC officials; at their meeting with Zhou, the ambassador made the mistake of suggesting that the Tibetan problem had already been relegated to the past. Zhou's disagreement was swift, cutting:

> I cannot agree with the ambassador saying the Tibetan problem is already past. Why? Because to this day, the Dalai Lama still conducts activities opposing the motherland in your place. This does not accord with the oral promises made by the Indian government in 1951 and 1956. Then, you often said that on no account would you grant the Dalai Lama asylum in India; he could only come as a Buddhist believer; moreover, [his] conducting political activities that destroy Sino-Indian friendship would not be permitted [by you]. But now the Dalai Lama's repeated activities opposing the motherland have not ceased; moreover, [he] has raised the so-called Tibet problem with the UN.[15]

Still that fear of the UN, of what its involvement with the Tibetan problem might mean. As long as a Tibetan leader could use India as a political base from which to appeal to the international community, New Delhi's stance on Tibet was not going to satisfy Beijing. And it was not, Zhou added, "just the Dalai; there are also the people belonging to a group opposing China who fled to Kalimpong. . . . If China permitted a large group from India to exist in China's territory, often reaching out abroad and to the UN, entering and leaving China as it pleased—what would the impressions of the Indian people be; what would the impressions of the Indian government be? I am willing to state this once again: if the Indian government just lets them [the Tibetans] take asylum and does not permit them to conduct political activities, we could not oppose it."[16] There was the PRC's view: India was harboring enemies of the Chinese state, enemies who incited rebellion and challenged the state's legitimacy in the international arena. As long as that situation endured, the Tibetan problem was very much a problem of the present. And perhaps, Zhou went on to suggest, a darker, more sinister reason lay behind India's permissive attitude toward the Tibetans: "Second, there is the border problem. . . . We cannot recognize the secret agreement signed between Britain and the Tibet regional government; we need to go through negotiations to decide the [status] of the places controlled by India south of the McMahon line. . . . *The Indian government had never raised the problem of the western border, that is, the problem of the Aksai Chin area. This problem was raised suddenly after the border problem was raised in 1959* [meaning it had not been raised when India had brought up disputed territory in prior years]."[17]

1959—the year raised a host of questions. Why had the problem been raised then? Was it because India had seen China struggling to contain the violence in the Tibetan borderlands? And why the emphasis on the Aksai Chin corridor? Could it be because India realized, as the PRC did, that that strip of territory was an important link between Xinjiang and Tibet, crucial to securing control of the Tibetan plateau? And why, as Zhou pointed out, had India rejected China's proposal for troops from both sides to withdraw a certain distance from the border?[18] There had been a way of dealing with the uncertain border: patient negotiation over the long term, with a willingness to compromise, to exchange; an understanding that ratcheting up nationalism by making territorial claims vociferously was counterproductive; that the precise location of a line was something reasonable people could agree to disagree about. This was the approach the PRC had taken throughout the fifties—it would continue to do so with other countries into the sixties—and until 1959, there had been little reason to assume it was uncongenial to India. The timing of the territorial demands, coupled with reports of Indian behavior in Tibet, led to an obvious conclusion: a hostile India was taking advantage of China's troubles to seize Chinese territory. Therein lay the cause of the termination of the Tibet trade agreement with its five-principled preamble.

But the agreement and preamble were no longer about just China and India. Beijing had invested so much time and rhetorical energy in touting the dream of a third world free from empire, peaceful and united. What were countries like Indonesia and Algeria, Egypt and Vietnam, supposed to make of this sudden, bitter fallout between the two countries that had pushed so hard for third world unity at Bandung? Beijing had long been aware that it needed to justify its conduct with India to the rest of the third world; hence the effort Chinese diplomats put into briefing their foreign counterparts on the dispute.[19] But the hope those briefings had raised for a quick solution was now gone. Beijing would have to make sure that the third world did not blame it for this change, that the third world realized that it had been India that had persisted in violating the five principles, while the PRC had only claimed its rightful territory.[20]

So Zhou Enlai wrote letters to third world leaders explaining what had happened. One such letter was sent to the Indonesian president Sukarno. Indonesia was not a country to be taken lightly: large, ambitious, with huge numbers of Chinese who had had to choose between citizenships; most important, perhaps, as the home of Bandung, it symbolized third world unity—a symbolism of which it was well aware and which it would try to use.[21] The PRC understood this, and Zhou's letter was a careful, meticulous defense of Chinese conduct.

Writing to Sukarno, Zhou drew the same connection between the Tibetan crisis and the Sino-Indian border conflict that he had with R. K. Nehru in 1961:

In March, 1959, a serf owner insurgency broke out in China's Tibet region. Not only did the Indian government support and encourage this insurgency, but after the insurgency had been pacified, it took in the remaining insurgents; they were at leisure to conduct political activities opposing China in India. Not long after the eruption of the Tibetan insurgency, Prime Minister Nehru formally raised large-scale territorial demands with the Chinese government. Not only did he demand that the Chinese government recognize as lawful India's already [accomplished] occupation of Chinese territory on the eastern sector of the Sino-Indian border, but he also demanded that that the Chinese government recognize that the Aksai Chin territory in the western sector of the Sino-Indian border, which India had not yet occupied, belongs to India.[22]

So much for Nehru's territorial claims; they violated, so the PRC was arguing, the essence of the five principles. They had begun with interference in China's internal affairs, when India chose to support the Tibetan rebels and their political activities. They had taken advantage of China's troubles to raise new territorial claims. They were, in short, a rejection of peaceful coexistence.

The reminder that Tibet was a region of China was important, for it gave Zhou solid grounds for China's assertion of territorial rights. The PRC had long maintained that Tibet was an integral part of China; what Zhou did in his letter to Sukarno was to take the claim one step further. Since Tibet had always been part of China and Tibetans therefore Chinese by citizenship, it followed logically that areas historically populated by Tibetans belonged to the PRC: "In the eastern sector, the territory north of the traditional line disputed by the Indian government has always belonged to China. This territory includes three parts of the Tibet region: Menyu, Luoyu, and Xiachayu. The area comes to 90,000 square kilometers, equal to three Belgiums or nine Lebanons. The long-time inhabitants of this place are Tibetans or people with intimate blood ties to the Tibetans. For example, the Ba people use Tibetan and follow Lamaism. For example, people here call rivers 'qu.' . . . They call mountain passes 'la'; Se mountain pass is called 'Sela.' "[23]

The same logic would apply to the other disputed sectors:

In the central sector, all the places disputed by the Indian government east of the traditional line have always belonged to China. The area comes to 2,000 square kilometers. The inhabitants of these places are virtually all Tibetans. These places have always been under the administration of the Tibetan regional government. The Tibet regional government retains, up to now, documents concerned with the performance of administration in these places.

In the western sector, the territories disputed by the Indian government east and north of the traditional line have always belonged to China. This territory chiefly comprises the Aksai Chin territory, of China's Xinjiang, and a part of Ali, Tibet. The area comes to 33,000 square kilometers, approximately one Belgium or three Lebanons. Although signs of habitation are scarce in this place, it has always been an important traffic line connecting Xinjiang and Ali, Tibet.[24]

Zhou was issuing a declaration of what China was: who its peoples were and where the state's frontiers lay. But where historians generally believe that the logic of self-determination and the nation-state underpinned the international system during the twentieth century, Zhou was using a very different conceptual framework—the framework of a multination state, something the Qing or Tang dynasties could have recognized as kin.[25] Zhou was defining a people—the Tibetans—and searching for traces of that people: language, traditional rites of passage, religion. But while the Tibetans did indeed exist, they had existed as part of the fourth world; for much of the past half century, they had been largely stateless. Zhou, however, was defining them as part of a third world state. For the purposes of demarcating the PRC's frontiers, the Tibetans—with their language that Zhou did not speak, their faith that was incompatible with his communism, their misguided independence movement and rebellion that he as much as any CCP leader had fought to quell—were every bit as Chinese as the Han. The Tibetan frontier, that wild fourth world area, was shaping the self-conception of a third world country. The nationalism of the Chinese state had absorbed and would now use Tibetan ethnic nationalism. By moving from empire-lite to a harder imperial structure in the Tibetan borderlands, the PRC was proclaiming itself clearly, for the entire world to hear, as a multination state, though it would remain unaware that it had become an empire.

Now that the claim was being made, it would be unyielding. Before 1962, there had been room to acknowledge uncertainty about where the boundary lay and a corresponding willingness to compromise; Zhou could offer a territorial exchange to Nehru, recognizing Indian sovereignty over the eastern sector in exchange for recognition of China's right to Aksai Chin.[26] That was no longer the case. Even as China withdrew troops from some of the territories it had won beyond the customary line—perhaps because the PLA was overstretched and did not need to hold those territories, perhaps because this would allow China to appear reasonable in the

eyes of the world—Beijing would remain unflinching in its assertion of sovereign rights in the region. That word "always" sounded a
new, implacable note. All the disputed areas had *always* been part of
China; there is little room for compromise on what has *always* been.
As much as the physical territory held, it was what the status of the
frontier said about Chinese strength that mattered to the PRC. When
the British had violated it and signed an agreement with the Tibetan
regional government, the frontier had been a symptom of Chinese
weakness. When the Indians had negotiated an agreement with
a legitimate Chinese government, the frontier had shown China's
goodwill toward the third world. In an unrelenting crisis, the frontier
was a challenge—a challenge that called on the PRC to prove that it
was willing and able to defend its territory, to show just how far its
realm extended. Rising to such a challenge left little room for ambiguity; what had once been a malleable idea would have to become
a claim set in stone. The diplomacy, henceforth, would be that of a
hardened empire.

The diplomacy needed to be successful, for third world en-
dorsement of Beijing's position was far from a foregone conclusion. Vietnam came out in strong support of the PRC; Ho Chi
Minh expressed his hope that the dispute would be resolved by
India accepting China's proposals (presumably, he meant the
proposal calling for a demilitarized zone and negotiation);[27] later,
he would describe Nehru as already a patrician, completely different from the man he had been before Indian independence.[28]
But other third world states remained undecided. In December,
six countries—Ceylon, Indonesia, Burma, Egypt, Cambodia, and
Ghana—convened in Colombo to see if they could devise means
for reconciling China and India. They issued proposals for peace
in 1963. India was willing to accept the recommendations in their
entirety, but China was not.[29]

The proposal that gave Beijing pause was the one that called for a
Chinese withdrawal from the western sector, while allowing Indian
troops to remain where they were. This was unfair, Zhou explained
to the Indonesian foreign minister, and unacceptable to the PRC;
the proposal should call for a withdrawal from both sides and along
the entire disputed line, not just the western sector. Besides, China

had already done more than the Colombo proposals called for: it had withdrawn twenty kilometers from the disputed line and released Indian troops and weapons apprehended in the war, only to find its goodwill unreciprocated by India.[30] There was some truth to this claim, perhaps, but security concerns played a role in Beijing's decision too. Hostile aircraft, as Zhou reminded the Indonesian foreign minister, were circling the area;[31] Chinese troops had to be there to make sure that danger did not return. How could the PRC withdraw from the frontier leaving Indian troops in place unmonitored? How could it know that nomads claiming sovereign rights for India would not wander into the void they left? How could they make sure that new rumors, new incitements to rebellion, would not be circulated among still restive Tibetans? To accept the Colombo proposals completely would jeopardize China's national security. (Rumors in the Indian press that the Colombo countries were considering bringing the matter before the UN General Assembly did not help. Beijing simply instructed its ambassadors to clarify that this was unhelpful—not least because while India was represented at the UN, the PRC was not. Whether it was the General Assembly or any other organ of the UN, it could not provide a just solution to the Sino-Indian dispute. Indeed, the UN might do quite the opposite, authorizing international police action against the PRC.)[32]

So the Colombo proposals went nowhere. And the third world reacted to a third world failure to resolve a third world quarrel predictably: it shattered, and the pieces flew in several different directions, exposing, yet again, the myth of third world unity. Indonesia urged China to take a step toward reconciliation so that it could urge New Delhi to do the same; Ghana came around to the Chinese position, agreeing that outsiders could not do much and that the dispute would require direct negotiations between India and the PRC. Cambodia felt that if India and China conferred, India would not turn to the west for help, but also acknowledged China's concerns about unilateral withdrawal. Burma wished to avoid complicating the situation further; Tanzania hoped China would change its stance and accept the Colombo proposals; Nepal told Beijing of its worries that Sino-Indian conflict would threaten Nepal, before telling India that Beijing was willing to hold direct negotiations. The Arab League tried to maintain pressure on Beijing, while Pakistan simply criticized India for receiving American aid.[33] On the Sino-Indian conflict, as on so much else, the third world could not find a united front.

There were some third world countries, however, which were far from averse to the end of the Sino-Indian entente. Back in 1954, Zhou and Nehru had realized that one of the reasons smaller third world countries courted American aid and influence was their fear of China and India uniting;[34] there was no room, when behemoths worked together, for practicing the balance of power politics that small states relied on for security. The Tibetan crisis changed all that. For Nepal and Pakistan, in particular, the geopolitical situation had never been better than it was by the end of 1962.

For Nepal, the end of the Sino-Indian trade treaty meant commercial opportunity. The PRC was now heavily dependent on Nepali trade for supplying Tibet—and Nepali traders and officials knew it. Trade with Nepal grew steadily over the years, but so too did the leverage Nepali traders had on their Tibetan counterparts. In 1963, Tibetans suddenly found that salt was fetching far less grain than it once had; indeed, prices for everything had gone up dramatically. The Tibetan nomads were not happy about this,[35] and complained to the Foreign Affairs Office—but there was little to be done about the matter. In 1965, Nepali authorities decided to increase the taxes levied on the trade. As local officials pointed out to their superiors in Beijing, this was not conducive to the grain-for-salt trade. Beijing promised to research the matter; in the meantime, however, the traders just had to be taxed.[36] It was a classic case of a small country manipulating a larger one—and if the effects for the Chinese economy as a whole were insignificant, they made an already hard life harder for the Tibetans. But the Tibetans would, to use the Chinese phrase, have to "eat bitter"; it was better than not eating at all.

Nor was Nepal embarrassed about asking for Chinese assistance with security concerns. In the spring of 1963, for example, Nepali officials offered intelligence and a proposal to the Chinese embassy in Kathmandu. Tibetan rebels, probably supported by India, were creating trouble in Nepal's north. Nepal's military was too weak to launch an offensive against rebels in the mountains. Would the Chinese be willing to conduct joint activities to deal with these troublemakers at the appropriate time?[37] We do not know for sure if such operations were ever conducted, though the PRC—perhaps because it had been burnt by previous experience—declined a Nepali request to send in Tibetans with propaganda materials to convince the rebels to come home.[38] But that the Nepalis could make such requests and have them entertained, that the PRC, far from urging Kathmandu to mend ties with New Delhi, contemplated "deepening the contradictions" between those two countries, showed how dramatically the Tibetan crisis had transformed the nature of Asian geopolitics. The PRC, once so adamant on the need for Asian unity, was acknowledging that intra-Asian tensions could serve its national interests. The quest for an elusive, mythical unity had ceased to be the guiding star of China's third world policy.

Perhaps no country took to this change quite as gleefully as Pakistan. Like Nepal, Pakistan had a tense relationship with India; unlike Nepal, it was a member of the American-sponsored anticommunist military pacts SEATO and CENTO. Throughout the fifties, Beijing had voiced deep apprehension about Pakistan's membership. These organizations were, after all, directed against an ideology by which the PRC defined itself; besides, they were detrimental to the cause of third world unity, pitting third world countries against third world countries. Pakistan had its own porous, undemarcated boundary with the far western PRC borderlands of Xinjiang, and it was host to an American military base. To have such a neighbor subscribing to such pacts was bound to make Beijing nervous.[39]

Pakistan was quick to reassure Beijing that its membership in SEATO and CENTO did not mean that it would attack—or support an attack on—the PRC. Karachi chose to participate in the pacts, Pakistani diplomats explained, solely as a defensive measure against a potential Indian attack. This line of reasoning did little to ease Beijing's concerns. From 1954 onward, Zhou Enlai would continually request that Pakistan opt to resolve its differences with India directly, without courting American influence and support. When first raising the problem with a Pakistani women's delegation in 1954, he also asked that Pakistan sign a statement with China based on the five principles. This the Pakistanis declined to do—presumably because they realized that the principle of mutual nonaggression might be incompatible with membership in SEATO and CENTO. Talking to the Pakistani ambassador to China in 1956, Zhou suggested expanding SEATO and CENTO to peaceful pacts that would include the entire Asian region and the Pacific, an expansion that would have been bound to include the PRC. It was a remarkable suggestion, akin to the Soviet request to join NATO—and one that the Pakistani ambassador felt ill equipped to carry out.[40] So things settled into a familiar pattern. China would chide Pakistan for violating the principles of Asian unity and being unfriendly to Beijing. Pakistan would reply that it had no intention of ever attacking the PRC, but only wished to defend itself against India, and that Beijing should get New Delhi to see reason. Then Beijing would respond that there was no need for such distrust if only Pakistan would embrace the five principles and the Bandung spirit, and the argument would circle wearily back to where it had started.

The impact the Tibetan crisis had on the Sino-Indian entente changed all this. Beijing probably remained suspicious of Pakistan's true intentions—if you were Chinese in the Cold War, it was only prudent to suspect everybody—but it gradually ceased to castigate Pakistan for participating in SEATO and CENTO. The two countries managed to build a large measure of trust by concluding a border agreement. The PRC had been considering negotiating a border with Pakistan since 1961; one problem, however, was that some of the territory in question was territory controlled by Pakistan, but claimed by India. When R. K. Nehru visited Beijing in 1961, Chinese officials told him that, given the reality on the ground, they could not negotiate the border west of the Karakoram pass with India;[41] if it wanted to settle the status of the border regions, the PRC would have to talk to the country in de facto control of those regions: Pakistan. The Chinese were frank about this in their discussions with Nehru, but somehow, the Sino-Pakistani boundary agreement was not finalized till 1963, when all hope of a Sino-Indian rapprochement had faded.

Some of the territory Pakistan ceded to the PRC was territory claimed by India. That it did so despite American objections proved to Beijing that Pakistan could act independently of its fellow SEATO and CENTO member. The claim that membership was a safeguard

Map 6. The western sector of the disputed Sino-Indian boundary and the Sino-Pakistani border. Note the territory ceded to China by Pakistan but claimed by India, which maintained that Pakistan had no right to cede it in the first place.

against Indian aggression garnered more empathy from the PRC too. "Long-term experience has proven you to be correct," Zhou would tell a Pakistani who was with a group of journalists from other Afro-Asian countries. "When we experienced invasion, we too understood."[42] Liu Shaoqi would make the same point in conversation with Pakistan's foreign minister Zulfikar Ali Bhutto; Pakistan's willingness to sign a border treaty despite American and British objections, Liu said, showed that its membership in those organizations was not meant to oppose China—indeed, was friendly to China.[43] And with the understanding that Pakistan's membership in SEATO and CENTO was not hostile, why not turn the membership to advantage? Why not ask Bhutto to espouse China's case at SEATO? Zhou would raise that hope in public: that by being present in SEATO and CENTO, Pakistan could be a voice of reason in those pacts, advocating for China. This was good not only for the PRC, but also for the "common interests of every Afro-Asian country, for Afro-Asian friendship."[44]

It was an astonishing development—a communist country lauding an ally for being a member of an anticommunist pact—and it showed just how many different parts China had to play on the world stage. Like the Qing Empire before it, the PRC was many different countries rolled into one, with a set of diverse interests to match. It was a communist country, but it was also a multinational state with security concerns independent of the capitalist-communist conflict; it was an aspiring third world leader with an audience outside the communist world. The sources of China's Cold War conduct went beyond ideology here. It had needed to protect restive borderlands. It had wanted to do so while remaining credible as a force for peace in the third world. These were the considerations that underpinned its dealings with Pakistan, as well as with other Afro-Asian countries.[45]

The emerging Chinese foreign policy differed radically from the one Beijing had pursued in the fifties. Then, it had sought to work with India to unite the Afro-Asian world against imperialism. It was to be the dawn of a glorious postcolonial age for countries that had suffered oppression, an age when relations would be based on the five principles and the Bandung spirit, instead of the wars and invasions so common in the past. The third world had its differences, but these could be overcome.

As the Tibetan crisis developed, however, Beijing moved toward an older, perhaps more cynical third world policy. In the new third world, Beijing would use contradictions between states instead of trying to resolve them. In the new third world, a country's participation in anticommunist pacts was not a betrayal, but a potential tool. In the new third world, Beijing would accept and even delight in the competition between states, instead of trying to forge a single bloc. The geopolitical arena demanded traditional balance-of-power politics, not facile calls for unity. It was a colder worldview—and it was far removed from the Bandung spirit. Between 1959 and 1962, that spirit sickened and died, though the five principles that had gone with it would be reincarnated, put to other rhetorical use.[46]

It was the Tibetan borderlands that had brought the curtain down on China's third world project with such acrimonious, carping finality. Absent the plateau-wide crisis of 1959, Beijing could have continued dealing with the third world the way it always had. The border crossers would have been a natural feature of the landscape, not a cause for alarm. India would not have become a safe haven for enemies of the Chinese state, and Nehru's intransigence on the boundary issue would not have seemed quite as pressing. Improving relations with Nepal and Pakistan would not have been quite as important; whatever happened with the boundaries, Beijing could have continued to urge them to resolve their differences with India, to adhere, as all good Asians should, to the Bandung spirit.

But the changes in the borderlands meant that the old way of doing things was no longer sustainable. What the Lhasa uprising and the ensuing chaos across Tibet did was to render a model of empire-lite unviable. The PRC would have to strengthen state control of the borderlands, and in doing so, it was bound to alter its relationships with its neighbors. Those relationships could have changed for the better, as they did, bit by agonizing bit, with Nepal, or spiraled into recrimination, as they did with India. But understandings based on empire-lite could not have survived 1959. And because those understandings had been so central to China's third world policy, their termination meant that a different third world policy, indeed a different third world, would be forced into being. The failure to unite third world countries, the acceptance that Asian countries had competing interests—these were changes wrought by developments in the fourth world. Non-state actors moving, uncontrolled, across the frontiers of a weak state brought about a major Chinese foreign policy shift.

The impact of the frontier on the Sino-Soviet relationship is harder to gauge. As we have already seen, the Tibetan crisis did initially push Beijing closer to Moscow; the USSR, after all, was a reliable veto holder in the UN Security Council. During the Sino-Indian border war, the USSR shared intelligence with Beijing; both sides still felt there was an interest in maintaining sound relations. But after Beijing had declared a cease-fire (and denounced Khrushchev for withdrawing Soviet missiles from Cuba), Moscow promised military aid to India. Beijing would look back at this decision as one of many instances of Soviet treachery.[47] The fourth world had kept the two communist countries together for a while. Now, it would provide yet another justification for their coming apart.

■ These were dramatic changes, both in the nature of modern China and in its foreign policy during the Cold War. They are changes missed by the existing historiography, largely because that historiography remains state-centric. We tend to take the state for granted; we assume, implicitly, that the PRC was the PRC, and that it ruled all the lands it claimed to control. Our stories rarely show sensitivity to the gaps within state power: the gaps between center and periphery, between provincial governments and fourth world peoples. But such sensitivity is crucial to a full understanding of modern China and the Cold War. The Chinese government was well aware of the state's weakness in the Tibetan borderlands—and it acted accordingly.

This book has drawn on new sources to chart the impact of the Tibetan borderlands on Chinese foreign policy. By paying attention to both local reporting and global diplomacy, it has shown how closely connected the local and global levels of the Cold War were: events in a place like Dingri could bubble up and reshape grand strategy in Beijing. The new documents show just how weak Beijing's rule of the Tibetan plateau was. The central government had no idea of who its citizens were, or where its boundaries lay.

It relied, for as long as it could, on a model of empire-lite, which permitted local collaboration and autonomy. And it based its policy toward the third world, as we have seen, on that imperial model.

The course the Tibetan crises took in 1959 rendered the empire-lite model of governance unviable. This book has shown how in dealing with the weakness exposed in Tibet, the PRC moved from empire-lite to a heavier, harder imperial formation—in the tone it took in international diplomacy, in its attempts to draw lines between countries and peoples, and in its final decision to put an end to trade flows that had sustained the Tibetan plateau for generations. The PRC response to a local crisis resembled that of empires before it; as with other empires, the response had ramifications for foreign policy. Given the Indian reaction to the new model of Chinese rule in Tibet, the Bandung spirit had to change. Instead of Sino-Indian friendship and unity across the third world, Beijing's policy would rest on the shrewd practice of balance-of-power politics. The results of these changes still mark Tibet, China, and the third world as we know them today.

All this happened because of non-state actors ranging uncontrolled across borderlands. And the impact they had suggests that historians should take them as seriously as anthropologists writing about Zomia have. This book should stimulate an interest in how the fourth world shaped other parts of the Cold War. The Pathan and Baluch movements on Pakistan's western frontier, the nomads of Soviet Central Asia, the Hmong of Laos—one suspects that their stories have much to tell us about international history.[48] As previously closed archives open, there is no reason for those stories to remain untold.

The Boy in the Mountains

There were many reasons to come back to Tibet, but there were many reasons to leave too. The boy in the mountains had learned to kill birds and he had learned other things that made him long to go away: the painful, unabating hunger that land reform brought, the way patriotic education sessions could crush a human soul, the heartbreak of hearing dead friends call to him from familiar paths. He was fortunate in that he was a hunxue'er; his mother told him that his father was Nepali, and that he could and should leave. So he declared himself a Nepali citizen and made his way to the world beyond the PRC.

I sit with him in a Kathmandu café, sipping cups of tea as his dogs frolic around us. He tells me what he remembers of Tibet as it was: the unexpected kindness of Chinese soldiers, the vistas around Lhasa he would bicycle to, the lessons on good Tibetan Muslims that he was taught in school. He remembers how, in the first days following the Dalai Lama's flight, he and his brother had marched to the Barkhor, holding aloft banners that called on their spiritual leader to come back. The soldiers had not stopped them—perhaps because at the time, the PLA was also hoping for the Dalai Lama's return.

In the eighties, he went back home to visit his family. His mother had died in the Cultural Revolution; his siblings had been unable to let him know. Home was no longer what it used to be, so he said goodbye to his brother and sister and made his way back to Kathmandu

"Do you still go back to visit them?" I ask.

"No," he says. He tears up easily, this man who has been through so much, and he does so now. "They told me not to. We keep in touch, but we have to be careful. You never know. . . ."

He sighs, and looks at the picture of snow-capped mountains on the wall. For him, I realize, the passes home have closed.

Notes

1. Interview with a Tibetan in Kathmandu who asked to remain anonymous. Interviews conducted in July 2010.

2. Geographers and Americanists sometimes differentiate between the terms "frontier" and "borderlands," but I use them interchangeably here; the characters in this book, like most laypeople, would not have made the distinction, and the distinctions do not materially alter the substance of my stories. I borrow the terms "official mind" and "local crisis" from the invaluable Robinson and Gallagher, with Denny, *Africa and the Victorians*. The term "fourth world" was first popularized by Manuel, *The Fourth World: An Indian Reality*, and used to describe stateless tribes. In applying the term to a time before Manuel was writing, I do not think I am doing it too much violence: there were, after all, stateless tribes before the term was coined, and a careful historian may apply it to them.

3. The description of China as an empire is controversial, but no longer unprecedented. See Westad, *Restless Empire*, for a starting point. Carole Mc-Granahan's magnificent "Empire Out of Bounds" makes the case that Chinese rule in Tibet was imperial; McGranahan explores that imperialism from a Tibetan perspective. For the historiography on the Qing Empire, see Perdue, *China Marches West*, Waley-Cohen, *The Sextants of Beijing*, and Rowe, *China's Last Empire*. The original contribution of this book is to point out that the empire was a changing one—it shifted from empire-lite to something heavier, harder—and to analyze, at some length, the motives, security concerns, and policies of the empire. The term "empire-lite" is used by Michael Ignatieff in *Empire-Lite: Nation-Building in Bosnia, Kosovo, Afghanistan* to describe nation-building missions such as those by liberal interventionists in the Balkans; I use it, instead, as defined in the text. The term "sub-imperialism," used in Bulag, *Collaborative Nationalism*, does not appeal to me, for it implies that Chinese rule in the borderlands was something other than imperialism.

4. A few words are necessary here about what historians describe as the third world project—partly because the term "third world" is susceptible to many definitions and partly because the PRC often changed its understanding of what the third world encompassed. The third world refers both to the African, Asian, and Latin American countries once subjected to western empires and to the movement that sought to find a third way between the American and Soviet blocs during the Cold War. See Westad, *The Global Cold*

War, for more on this point. For China, the idea of third world unity often shifted between pan-Asian unity and Afro-Asian unity (sweeping out every now and then to encompass Latin America too), an ambiguity that deserves far more scholarly attention than it has thus far received. For the purposes of this book, China's policy in the third world means China's policy toward Afro-Asian countries; the idea of third world unity is as ambiguous as it was for Beijing.

5. For an overview of China's Cold War, the reader should start with Chen Jian, *Mao's China and the Cold War*. Examples of the new Cold War history on China include Luthi, *The Sino-Soviet Split*, Radchenko, *Two Suns in the Heavens*, and, in Chinese, Shen Zhihua, *Mao Zedong, Sidalin yu Chaoxian zhan zheng*. See also Christensen, *Useful Adversaries*. The remarkable work of Xiaoyuan Liu on China's frontiers is perhaps best represented by his latest collection of essays, *Recast All under Heaven*. On frontiers approached from a different vantage point, see Lin, *Modern China's Ethnic Frontiers*. Interpretive emphasis aside, the present book differs from Liu's and Lin's in several respects. It is based on new sources, and, therefore, manages to draw a more comprehensive picture of life in the borderlands, especially in the era following 1955. Where previous work on China's frontiers has emphasized central decision making, the vantage point here shifts frequently, from periphery to center and back again, a move made possible because of the wealth of new sources from the Chinese government in Tibet. A special issue of the *Journal of Cold War Studies* (Summer 2006) did focus on Tibet, but it was devoted largely to discussing CIA links with Tibetan rebels and to the impact of the Tibetan crisis on Sino-Soviet and Sino-Indian relations. As the current book shows, Tibet's significance for China and its foreign policy went much deeper and much farther than scholars previously thought. For work by Tibetologists, one must start with Melvyn Goldstein's monumental three volumes on Tibetan history: *The Demise of the Lamaist State*, *The Calm before the Storm*, and *The Storm Clouds Descend*. The fourth and final volume, which Goldstein says will take the story to 1959, is much anticipated. See also Goldstein, *The Snow Lion and the Dragon*, the stunning *Arrested Histories* by Carole McGranahan, and Tuttle, *Tibetan Buddhists in the Making of Modern China*.

6. Gaddis, *We Now Know*.

7. The classic case for the latter half of the twentieth century bringing an end to empire is Mazower, *No Enchanted Palace*. A close comparison of the Chinese case with those of earlier empires should suffice to call the "end of imperialism" line of thought into question. In addition to the work of Robinson and Gallagher, with Denny, referred to above, see Porter, *The Lion's Share*, and Maier, *Among Empires*.

8. I acknowledge here a profound debt to work by anthropologists, in particular to two books by James Scott, *Seeing Like a State* and *The Art of Not Being Governed*. Anthropologists working on contemporary Tibet have done some extraordinary work; see in particular the work of Sara Shneiderman and Carole McGranahan.

9. The claim made in Zhonggong Qinghai difang zuzhi zhi bian zuan wei-yuanhui bian [zhu bian Yao Xiangcheng], *Zhongguo gongchandang Qinghai difang zuzhi zhi*, 485, that the Dalai Lama "clique" was behind the Khamba rebellions of 1956, for example, is contradicted not only by Tibetan sources, but also by Chinese documents.

CHAPTER 1

1. Yang Gongsu, *Cang sang jiu shi nian*, 194.

2. Ibid. If, as seems probable, Yang saw Himalayan griffons, one can understand how they could seem so large.

3. The best discussion of Chinese imperialism is the magnificent Westad, *Restless Empire*. Carole McGranahan explores Chinese imperialism in Tibet from a Tibetan perspective in her "Empire Out of Bounds: Tibet in the Age of Decolonization." The description of Tibet as empire-lite has not been made previously; the term is used by Michael Ignatieff, but where Ignatieff uses it to describe liberal intervention, I am employing it to define an imperial structure that rests on the principle of minimal interference with local autonomy and ways of life.

4. The collaboration has been remarked on by Melvyn Goldstein in *The Calm before the Storm* and in *The Snow Lion and the Dragon*. The impact of Tibet on broader Chinese foreign policy, however, has remained largely uncharted by historians. Explanations of China's Cold War conduct generally focus on ideology; see for example, Chen Jian, *Mao's China and the Cold War*, and Luthi, *The Sino-Soviet Split*. Yet the "five principles of peaceful coexistence" did not emerge in a vacuum; they were a direct outgrowth of acquiring Tibet. This chapter shows that geography and frontiers mattered as much as, if not more than, ideology.

5. The best study is Beckwith, *The Tibetan Empire in Central Asia*.

6. For details, see Smith, *China's Tibet? Autonomy or Assimilation*.

7. On Qianlong's Buddhism, see Elliott, *Emperor Qianlong*, 72–74. Information on the general relationship drawn from Waley-Cohen, *The Sextants of Beijing*, and Chen Jian, "The Tibetan Rebellion of 1959 and China's Changing Relations with India and the Soviet Union."

8. See Lamb, *British India and Tibet, 1766–1910*, and Fleming, *Bayonets to Lhasa*, for accounts of the Younghusband mission.

9. On cultural and religious connections, see Tuttle, *Tibetan Buddhists in the Making of Modern China*.

10. The term was coined by Willem Van Schendel in "Geographies of Knowing, Geographies of Ignorance," but it has been explored most fully by James C. Scott in *The Art of Not Being Governed*. Melvyn Goldstein, in his monumental work on Tibetan history, calls it a state ("lamaist state" as *The Demise of the Lamaist State* has it), but his own evidence points in the direction of statelessness: foreign policy initiatives taken by several different factions, troops uncontrolled by the putative government, and general chaos abound in his narrative, much of which is set in Lhasa alone. Goldstein's own work thus makes the case for reclassifying Tibet as a realm in which statelessness prevailed. See also Samuel, "Tibet as a Stateless Society and Some Islamic Parallels." Samuel's argument is thoroughly convincing, though in making the case for Tibetan statelessness, I would place more emphasis on the absence of the capacity to conduct a single, cohesive foreign policy. In thinking of what makes a state, I am inclined first to the "Who do you call?" test that Henry Kissinger famously applied to Europe. Who would one call if one wanted the Tibetan government to undertake a certain foreign policy or keep its domestic house in order? The answer would be not the government claiming to represent Tibet, nor yet the Chinese government; it would be any number of local chieftains or lamas, depending on what one wanted done and where. Frequently, these people could be played off against one another, as Chinese practice with the Dalai and Panchen Lamas showed; none of them had a monopoly on the use of force. Bluntly stated, Tibet was too lacking in cohesion to qualify as a nation-state. McGranahan, *Arrested Histories*, argues that Tibet was a different type of state from that seen in Europe, but it also documents the lack of cohesion with regard to foreign and military policy. For my purposes here the description of Tibet as a stateless realm thus seems valid.

11. Chiang Kai-shek, *China's Destiny*, 39–40.

12. The best account is the exhaustively researched Lin, *Tibet and Nationalist China's Frontier*. Numerous secondary sources mention the Kashag's message to FDR, including Dunham, *Buddha's Warriors*.

13. See the invaluable Liu, *Frontier Passages*.

14. For an introduction to the Chinese civil war, see Westad, *Decisive Encounters*.

15. The episode is discussed in Lin, *Tibet and Nationalist China's Frontier*. Lin suggests that the Tibetans were afraid that the Chinese Communists would replace existing Nationalist officers with Communist ones; this could be the case, but the Tibetan telegram quoted below seems to make the case only for the difficulty in telling Communists from Nationalists.

16. Archives of the Ministry of Foreign Affairs of the Republic of China, Academia Sinica, 11 EAP 02941, Telegram from Kashag to Li Zongren, then President of the Republic of China, July 19, 1949, original in English. "Kuomintang" is the way the party's name is spelled in the original document; I have used "Guomindang" in the rest of the text. British documents suggest that the "barbas" in question were probably Kazakhs. Ethnic tension between Kazakhs and Tibetans did flare up at this time, with deadly consequences for the former. Disputes between Tibetans and the various ethnic groups of western China merit further scholarly investigation.

17. Xizang Zizhiqu zhengxie wenshi ziliao yanjiu weiyuanhui, *Xizang wenshi ziliao xuan ji*, vol. 17, 65.

18. National Archives, Kew, Britain (hereafter PRO), FO 371/ 76316, Note from Kashag to High Commissioner of United Kingdom in New Delhi, January 20, 1949. The British did indeed share intelligence with the Kashag; they also assisted with transit visas for the deported Chinese officials. For information about that dashing figure, Ma Bufang, see Liu, *Frontier Passages*.

19. Cited in Chen Jian, "The Chinese Communist 'Liberation' of Tibet," in Brown and Pickowicz, *Dilemmas of Victory*, 136.

20. Zhonggong zhongyang tongzhan bu, ed., *Minzu wenti wenxian huibian*, 210–11.

21. Ibid., 1267.

22. Hence the, to my mind, sincere insistence on expelling imperialism from Tibet that marked Chinese statements and indeed the eventual accord between China and Tibet. The geostrategic significance of Tibet is discussed in Garver, *Protracted Contest*, 32–78.

23. I am using the idea of anti-imperial imperialism differently from Niall Ferguson in *Colossus: The Price of America's Empire*, in that I am arguing that anti-imperialism can be a force for acquiring an empire.

24. Zhonggong zhongyang wenxian yanjiu shi, zhonggong Xizang zizhiqu weiyuanhui, zhongguo zang xue yanjiu zhongxin, eds., *Mao Zedong Xizang gongzuo wenxuan*, 3–7.

25. Xizang Zizhiqu difang zhi bian zuan weiyuanhui, *Ali diqu zhi*, 1359–71. The literature barely remarks on this expedition, and it deserves more attention, not least because of Ali's strategic importance and because the multiethnic contingent made its way through. Unfortunately, sources are hard to come by.

26. The decisions are covered in *Mao Zedong Xizang gongzuo wenxuan*. Yang's memoir also mentions them. See also Goldstein, *The Calm before the Storm*, 19–40, and Chen Jian, "The Chinese Communist 'Liberation' of Tibet."

27. See Chen Jian, "The Chinese Communist 'Liberation' of Tibet." This sections draws principally on Chen's work.

28. These twists and turns are covered in Goldstein, Sherap, and Siebenschuh, *A Tibetan Revolutionary*, 147–48.

29. *Mao Zedong Xizang gongzuo wenxuan*, 23.

30. See here Chen Jian, "The Chinese Communist 'Liberation' of Tibet," and Goldstein, *The Calm before the Storm*, 84.

31. Goldstein, *The Snow Lion and the Dragon*, and Chen Jian, "The Tibetan Rebellion" both emphasize the point.

32. The events are well covered by Chen Jian, "The Chinese Communist 'Liberation' of Tibet". Deng's role is emphasized by Yang, *Cang sang jiu shi nian*, 188–91.

33. Goldstein, Sherap, and Siebenschuh, *A Tibetan Revolutionary*, 148.

34. Yang, *Cang sang jiu shi nian*, 188–91. The parallel is, to the best of my knowledge, unexplored in most of the English-language literature, including Ezra Vogel's monumental new biography of Deng, *Deng Xiaoping and the Transformation of China*. This is a pity, as Deng's experiences in Tibet did much to inform his policies in years to come.

35. My concern here is with the practical aspects of collaboration, rather than with the tangled ways in which the PRC defined its minorities. But the subject of PRC policy toward minorities is fascinating, and has been well served by the literature. Mullaney, *Coming to Terms with the Nation*, is especially good on the evolution of a minorities policy, exploring just how the new state tried to define and count the ethnicities it contained. For encounters with minorities, Xiaoyuan Liu is the best guide; see Liu, *Recast All under Heaven* and *Frontier Passages*. Where both Liu and Mullaney see the policy as marking a transition from empire to nation-state, I see it rather as the reemergence of a Chinese empire. Guldin, "Anthropology by Other Names," argues that Chinese minority policy was heavily influenced by the Soviets, but the works by Mullaney and Liu show, among other things, how Chinese the origins and impetus of minority policy were. The truth seems to have depended on where one was at a particular time; Xikang officials, for example, cited Stalin's works "on the minority question" approvingly. Some of the preferential policies the state adopted toward minorities bring to mind Terry Martin's description of the Soviet Union in his *The Affirmative Action Empire*. For further case studies in China, see Brown, *Negotiating Ethnicities in China and Taiwan*.

36. *Mao Zedong Xizang gongzuo wenxuan*, 45–46. On Mao's experiences with Tibetans, see Liu, *Frontier Passages*. The warnings against Han chauvinism abound; for Mao's call to avoid such chauvinism in dealing with Vietnam, see Zhai, *China and the Vietnam Wars*.

37. On the Dalai Lama's interest in communism, see Goldstein, *The Storm Clouds Descend*, 17.

38. Yang's memoir recalls language training and the attempt to be sensitive to local customs.

39. Interview with an anonymous Tibetan in Kathmandu.

40. My discussion here is drawn from Chen Jian, "The Tibetan Rebellion." The question about Mao's long-term intentions is ultimately unanswerable. It is true, as Chen Jian documents, that he repeatedly told fellow CCP members that reform would come eventually; it is also conceivable that he might have done so only to cement his political standing, all the while intending to let Tibet run its own course and relate to the PRC in a "one country, two systems" model. His international policy at the time was based on the idea that different systems could coexist; a similar strain of thinking might have defined his innermost thinking on Tibet. We cannot know what he planned, but we do know what he did—and what he did is consistent with an approach based on respecting and perpetuating Tibetan mores.

41. Ibid.

42. Ibid.

43. See here Gao Wenqian's biography of Zhou, *Zhou Enlai: The Last Perfect Revolutionary*.

44. The Dalai Lama's trip to India is covered by the excellent Tsering Shakya, *The Dragon in the Land of Snows: A History of Modern Tibet since 1947*, which relies on the Dalai Lama's memoirs to reconstruct the conversation with Zhou Enlai. I am drawing on a recently declassified Chinese document: Zhou's report of his conversation, which was filed almost immediately. The Dalai Lama's account differs remarkably—he claims that he was sharp with Zhou and did not trust him at all. Zhou's account appears more convincing to me because it was not written in retrospect and was targeted to an internal audience that needed and demanded accurate information on the meeting. Zhou's account shows both how loosely the Chinese felt it necessary to govern Tibet and how valuable a source of information the Dalai Lama was for the PRC. Goldstein, *The Storm Clouds Descend*, 373-78, also draws on Chinese sources to give an account much the same as that given here.

45. Foreign Ministry of the People's Republic of China (hereafter FMPRC) 203-00018-04, Memcon of Zhou Enlai's talks with the Dalai and Panchen Lamas on his visit to India, December 7-25, 1956; conveyed in a memorandum from Zhou to the Chairman and the Central Authorities.

46. Ibid. Zhou's report does not mention whether or not the money was given as offered.

47. Ibid.

48. Ibid.

49. Ibid. That the Dalai Lama did not rush to accept either invitation suggests divisions within his staff.

50. Yang uses the term "diplomatic rights" over and over again. For a description that reveals the cosmopolitanism, see Harrer, *Seven Years in Tibet*. Surprisingly, the idea of Tibet as an isolated place persists even in scholarly works.

51. See Garver, *Protracted Contest*, 46.

52. Ibid., 48–49.

53. FMPRC 105-00136-04, Memorandum of the fourth conversation concerning Sino-Indian relations in the Chinese region of Tibet, January 8, 1954.

54. In addition to the ones detailed in the memcon, officials took to adding "peaceful coexistence." The origins of the principles are often left unexplored in accounts of their general significance.

55. A point generally overlooked in analyses of Deng's fostering of reform and opening such as that by Vogel, *Deng Xiaoping and the Transformation of China*.

56. He started doing so at least as early as his 1954 encounter with a Pakistani women's delegation; FMPRC 204-0004-03, October 7, 1954.

57. For an analysis of the five principles, see Zhang, "Constructing 'Peaceful Coexistence.'" Bandung is best covered by Chen Jian, "China and the Bandung Conference," in Acharya and Tan, *Bandung Revisited*. For the ambition of Nehru and Mao, see Khan, "Cold War Co-operation."

58. Khan, "Cold War Co-operation."

59. For interpretations along this line, see Mullik, *My Years with Nehru*.

60. Jilin Provincial Archives, 77/4/1, Foreign Ministry to Work Committees and Foreign Affairs Offices of Jilin, Heilongjiang, Yunnan, Guangxi, Inner Mongolia, Xinjiang, and Tibet, April 25, 1958.

61. Guangxi Zhuang Autonomous Region Archives, Foreign Ministry Report on the Boundary Commission, July 16, 1958.

62. Guangxi Zhuang Autonomous Region Archives, 50/2/258, December 18, 1958.

63. The Kham upheavals have received a fair amount of attention. The best account is Li Jianglin's new book, *Dang tie niao zai tian kong fei xiang*. Goldstein, *The Storm Clouds Descend*, also offers a superb account.

64. The details of land reform in Qinghai, for example, including its Tibetan areas, are chronicled proudly in *Zhongguo gongchandang Qinghai difang zuzhi zhi*, 414–20.

65. Chongqing Municipal Archives, 1200/5/4, September 23, 1954.

66. *Mao Zedong Xizang gongzuo wenxuan*, 100.

67. Chongqing Municipal Archives, 1200/5/4, September 20, 1954.

68. Ibid.

69. Ibid., September 23, 1954, mentions that the minority issue is important because minorities lived on the frontiers, where enemies could provoke
them.

70. There are, as I discovered on a visit, documents on the Golok rebellion—much less studied than that of the Khambas—in the Qinghai Provincial
Archives, but these remain closed. Until these are declassified or fieldwork
becomes easier in the region, the subject will remain almost entirely unknown. The spread of the rebellion is covered in Li Jianglin, *Dang tie niao zai
tian kong fei xiang*, 169.

71. My discussion here draws on ibid., and Goldstein, *The Snow Lion
and the Dragon*, especially 53–56. It is Goldstein who uses that apt term,
"gradualism."

72. For an intriguing account of the relationship between Tibet and the
United States, see Knaus, *Beyond Shangri-la*. See also Goldstein, *The Snow
Lion and the Dragon*, 49.

73. Khan, "Cold War Co-operation."

74. Knaus, *Orphans of the Cold War*, and Dunham, *Buddha's Warriors*,
offer accounts.

75. Interview with an anonymous Tibetan in Kathmandu.

76. See Goldstein, *The Snow Lion and the Dragon*, especially 54, for a sense
of the mood in Lhasa.

77. My account of the revolt draws principally on Chen Jian, "The Tibetan
Rebellion of 1959." Chen Jian consulted a number of Chinese sources in piec-
ing together his narrative, and I cannot improve on his basic chronology and
narrative. I have, however, drawn on the Dalai Lama's memoirs to provide at
least some impression of what was happening in the Norbulingka. Based on
the evidence, I see the ultimate failure of China's empire-lite policy as due in
part to state weakness. Beijing simply could not exert control over soldiers far
from home. In fairness, this could have happened to any government—it is a
reminder of the many things that presidents, chairmen, and the very powerful
have little to no control over.

78. Chinese and Tibetan sources spent a good deal of time and space arguing about whether the shots were fired; I accept Chen Jian's account, which
seems the most likely. Chen Jian draws on Chinese sources that suggest that
the shots were fired by a soldier named Zeng Huishan, who was not autho-
rized to fire.

79. Dalai Lama, *Freedom in Exile*, 149.

80. Interview with an anonymous Tibetan in Kathmandu.

81. Interview with an anonymous Tibetan in Kathmandu.

82. Information drawn from McGranahan, *Arrested Histories*, 105–6, and Li Jianglin, *Lasa! 1959!*, which emphasizes how decentralized the violence was.

CHAPTER 2

1. On Gyalo Thondup's career, see the invaluable McGranahan, *Arrested Histories*, and Craig, *Kundun*. The CIA's assistance to Tibetan rebels is well documented in Dunham, *Buddha's Warriors*, and in Knaus, *Orphans of the Cold War*. Knaus, a CIA agent involved with the program, was on good terms with Gyalo, and the book offers some vivid portraits of their relationship.

2. Ministry of Foreign Affairs, Republic of China, Academica Sinica, 11-EAP-02900, Letter from Oland Tsang to Foreign Minister Huang, April 5, 1959; original in English. The relationship between Hong Kong and Taiwan during the Cold War remains surprisingly underexplored.

3. Ibid., Letter from Gyalo Thondup to Oland Tsang, September 27, 1959. The original document is in Chinese; the Tibetan was comfortable with Mandarin.

4. Ibid.

5. I am dancing over a whole library of literature here on what makes a state. A starting point is Max Weber, who provides that invaluable phrase, "monopoly of the use of force." Krasner, *Sovereignty*, lists some of the different attributes of statehood. My goal here is not to get into the endless—and rather dull—debate about the legal status of Tibet; rather, I am trying to describe how life and governance in the region worked at the time.

6. Tsang mentioned the parallels with Europe in his letter to Huang; 11-EAP-02900. A partial list of the new states that came into existence in the forties and fifties includes India, Pakistan, Israel, and Burma.

7. Krasner lists the ability to make and defend claims in the international system as an attribute of sovereignty.

8. FMPRC 105-00351-02, February 16, 1957. My gratitude to Charles Hill for explaining why the UN mattered.

9. The most accessible statement of this argument is Mazower, *No Enchanted Palace*. Decolonization in general has a rich historiography; see Louis, *Imperialism at Bay*, for a starting point. McGranahan, "Empire Out of Bounds," makes a brilliant case presenting China's relationship with Tibet as an imperial one. McGranahan, however, is using Tibetan sources and seems more interested in how the Tibetans saw and responded to China; the shifts in Chinese diplomacy Tibet caused and how those shifts found parallels in international politics is not her theme. Tibet's impact on Chinese diplomacy has been explored—see the special issue of the *Journal of Cold War Studies* on Tibet for a starting point—but the full extent of that impact has yet to be

gauged accurately. I have the advantage of new sources, only recently declassified by the Foreign Ministry of the People's Republic of China.

10. A copy of the Kalmyk appeal to the UN was kept in the ROC archives. In an interview with me, Knaus recalled marching with the Kalmyks. Documents containing information on British civil society initiatives supporting Tibet are available in the National Archives at Kew; these involved such luminaries as Peter Fleming. The folders at Hoover contain information on civil society initiatives in America.

11. FMPRC 105-00652-01, The Panchen Lama's Attitude Towards the Tibetan Rebellion, Telegram from Tibet Work Committee Confidential Office to Confidential Bureau of Party Central Committee, March 23, 1959.

12. *Mao Zedong Xizang gongzuo wenxuan*, 98.

13. FMPRC 105-00652-01, Letter from Panchen Lama, March 19, 1959.

14. FMPRC 105-00652-01, Telegram from Tibet Work Committee to Central Authorities, March 20, 1959, which mentions the request for information received the same day.

15. FMPRC 105-00652-01, Report from Shigatse Work Committee to Tibet Work Committee, March 19, 1959.

16. FMPRC 105-00652-01, Report from Tibet Work Committee Confidential Affairs Office to Central Confidential Affairs Bureau, March 23, 1959.

17. Ibid.

18. FMPRC 105-00652-01, Report from Shigatse Work Committee to Tibet Work Committee, March 19, 1959.

19. FMPRC 105-00652-01, March 23, 1959.

20. The main argument is that Tibetan leaders got support from India, and that the Soviet Union's attempt to remain neutral in the subsequent Sino-Indian dispute fueled PRC anger, thereby exacerbating tensions between the two communist powers. See Chen Jian, "The Tibetan Rebellion of 1959." A similar explanation is given in Luthi, *The Sino-Soviet Split*. The main problem with this interpretation is that it reads history backwards, drawing a straight line from the rebellion of 1959 to the Sino-Indian war of 1962. By doing so, it captures the PRC's anger at what was seen as a Soviet betrayal in 1962, but ignores the cooperation between Beijing and Moscow that was the hallmark of 1959. Like most relationships, the Sino-Soviet one had its good and bad moments; it oscillated from cordiality to rancor and back again, though a certain lack of trust seems to have been a perpetual undercurrent. (The term "split" obscures this changeability—and further research into the twisted tango between Beijing and Moscow therefore seems merited, despite the burgeoning literature.) What happened in 1962 did not *have* to happen—and PRC diplomacy on Tibet at the time reflects an attempt to avoid a final rupture, to gain Moscow's support for projects where interests coincided.

21. FMPRC 109-01354-04, Reactions of Soviet heads, masses, diplomats, etcetera to the Tibetan problem, and the Sino-Indian border and relations between the two countries, March 27, 1959 to December 3, 1959, Telegram to Foreign Ministry from Embassy in Soviet Union, March 27, 1959.

22. FMPRC 109-01354-04, Telegram from Embassy in Soviet Union to Foreign Ministry, May 14, 1959.

23. FMPRC 105-00652-01, Memorandum of Conversation, May 1, 1959.

24. Luthi assigns great importance to the ideological dispute; for an older view, see the still useful Zagoria, *The Sino-Soviet Conflict.*

25. A good overview of the Soviet-Indian relationship is Mastny, "The Soviet Union's Partnership with India."

26. FMPRC 105-00657-03, Indian Vice-President and others discuss the Tibet Problem with the Soviet Ambassador, Memcon, Vice-minister Chen Yi and Soviet ambassador to China, May 8, 1959, 1.

27. Ibid.; italics my own, showing the emphasis Chen placed on the difference between the publicity India gave to the Tibetan question and the discretion of the Chinese. Indian attempts to get Tibetans to register as Indian citizens are explored in Chapter 4.

28. FMPRC 109-01354-04, Telegram from General Staff Department, May 12, 1959.

29. UN Yearbook, 1959, http://unyearbook.un.org/unyearbook.html?name =isysadvsearch.html.

30. Author's interview with Knaus, Washington, D.C., May 3, 2011. The CIA's role in hiring Gross is also documented in the papers of CIA agent Bruce Walker, held at the Hoover Institution.

31. UN Yearbook, 1959.

32. Ibid.

33. The eastern bloc maintained the same line. An interesting variation on the theme was introduced by the Romanian representative, who, "among other things, questioned the validity of the argument of the sponsors of the item that attempts to destroy the traditional way of life in Tibet were contrary to the Universal Declaration of Human Rights. Serfdom, which was contrary to the Declaration, was a specific traditional way of life in Tibet, he stated." UN Yearbook, 1960.

34. I borrow the term "official mind" from Robinson and Gallagher, with Denny, *Africa and the Victorians.*

35. FMPRC 110-00466-01, Telegram from Embassy in Sweden to Foreign Ministry, August 25, 1959.

36. FMPRC 110-00466-01, Report on conversation with Danish foreign secretary general, August 29, 1959. The PRC diplomats took up their concerns with Stockholm too, but here they turned out to be irrelevant; newspaper

reports of Norbu having applied for a visa were apparently incorrect. The Swedes did point out that they would retain the right to decide on whom to issue a visa to, but that at present, there was no real problem (FMPRC 110-00466-01, Memcon, August 27, 1959).

37. See the epilogue for a further discussion of Sino-Pakistani relations.

38. FMPRC 113-00277-01, Memcon, Geng and Malik, October 15, 1960. Just why Pakistan chose to support the resolution is unclear, but it might have had something to do with the general conceptual rethinking of national security policy undertaken by the Ayub Khan regime. Khan was a creative man, a leader willing to consider a defense alliance with India, instead of against it; showing Beijing that he did not need its friendship would have been consistent with his unpredictability in foreign affairs. Further research would require access to Pakistani sources, which remain, unfortunately, hard to come by.

39. I am drawing principally on the remarkable scholarship of historians of imperial Britain. Robinson and Gallagher, with Denny, have drawn attention to the shift from "formal" to "informal" empire; there being nothing informal about PRC control of Tibet, the terminology does not transfer directly, though it offers a useful conceptual tool. Porter, *The Lion's Share*, makes the point that the expansion of "formal empire" reflected British insecurity. Again, the parallel is not exact, but the sense of crisis contributed to the urgency of PRC diplomacy and state-building.

40. The PRC was well aware of this, as several reports from the embassy in India to Beijing show.

41. I am thinking in particular of the recent scholarship on the human rights movement of the seventies. See the brilliant and far-ranging essay by Michael Morgan, "The Seventies and the Rebirth of Human Rights," and Snyder, *Human Rights Activism and the End of the Cold War*. Implicit in my discussion of Tibet here is that transnational civil society initiatives predate the seventies.

42. FMPRC 105-00722-01, Telegram to Embassy in India from General Intelligence Department, April 4, 1960.

43. FMPRC 105-00722-01, Telegram from Embassy in India to Foreign Ministry, April 12, 1960.

44. Ibid.

45. FMPRC 105-00722-01, Telegrams exchanged between Embassy in India and Foreign Ministry, April 4, 1960, and April 8, 1960.

46. 11 EAP 02902, Report on the Afro-Asian Convention on Tibet.

47. Ibid.

48. 11 EAP 02902, Chang Kuo-sin's Report on the Afro-Asian Convention, original in English.

49. Ibid.

50. Ibid.

51. Information drawn from FMPRC 105-00722-01, India's Plot to Carry Out an "Asian-African Tibet Conference," April 2–16, 1960.

52. 11 EAP 02902, Chang Kuo-sin's report.

53. Several parallels come to mind here, notably Poland's absorption of its Belarussian population after the successful revolution of 1989—vividly documented in Ascherson, "The Borderlands"—and Indian policy toward Nagaland, Goa, and Sikkim, to name but three. The fact that Poland had been a victim of Soviet oppression made it difficult to conceive of a Poland that would oppress ethnic Belarussians; India's experience of British imperialism made it hard, though not impossible, to think of its conduct toward restive territories and peoples as imperial in nature. One great exception exists to the general argument made here: imperial Japan, which was known to have been both a victim of western imperialism and an imperial power in Asia. Despite having given the matter much thought, I confess myself unable to explain why Japan was different.

An intriguing new book, Manjari Chatterjee Miller, *Wronged by Empire: Post-imperial Ideology and Foreign Policy in India and China*, makes the argument that the experience of imperialism caused India and China to "maintain an emphasis on victimhood and entitlement" (2). My argument differs: where Miller is trying to explain Chinese and Indian foreign policy, I am focusing on how other countries perceived China and on showing how victimhood *enabled* certain diplomatic moves.

54. See Mazower, *No Enchanted Palace*.

55. Historians of the pre-twentieth-century world are adept at recognizing this; for a study of the Chinese case, see Perdue, *China Marches West*, and the work of "new Qing" historians such as Joanna Waley-Cohen and William Rowe, who write of the Qing "empire." The work on the Mughal Empire also proves instructive in this regard; see Richards, *The Mughal Empire*.

56. UN Yearbook, 1959.

57. The relationships are astonishingly underexplored, despite the wealth of new sources in Beijing, London, and Paris.

58. PRO, PREM 11/4008, Record of Discussion between the Secretary of State, Mr. Herter, and M. Couve de Murville in New York on September 18, 1959.

59. Most notably the Tibet Society, which counted among its members such luminaries as Peter Fleming and Sir Olaf Caroe.

60. PRO, FO 371/158601, Stewart to A. J. De la Mare, January 31, 1961.

61. PRO, FO 371/158601, Campbell to DeLa Mare, February 11, 1961.

62. UN Yearbook, 1961.

63. PRO FO 371/158601, Letter from Narayan, February 25, 1961.

64. Thucydides, *The Peloponnesian War*, 351. The argument here is drawn from Krasner.

65. I am stealing the phrase from Langer, *The Diplomacy of Imperialism*, but using it differently. Langer was describing the diplomatic dance between the great powers as they scrambled for Africa; I am using the term to define what acquiring an imperial holding does to a state's diplomacy. My argument here has been deeply influenced by reading Porter, *The Lion's Share*.

CHAPTER 3

1. FMPRC 105-00732-04, Concerning the three border people of Dingri, Tibet, who went to Kongbu, Nepal, and were caught by Nepali troops. Information drawn from the telegram sent by the Tibet Work Committee and military region on September 10, 1960, appending the Telegram from the Dingri Border Defense Station sent on September 4, 1960. Most Tibetan names used here have been rendered into pinyin from Chinese characters, unless they survived in another form.

2. FMPRC 105-00732-04, Telegram sent on September 4, 1960; note from general staff department on 7; telegram sent from Tibet Work Committee to Foreign Ministry, on September 17, 1960.

3. FMPRC 105-00732-04, Telegram from Dingri November 2, 1960.

4. See, for example, Fravel, *Strong Borders, Secure Nation*, which makes the argument that China willingly compromised on its border claims with respect to Nepal to strengthen its hand dealing with Tibet. A similar argument is made in Rose, *Nepal*. This argument is correct as far as it goes, but obscures just how hard state weakness made it for China to reach that agreement. Fravel does discuss the challenges of containing ethnic minorities as a source of Chinese conduct in territorial disputes, but this constitutes only part of the picture. The lack of state cohesion—that is, the gulf between Beijing and Lhasa, and then Lhasa and Dingri—is of immense importance in understanding the PRC's experience at the time, as is its sheer lack of knowledge about the places and peoples it purported to govern. The actual response to state weakness, as this chapter shows, went well beyond the mere agreement to draw a line agreeable to both sides.

5. These documents were previously unavailable to scholars.

6. The best account in Chinese is Li Jianglin, *Lasa! 1959*. See also Goldstein, *The Snow Lion and the Dragon*. For more on divisions within the Tibetan resistance, see the impressive McGranahan, *Arrested Histories*. The preceding chapter in this volume shows the gap between Gyalo Thondup

and members of other Khamba groups when discussing the Afro-Asian Convention on Tibet.

7. The records used here, being from the FMPRC, do not provide any evidence of PLA involvement in such activities. I have little doubt that some PLA troops did as much as the Tibetans in this regard, simply because this is what troops generally do. The evidence, however, is unavailable—which means the portrayal of risk here remains one-sided (though that does not make that one side less real).

8. FMPRC 105-00950-04, The Nepali Ambassador calls for protecting foreigners in Tibet; concerning the establishment of a radio station in the Nepali consulate, March 7–25, 1959, Conversation with Nepali consul general about the present situation in Tibet, March 23, 1959, 10–11.

9. FMPRC 105-00950-04, March 13, 1959, 8–10. Interestingly, this suggests a breakdown before March 10.

10. FMPRC 105-00950-04, Foreign Ministry to Tibet Foreign Affairs Office, March 25, 1959.

11. FMPRC 105-00950-02, Telegram from Tibet Foreign Affairs Office to Foreign Ministry, April 19, 1959, 2.

12. FMPRC 118-00963-30, Telegram from Tibet Foreign Affairs Office to Foreign Ministry, October 20, 1960, 1. The report also mentions a Mongol and a Soviet citizen—unsurprising given the ties to Tibetan Buddhism that Mongols and Soviet Kalmyks had.

13. FMPRC 118-00963-06, Telegram to Foreign Ministry and Public Security Bureau from the Tibet Work Committee, Social Department, and Foreign Affairs Office, November 8, 1960, 2–3. As a condition of release, the bicycle thief had to promise to return the bicycle to the original owner and write a self-criticism promising that he would commit no more crimes. Most of the criminals whose cases made it into the documents appear to have been sent home eventually—mainly to keep on good terms with the neighbors, but perhaps also because prison space was at a premium.

14. See here the delightfully vivid memoir by Yang Gongsu, *Cang sang jiu shi nian*, 206–7.

15. Indeed, as the next chapter shows, people of mixed descent had come to occupy positions of authority in the PRC's emerging state apparatus.

16. FMPRC 105-00950-02, Telegram to Foreign Ministry from Tibet Foreign Affairs Office, June 6, 1959, 9.

17. FMPRC 105-00950-02, 7.

18. My thinking here has been shaped by reading a brilliant account of a similar hardening in the British Empire: Maya Jasanoff, *Edge of Empire: Lives, Culture, and Conquest in the East, 1750–1850*. On citizenship, see also Scott, *Seeing Like a State*, 32.

19. Information on Koirala's visit to Beijing is drawn from FMPRC 204-00101-03, Memoranda of conversations between Prime Minister Zhou Enlai and Nepali Prime Minister Koirala, March 12 to 15, 1960.

20. FMPRC 105-00728-03, Prime Minister Zhou Enlai Visits Nepal, May 10–16, 1960.

21. Note the emphasis placed on the five principles of peaceful coexistence and the reference to Bandung in the joint communiqué that resulted from Zhou's visit.

22. Whelpton, *A History of Nepal*, 98.

23. My discussion of Nepal's security policy is based on Rose, *Nepal*.

24. FMPRC 204-00101-03, Zhou-Koirala talks, memorandum of third conversation, March 15, 1960, 23.

25. FMPRC 204-00689-04, Nepali consul general in Lhasa's response after returning to Tibet, April 26, 1960. He reportedly said this on April 21.

26. Robin Winks, *Cloak and Gown*, shows Sherman Kent, one of the founders of American intelligence, arguing that 90 to 95 percent of what was needed to produce an intelligence estimate could be found in the public domain.

27. FMPRC 203-00129-01, The activities of Guomindang special forces and Tibetan rebels in Nepal, and telegrams exchanged between China and Nepal on the matter, March 28, 1960 to August 8, 1960; telegram from Chinese embassy in India to Foreign Ministry and Central Investigation Department, March 28, 1960, 1.

28. Whelpton, *A History of Nepal*, 106.

29. FMPRC 105-01138-02, March 23, 1962.

30. FMPRC 203-00129-01, Telegram from Chinese embassy in India to Foreign Ministry, March 28, 1960, 1.

31. On Chinese awareness of weapon drops, see Khan, "Cold War Co-operation." On CIA recruitment in Qinghai, see Dunham, *Buddha's Warriors*, and Knaus, *Orphans of the Cold War*.

32. FMPRC 203-00129-01, Telegram from Chinese embassy in India to Foreign Ministry, March 28, 1960.

33. Ibid.

34. FMPRC 105-01002-02, Concerning the activities of the Chairman of the Nepal "Tibet Refugee Association" Prasad going to Taiwan, June 30, 1960 to August 3, 1960.

35. FMPRC 203-00129-01, Telegram from Chinese embassy in India to Foreign Ministry, March 28, 1960.

36. FMPRC 203-00129-01, Chinese dispatch to Nepali Foreign Secretary in English, undated.

37. FMPRC 203-00129-01, Telegram from Chinese embassy in India to Foreign Ministry, March 28, 1960.

38. An official chronicle, *Zhongguo gongchandang Qinghai difang zuzhi zhi*, 486, for example says that Taiwan parachuted special forces, communication equipment, and weaponry to Qinghai ten times between May 1959 and April 1960. Allen Whiting, prescient as ever, did suspect Guomindang-Tibetan links in *The Chinese Calculus of Deterrence*, but later scholars doubted their significance; they do not garner much attention, for example, in the special issue of the *Journal of Cold War Studies* devoted to Tibet. Lin's *Tibet and Nationalist China's Frontier* and *Modern China's Ethnic Frontiers* draw on Taiwanese sources to show that Chiang did have ties with Tibetan rebels, though the author's sources are generally confined to the years prior to 1959. Goldstein in *The Storm Clouds Descend*, also mentions Tibetan links with the Guomindang in the years leading up to 1957, though Chiang's motives are not Goldstein's subject. Jay Taylor mentions Chiang's musings on Tibetan autonomy in *The Generalissimo* and the U.S. refusal to help Chiang on Tibet in *The Generalissimo's Son*. To my mind, however, Taylor misreads Chiang's intentions. He portrays Chiang as genuinely interested in Tibetan autonomy; Chiang's diary suggests that he saw the 1959 uprisings chiefly as something to be exploited in taking back the mainland.

39. Information on Chiang's thinking is drawn from the Chiang Kai-shek diaries, hereafter CKS, with box and folder numbers in that order; CKS 67.7, March 21–24, 1959, kept at the Hoover Institution. The Chiang family does not allow direct quotations from the diaries without permission; since Chiang was not the most elegant or quotable of writers, I opted to paraphrase.

40. For a summary based on American sources, see Taylor, *The Generalissimo's Son*.

41. The diary entries for March 26 and May 3, 1959, provide examples.

42. CKS 67.7, March in review; the resistance fighters come up again in 67.8, on April 10.

43. CKS 68.5, November 15, 1960.

44. CKS 67.7, March 22, 1959.

45. 11 EAP 02901, from the archives of the Ministry of Foreign Affairs of the Republic of China, now housed at Academia Sinica.

46. Ibid.

47. FMPRC 203-00129-01, Telegram. The use of Nepali suggests that Nepalis as much as Tibetans were a target of the propaganda effort.

48. Two excerpts from *Gongshehua xia de qiao xiang lin zhao*, 25–26.

49. The discussion of land reform is drawn from FMPRC 105-0060-01, Telegram sent by Tibet Committee to Central Authorities, August 27, 1959. For more on the sequencing of the land reform program in Tibet, see epilogue.

50. See FMPRC 118-00974-04; full discussion in chapter 4. Information on Chou Shu's movements and background in this paragraph come from FMPRC

203-00129-01, Telegram from Central Investigation Department to Chinese Embassy in Nepal, August 20, 1960. The date at which the information on her was communicated to the embassy suggests that she remained on the central investigation department's mind even after Zhou's visit. I use a non-pinyin romanization of Chou Shu's name for consistency's sake: this is the version the PRC used in communicating her name to Nepal.

51. Bruce Walker's introduction to his papers at the Hoover Institution: Bruce Walker papers, box 1, folder 1.

52. FMPRC 203-00129-01, Telegram from Embassy in India to First Asian minister of Foreign Ministry, enclosing communication to Nepali foreign secretary; original in English. "Kansu" is the transliteration in the original; I have used the more common "Gansu" elsewhere.

53. As an aside, this is one of the few times in Cold War history when we can see Chinese intelligence in action.

54. FMPRC 105-00728-03, Premier Zhou Enlai Visits Nepal, Telegram from Embassy in India to Foreign Ministry, May 13, 1960, 4.

55. FMPRC 105-00728-03, Telegram from Embassy in India reporting conversations with officials after Zhou's departure, May 10, 1960, 6–7.

56. FMPRC 203-00035-01, Zhou-Koirala Memcon, April 27, 1960, 12–14.

57. Rose, *Nepal*, 225–26.

58. My interpretation here differs from that of Rose. Rose sees the Chinese infringement of the border as a Chinese threat display, designed to convey to the Nepalis just how displeased Beijing was by Koirala's intransigence on the outstanding border issues. Following the telegrams between Beijing and Lhasa, however, I am convinced that it was a blunder: PLA troops, not knowing or even caring where the border was, trespassed without Beijing even being aware. I have had access to new documentation from the PRC which Rose could not use. Even assuming, however, for the purposes of argument, that Beijing forged these documents to trick historians into believing that it did not sanction the PLA trespass, or, more benignly, lied to its own provincial government about what it knew and when, the facts are inconsistent with the idea of teaching Nepal a lesson. If such had indeed been Beijing's objective, there would be no need for apologies in exchanges with Koirala, and even less need to provide compensation. One does not apologize or compensate for a lesson well taught.

59. FMPRC 105-00730-03, Telegram from Foreign Ministry to Ambassador Pan and Tibet Foreign Affairs Office, June 30, 1960, 1; Telegram from Embassy in India to Foreign Ministry communicating Pan's actions, June 30, 1960, 2.

60. FMPRC 105-00730-04, Telegram from Ambassador Pan to Foreign Ministry, dispatching letter, June 29, 1960.

61. FMPRC 105-00730-04, Pan Zili's talks with Nepali ambassador, June 29, 1960, p.3.

62. FMPRC 105-00730-04, Zhou letter to Koirala, July 2, 1960, 10. This stands in stark contrast to the Chinese response when Basnyat asked for compensation for losses suffered in Tibet in 1959. Lhasa's authorities were told to tell the Nepali consul general that while he could submit a letter describing losses, compensation was uncertain; the responsibility for the damage rested with the rebels. See FMPRC 105-00950-07, Telegram from Foreign Ministry to Tibet Foreign Affairs Office, April 10, 1959, 10–11.

63. FMPRC 105-00730-04, Pan Zili's talks with Nepali ambassador, July 3, 1960, 13.

64. FMPRC 105-00951-02, Report from Tibet Foreign Affairs Office to Foreign Ministry, October 27, 1959.

65. On the Mustang guerrillas and the CIA, the best starting points are Knaus, *Orphans of the Cold War*, and Dunham, *Buddha's Warriors*. McCarthy, *Tears of the Lotus*, offers a personal account from the CIA officer who helped train the Tibetans. Whether or not the Chinese were aware of the program has long been a subject of debate, though the capture of some of the Tibetans made it almost certain that the PRC would have gotten this information. The intelligence reports from Nepal are in FMPRC 105-01005-01, Reports from Ambassador Zhang, October 7–13, 1960; telegram from general intelligence department to Xinjiang and Tibet commanders, December 24, 1960, 9–24. The reports also note American involvement with the Khambas; the PRC was aware of the programs chronicled by Knaus, Dunham, and McCarthy.

66. At least it is said to be Chinese territory in the report: FMPRC 105-01005-02, June 10, 1960, 1–2.

67. Here I am only speculating as to what the soldiers felt. But the speculation is based on a number of documents that suggest frustration at the gap between center and periphery; see, for example, the reports from the military command at Ali, FMPRC 118-00955-14.

68. FMPRC 105-00730-05, Zhou's letter to Koirala, July 12, 1960, 14.

69. FMPRC 105-00730-08, Koirala letter to Zhou, July 24, 1960, 2; Zhou's letter to Koirala, July 28, 1960, 5

70. FMPRC 105-00730-06, Pan's report on talk with Nepal, July 7, 1960, 8–11.

71. FMPRC 105-01063-07, March 26, 1961.

72. The literature on Nehru here is ample. The best treatment is still Whiting, *The Chinese Calculus of Deterrence*, but see also Garver, "China's Decision for War with India, 1962," and Fravel, *Strong Borders, Secure Nation*. One might argue that Nepal, being small, would be less willing to challenge China than India, but the Nepalis had a strong record of martial success—one that

both they and the Chinese were aware of. Some Nepali politicians argued for military action against the PRC.

73. FMPRC 105-00730-11, Ambassador Pan's talks with the Nepali king, July 21–23, 1960.

74. Again, I acknowledge the debt to Jasanoff, who discusses similar moves undertaken by the British Empire. On PLA actions in Tibet, the sources and literature are voluminous—and to be treated cautiously: official publications, scrupulously edited, lie at the core of both. Han, Huaizhi, Tan, Jingqiao, Liu, Kai, eds., *Dangdai zhongguo jundui de junshi gongzuo*, is a valuable, if potentially misleading, primary source. Goldstein's many books offer a good secondary account.

75. FMPRC 105-01857-01, March 6, 1963. Garver, *Protracted Contest*, 148, mentions a top-secret joint operation prior to this, but the claim, though conceivably true, does not appear in the archival record.

76. This theme and the further movements hinted at in final paragraph are addressed in the next chapter.

77. The third was due to return shortly, but no final word of his arrival can be found.

CHAPTER 4

1. FMPRC 118-01048-17, Report from the Tibet Foreign Affairs Office Concerning Suonan Daji's Report on the Situation of the Wure Exchange Market, and Replies, October 4, 1962 to October 23, 1962; Report to Foreign Ministry from Tibet Foreign Affairs Office, October 4, 1962, 1.

2. Ibid., 1–2.

3. Ibid., 3.

4. The classic account of the Sino-Indian War remains Whiting, *The Chinese Calculus of Deterrence*, which does not, unfortunately, pay much attention to the cross-Himalayan trade and its importance for the region. See also Maxwell, *India's China War*. Garver, *Protracted Contest*, discusses both Tibet and the border dispute, but it does not track how Tibetans were seen as agents of aggression there; see also Garver's article, "China's Decision for War with India in 1962." The links between the Tibetan rebellion and Chinese policy toward India are explored in a special volume of the *Journal of Cold War Studies* devoted to Tibet. See also Fravel, *Strong Borders, Secure Nation*. Dai Chaowu's superb account of the Sino-Indian trade does not go beyond 1959. The border dispute and the war also get some attention in Luthi, *The Sino-Soviet Split*, Radchenko, *Two Suns in the Heavens*, and Chen Jian, *Mao's China and the Cold War*. All these accounts focus on decision-making by central authorities, thereby missing the frontier developments to which those authorities responded. The

current work is, to my knowledge, the first attempt to tell the story from the ground up: that is, to track the movements of actors in the disputed regions and the impact of those movements on the policy of faraway capitals.

5. On the Great Leap Forward, see Becker, *Hungry Ghosts*, Dikotter, *Mao's Great Famine*, Manning and Wemheur, *Eating Bitterness*, and Luthi, *The Sino-Soviet Split*. Neither of the latter two accounts pays much attention to Tibet—which is perfectly justifiable given that the famine was different from that caused in China proper and that sources have only recently become available. For an overview of some of the political controversies surrounding the discussion on Tibet, see Barry Sautman, " 'Demographic Annihilation' and Tibet" in Sautman and Dreyer, *Contemporary Tibet*.

6. For a full account of PRC conduct on contested borders, see Fravel, *Strong Borders, Secure Nation*.

7. Garver, *Protracted Contest*, 100–101, covers this. For a detailed account drawing on new Indian sources, see Miller, *Wronged by Empire*, 55–81.

8. Zhou's remarks to reporters in Waijiaobu, zhonggong zhongyang wen-jian yanjiu shi, *Zhou Enlai waijiao wenxuan*, Press Conference in New Delhi, April 25, 1960, 282.

9. Note from Government of China to Ministry of External Affairs, April 27, 1959, in *Indian Ministry of External Affairs, Notes, Memoranda and Letters Exchanged Between the Governments of India and China, White Paper I*, 70; original in English.

10. FMPRC 105-00653-01, Concerning the Affair of the Tibetan Living Bud-dha Duojie Pamu who fled to India returning home; Telegram from Chinese Embassy in India to Foreign Ministry, July 10, 1959, 1–2.

11. Ibid., 30–32.

12. Ibid., 32–33. Note the distinction Pamu drew between Khambas and Tibetans; Tibetans drew it then and continue to draw it now. The Khambas are known for their marksmanship and their lawlessness.

13. FMPRC 105-00653-01, Report from Tibet FAO to Foreign Ministry, July 29, 1959, 9–10.

14. FMPRC 105-00653-01, Telegram to Chinese Embassy in India from For-eign Ministry, August 14, 1959.

15. The details here are taken from her subsequent recollections in *Xizang wenshi ziliao*, vol. 2, 126–27.

16. FMPRC 105-00653-01, Telegram to Foreign Ministry from Embassy in India, February 22, 1960. The Chinese word for refugees (*nanmin*) appears, as it so often does in these documents, in quotation marks to emphasize that these were not—as PRC officials saw it—real refugees at all.

17. Information drawn from FMPRC 118-00974-04, May 18, 1960 to Sep-tember 6, 1960. The Chinese note of complaint and the Indian response

are included in a compilation of white papers and memoranda published by the Indian Ministry of External Affairs, but this obviously does not include the correspondence between the Chinese embassy and the Foreign Ministry.

18. FMPRC 118-00974-04, 28. For more on the conference and Taiwan's conduct there, see chapter 2.

19. FMPRC 203-00309-03, Note to FMPRC from Embassy in India, April 6, 1960, 1.

20. FMPRC 203-00309-03, Note to Embassy in India from Central Investigation Bureau, April 6, 1960, 2.

21. FMPRC 203-00309-03, April 7, 1960, 5.

22. FMPRC 203-00125-01, Telegram to Foreign Ministry from Embassy in India, March 29, 1960, 15.

23. CKS 67.19, February 1960, and CKS 67.20, March, 1960.

24. FMPRC 118-00961-04, Telegram to Foreign Ministry from Embassy in India, August 1, 1961, 1.

25. FMPRC 118-00961-04, Tibet Foreign Affairs Office to FMPRC, September 5, 1961, pp.3-4. Note the presumed equality of branches: the FAO could reject a request made by an ambassador and tell him how the matter should have been handled.

26. R. K. Nehru visited Beijing in 1961; his discussions with Zhou mark one of the last attempts to resolve Sino-Indian differences. India objected to China's attempt to negotiate a border with Pakistan because the prospective border lay in territory claimed by India; FMPRC 105-01774-03, July 16, 1961.

27. Whiting, *The Chinese Calculus of Deterrence*, describes the risk China apprehended, though he frames it in less stark terms. I had the advantage of new documentation from the Chinese side.

28. FMPRC 118-01048-24, Telegram from the Work Committee in Ali, February 19, 1962.

29. Ibid.

30. Ibid.

31. Ibid. On mapping people as a form of state strengthening, see Scott, *Seeing Like a State*.

32. This offers one answer to a question about the impact of nomads on sedentary society posed by A. M. Khazanov, "Nomads in the History of the Sedentary World," in Khazanov and Wink, *Nomads in the Sedentary World*. The Tibetan case at this time suggests that nomads can cause the state to become stronger, heavier. This problem was not limited to China and the Tibetan plateau; for an insightful look at similar dynamics in the Middle East, see Bassam Tibi, "The Simultaneity of the Unsimultaneous: Old Tribes and

Imposed Nation-States in the Modern Middle East," in Khoury and Kostiner, *Tribes and State Formation in the Middle East.*

33. FMPRC 118-00963-10, October 10, 1961.

34. Information on Fox and British denials of his affiliation drawn from PRO, which gives some detail on other citizens of British descent working with Tibetans. Information on Hamite and Fox's cooperation with him drawn from FMPRC 118-00963-10.

35. FMPRC 118-00963-10, October 10, 1961. The diary, presumably, remains somewhere in China and might surface in an antique market someday.

36. The literature on Tibetan Muslims is sparse; one may start with Akasoy, Burnett, Yoeli-Tlalim, *Islam and Tibet*, and the brief introduction by Alexander Berzin at www.berzinarchives.com (November 23, 2011). The subject cries out for further research. This chapter provides the first account of Tibetan Muslims in the era of the PRC and of their role in the Cold War.

37. The Hui, one of the many ethnic groups in China, are for practical purposes indistinguishable from the majority Han, except for the fact that they happen to practice Islam.

38. Information on the Kaji population and Chinese reasons for rejecting Indian claims are taken from Yang Gongsu, *Cang sang jiu shi nian*, 207–9. Interestingly, Yang claims that the Kajis were asking, in response to Indian instigation, to become Indian as early as 1956, though the peaceful approach of authorities allowed these activities to die down of their own accord. FMPRC archival documents from 1961 and 1962 speak of Kaji demonstrations in 1960 (not given much attention by Yang). Further details on the demonstrations of 1960, however, were not available in 2011 when I was doing my research on the subject. See also the extensive notes exchanged on Kajis between Chinese and Indian governments in *Notes, White Paper IV* (originals in English).

39. One example of an outright rejection of such a claim occurred in talks in Lhasa: FMPRC 118-00963-17, Tibet FAO Report on Talks with Indian Consul Gauher on Kajis, December 24, 1960, 2. See also *Notes, White Paper IV.*

40. FMPRC 118-00963-10, October 10, 1961.

41. FMPRC 118-01046-11, Telegram to FMPRC from Tibet FAO, July 14, 1962, 1–2.

42. FMPRC 118-01046-10, Central Tibet Work Committee concerning some Hui of Lhasa who want to become foreigners, April 9, 1962.

43. Interview with an anonymous Tibetan in Kathmandu, summer 2010.

44. FMPRC 118-01046-01, Telegram from Tibet Foreign Affairs Office to Foreign Ministry, December 22, 1960, 3.

45. Ibid.

46. Ibid.; emphasis in original. At least one Muslim from Xinjiang, presumably neither Hui nor Kaji, was caught attempting to claim Kaji descent.

47. *Xizang wenshi ziliao*, vol. 3, 92.

48. Details on trade and trade plans here are drawn from FMPRC 105-00997-02, The Situation and Existing Problems of Our Trade with India, Report from the First Asian Minister of the Foreign Ministry, April 1, 1960.

49. FMPRC 118-01366-04, Telegram from Ali Foreign Affairs Division Office to Tibet Foreign Affairs Office, December 20, 1960.

50. FMPRC 118-00955-05, Telegram from Tibet Foreign Affairs Office to Foreign Ministry, March 29, 1961.

51. FMPRC 105-01123-04, Telegram from Tibet Foreign Affairs Office to Foreign Ministry and Southwest Department, Concerning the trends of the Indian official structures, May 5, 1962, 36.

52. FMPRC 105-01123-04, Telegram to Foreign Ministry from Tibet Foreign Affairs Office, The reaction of merchants and masses to the expiration of the Sino-Indian agreement, June 6, 1962, 47.

53. For a starting point, see Zhang, *Economic Cold War*.

54. FMPRC 105-01123-04, Tibet Foreign Affairs Office Report on Yadong masses to Tibet Work Committee and Foreign Ministry, May 29, 1962, 38–39.

55. FMPRC 105-01123-04, Report from Tibet FAO to General Staff and Foreign Ministry, 45.

56. FMPRC 105-01123-04, FAO to Foreign Ministry, June 7, 1962, 49. It is completely possible, of course, that Gyantse was putting a positive spin on the situation—perhaps being the place the Dalai Lama had transited en route to India still rankled.

57. For an example of the PRC claim that India rejected Chinese proposals to reach a new agreement, see Yang Gongsu, *Cang sang jiu shi nian*, 231; the Indian language is drawn from a note the Indian Ministry of External Affairs sent to the Embassy of China in India on July 11, 1962, published in *Notes*, White Paper VI, 215; abbreviation "govt." in original title.

58. *Notes*, White Paper VI, Note given by the Ministry of External Affairs, New Delhi, to the Embassy of China in India, 189, and Note given by the Ministry of External Affairs, New Delhi to the Embassy of China in India, 193–96.

59. FMPRC 105-01131-01, Telegram to Foreign Ministry from Chinese Embassy in India, June 6, 1962.

60. He is identified on the website of the Sichuan Provincial Government, Foreign Affairs Office at http://www.scfao.gov.cn/info/detail .jsp?infoId=B000000605. Goldstein, *The Calm before the Storm*, also discusses Sinha's role as the Indian representative to Lhasa in the early fifties. Whether or not this particular role made him especially suspicious to the Chinese is difficult to say; by this point, I suspect they would have reacted to the proposal to renew the agreement in the same way, regardless of which particular Indian diplomat was making it.

61. FMPRC 105-01131-01, Telegram to Foreign Ministry from Chinese Embassy in India, June 6, 1962. Just why the Indians would move from imposing a blockade to asking for a renewal of the agreement is unclear, but there was nothing consistent about their approach to China in general at this time.

62. FMPRC 105-01131-01; cause for apprehension can be gleaned from Telegram to Foreign Ministry from Chinese Embassy in India, May 23, 1962.

63. FMPRC 118-01368-03, December 28, 1960 to August 18, 1961.

64. FMPRC 118-01048-01, Chinese ambassador to Nepal on food export, January 16, 1962.

65. FMPRC 118-01048-03, Telegram from Tibet Foreign Affairs Office to Foreign Ministry, Concerning prohibition of food exports from Nepal, April 16, 1962. "Rongba" is a word for the people who live in the lowlands of Nepal.

66. Ibid.

67. FMPRC 118-01048-04, May 9, 1962.

68. *Notes*, White Paper VI, Note given by the Ministry of External Affairs, New Delhi, to the Embassy of China in India, July 11, 1962, 215.

69. Sautman, " 'Demographic Annihilation,' " and Becker, *Hungry Ghosts*, both dismiss the idea of ethnic cleansing, but they disagree on the number dead. Sautman is especially harsh on Becker's reliance on figures given by Tibetan refugees. Of course, other figures are not available; Becker worked with the best data he could get. Absent further archival opening, we will never know.

70. In addition to the works by Sautman and Becker cited above, more information on the famine can be found in Dikotter, *Mao's Great Famine*, and in Yang, *Tombstone*.

71. FMPRC 118-01046-12, June 28, 1962.

72. FMPRC 105-01123-01, June 19, 1962.

73. FMPRC 118-01048-08, Report from Ali Foreign Affairs Office on the trade situation vis-à-vis our masses after the expiration of the Sino-Indian agreement, July 2, 1962. There is a blacked-out line in the document before the idea of breaking the blockade is aired; presumably, it contained some thoughts on just how that blockade was to be broken. On the difficulty of transporting imported grain, see Dikotter, *Mao's Great Famine*. It is worth remembering that when food was shipped from China to Tibet in the early fifties, it had to go via ship to Calcutta, from where it was then sent overland to Tibet. This was quicker and easier than sending it to Tibet "straight" through Sichuan, Yunnan, Qinghai, or Xinjiang. I have given the weights in the Chinese unit of *jin*, as the original report did; 1 jin is about 1.1 pounds.

74. See Sautman, " 'Demographic Annihilation,' " for a conservative estimate.

75. Interview with anonymous Tibetan in Kathmandu.

76. FMPRC 105-01123-04, Telegram to Foreign Ministry from Tibet Foreign Affairs Office, June 6, 1962.

77. FMPRC 118-01048-17, Telegram from Foreign Ministry to Tibet Foreign Affairs Office, October 23, 1962, 4.

78. It is still difficult to improve on Whiting's classic account, *The Chinese Calculus of Deterrence,* but see also Maxwell, *India's China War,* and Fravel, *Strong Borders, Secure Nation.* Garver, "China's Decision for War with India in 1962," does try to take us inside the Chinese politburo, but he lacks archival soures, and the volumes he draws on for his account are not reliable enough to permit full confidence. Whiting and Garver agree on the PRC's basic motives—to prevent India from undermining Chinese control of Tibet and, perhaps, to deter India from border aggression; the key unresolved question is why the war happened at the precise moment it did. Garver suggests that the PRC's perceptions regarding Indian policy toward Tibet were inaccurate; China blamed India, he suggests, for problems that China itself had caused in Tibet. Based on the new documents used in this chapter (which Garver did not have access to), particularly the reports from the frontier, this argument seems untenable. The PRC had reason to be suspicious of Indian policy toward Tibet.

EPILOGUE

1. Details on refugee life are drawn from interviews with anonymous Tibetans in Kathmandu in 2008.

2. *Dangdai Zhongguo de Xizang,* vol. 1, 275–84. This official volume can be a bit misleading, often omitting mention of difficulties, but carefully used, it is the only and therefore best source available on certain key questions about official policy in Tibet.

3. FMPRC 118-01808-03, Telegram from Central Committee to Tibet Work Committee, August 29, 1965.

4. Dikotter, *Mao's Great Famine,* 47. Dikotter, like most scholars of Mao's agricultural policies, does not have much to say about Tibet—understandably given the lack of sources. The small historiographical contribution to that particular subject made in the opening of this chapter is to emphasize how gradual the change was. Historians tend to think of Mao's China as bold to the point of being foolhardy on such questions, but in the Tibetan borderlands, at least, there was some caution about the pace of change. Warren W. Smith, *China's Tibet?,* offers a chapter on the reform, but, lacking Chinese sources, fails to give a nuanced account of how reform was supposed to proceed. Becker, *Hungry Ghosts,* still remains the best account of the famine in Tibet.

5. FMPRC 118-01808-03, Telegram from Southwest Bureau to Central Committee, August 20, 1965.

6. Ibid.

7. The brilliant and meticulous Liu, *Recast All under Heaven*, 207, draws attention to "the completion of China's domestic sovereignty" in its border-lands. Liu sees this as a gradual shift from empire to the nation-state, starting in the nineteenth century; my analysis differs in two key respects. First, I see the cause not as a process beginning in the nineteenth century, but as a set of local crises that erupted in 1959 and triggered a specific set of responses: drawing borders, regulating movement, defining citizenship, and defending claims on the global stage. Absent the events of 1959, Mao's China would not have undertaken the state-building measures it did in the way it did and when it did. Second, where Liu sees China emerging as a modern nation-state, I see it as a reincarnation of empire in the form of a multination state. The change was not from empire to nation-state, but from empire-lite to a harder imperial structure; the latter defined itself as a multination state.

8. Cited in Goldstein, *The Snow Lion and the Dragon*, 59.

9. FMPRC 203-00006-01, Memoranda of the Conversations between the Two Prime Ministers on Zhou Enlai's First Visit to India, First conversation, June 25, 1954, 23.

10. For a survey of the evolution of the five principles over time, see Chen Jian, "China and the Bandung Conference," in Acharya and Tan, *Bandung Revisited*.

11. For a more thorough exploration, see Khan, "Cold War Co-operation."

12. Chen Jian, "China and the Bandung Conference."

13. Without further access to Indian sources, we cannot know for sure why such measures were not taken, or what alternatives New Delhi considered. Domestic politics and cultural sympathy for the Tibetan plight were certainly factors in India's disenchantment with Beijing, but the full impact they had on policymaking remains to be explored.

14. The best exploration of PRC threat perceptions is still Whiting, *The Chinese Calculus of Deterrence*. But see also Garver, "China's Decision for War with India in 1962" and Fravel, *Strong Borders, Secure Nation*. Garver's article suggests that the Chinese perceived threats inaccurately and that India and China both bear responsibility for the war. This might well be correct—absent full declassification of Indian sources we cannot know for sure—but given the weight of reporting from Tibetan outposts, one can understand why Beijing perceived India the way it did. My purpose here is not to condemn India for the war, or to judge between two claimants to territory; it is simply to try to see what the PRC saw at the time and understand the consequent reactions and policies. Garver did not have access to the newly declassified Chinese sources that form the core of this book.

15. FMPRC 105-01774-03, Memcon, R. K. Nehru and Zhou, July 16, 1961.

16. Ibid.

17. Ibid.; my italics for emphasis.

18. Ibid.

19. FMPRC 109-000870-03, October 26, 1959.

20. For all the literature on the Sino-Indian relationship, there is surprisingly little written about the impact of that dispute on the broader third world. The literature on the third world project tends to mention the dispute only in passing. Scholars debating when the dream of a unified third world ended generally look to the late sixties and seventies; for an overview, see Kalinovsky and Radchenko, *The End of the Cold War in the Third World*. One of the key historiographical contributions of this chapter is to explore how events in the Tibetan borderlands undid the third world project. The Bandung spirit had dissipated by 1962 because of the way the fourth world shaped the choices made by China and India, as well as by other countries like Pakistan and Nepal. Chinese foreign policy toward the third world before the Tibetan crisis differed markedly from what it became after that crisis had played out: where Beijing had once claimed interest in uniting the third world against imperialism, it began to see the divisions within the third world as useful to PRC national security. On China and the third world project, see Chen Jian, "China and the Bandung Conference," and Zhang, "Constructing Peaceful Coexistence," as well as Westad, *The Global Cold War*.

21. The Sino-Indonesian relationship requires further research. For Indonesia's third world policy, see Acharya and Tang, *Bandung Revisited*.

22. FMPRC 105-01786-02, Zhou Enlai's Letter to Sukarno, November 15, 1962.

23. Ibid.

24. Ibid. Zhou went on to mention that ethnic groups from Xinjiang used and had names for the Aksai Chin area—a use of evidence that paralleled his reasoning on the eastern sector. One of the topics I have had to leave unaddressed in this study is the connection between Xinjiang and Tibet. The sources are simply not available. But the topic is intriguing and important. As Zhou pointed out, a corridor of traffic existed between the two places, and Chinese security concerns in Xinjiang were similar, though not identical, to the ones stemming from Tibet. Xinjiang obviously raised some concerns about Sino-Indian relations, though again, documents on the subject remain unavailable. Should the requisite sources become accessible, further research is well merited.

25. Liu, *Recast All under Heaven*, argues that China shifted from an empire to a modern nation-state from the nineteenth century to the twentieth, and that policy toward Tibet after 1959 marked a departure from the practices of the Qing. To my mind, however, the assertion of sovereignty involved a shift from one form of empire to another: Mao's China mapped itself onto

what had been part of the Qing Empire, and the claims it made were those of a multination state. The similarities to the Qing—in the regions encompassed, in the use of the Panchen Lama, in the attempt, even as late as the early sixties, to provide for some religious autonomy—appear striking. For more on the Qing, see Westad, *Restless Empire*. The literature on the nation-state is vast; I am grateful to Ryan Irwin, Chris Miller, and Sara Silverstein for a discussion on the subject. Historians of Eastern Europe see the origins of the nation-state in the challenges to the large empires that existed there: see Mazower, *Balkans*, and the fascinating Snyder, *The Reconstruction of Nations*. For language—specifically print—as the defining attribute of a nation, see Benedict Anderson, *Imagined Communities*. The idea of the multination state has generally been the province of Russianists and Sovietologists, but to my mind, the nation-state never really existed outside Europe. One could quite comfortably characterize India and—if one suspends belief in being Muslim equaling being a separate nation—its smaller sibling Pakistan as multination states; the same applies to Indonesia. That historians still see decolonization as representing the emergence of nation-states in the third world says more about the power of the myths perpetuated by third world leaders than the facts on the ground.

26. Curiously, Garver, *Protracted Contest*, 104–5, mentions that the Chinese suggested they might be willing to make certain concessions on the western sector in exchange for Indian flexibility in the east in 1986. This seems odd given the geostrategic value of Aksai Chin (though the construction of roads linking Qinghai, Sichuan, and Yunnan much more strongly to the Tibetan plateau did reduce the importance of the Aksai Chin corridor). Garver's sources are Indian and might well have misinterpreted the Chinese position. Until further documents become available, we cannot be quite sure what really happened. It is possible, of course, that given the way things had changed over time, Deng felt much more secure about China's grip on the borderlands than Mao had.

27. FMPRC 106-00729-04, Telegram to Foreign Ministry from Embassy in Vietnam, November 23, 1962.

28. FMPRC 106-00729-04, November 24, 1962.

29. The Colombo conference garners surprisingly little attention, perhaps because it was unsuccessful. For an introduction, see Fisher, "India in 1963." My understanding of the conference was deepened by reading Dai Chaowu's intriguing conference paper, "Sino-Indian Border War of 1962 and China's Response to the Colombo Proposals." Where Dai sees the war and the Chinese response as driven by shifts in Chinese ideology, however, I think that the security perceptions of the Indian role on the frontier were not particularly ideologically colored.

30. FMPRC 105-01837-01, Memcon, Zhou and Indonesian Foreign Minister, September 20, 1963.

31. Ibid.

32. FMPRC 105-01848-03, "Talking Points," September 14, 1963.

33. FMPRC 105-01638-01, "New Situation" March 9, 1963. This particular folder compiles press reports and diplomatic talks to chart Afro-Asian reactions to the Sino-Indian conflict, as well as the propaganda and diplomacy China and India engaged in.

34. Khan, "Cold War Co-operation."

35. FMPRC 118-01232-01, Telegram from Tibet Foreign Affairs Office to Foreign Ministry, August 23, 1963.

36. FMPRC 105-01742-01, Telegram from Tibet Foreign Affairs Office to Foreign Ministry, July 13, 1965, and Telegram from Foreign Ministry to Tibet Foreign Affairs Office, July 28, 1965.

37. FMPRC 105-01857-01, Telegram to Military Intelligence from Embassy in Nepal, March 6, 1963.

38. FMPRC 105-01857-01, Telegram from Foreign Ministry to Embassy in Nepal, January 3, 1964.

39. Zhou explained the problem clearly (and in terms he would use repeatedly throughout the years) in his conversation with a Pakistani women's delegation; FMPRC 204-0004-03, October 7, 1954. We still need a full exploration of PRC state-building in the fourth world of Xinjiang.

40. FMPRC 105-00351-01, January 4, 1956. Zhou's suggestion, I suspect, reflects China's search for a modus vivendi with the United States. Had the Pakistanis communicated the suggestion to Washington and had Washington seen here a means to reaching an accommodation with the PRC, the Sino-American rapprochement might have come about much earlier than it did. To me, the tone of Chinese diplomacy here suggests that contrary to Chen Jian's interpretation, the "lost chance" was not altogether a myth. As things turned out, we will never know for sure.

41. He complained about this to Zhou. FMPRC 105-01774-03, July 16, 1961.

42. FMPRC 105-01842-04, Abstracts of talks concerning Pakistan by Liu Shaoqi, Zhou Enlai, Chen Yi since 1963, May 17, 1963.

43. FMPRC 105-01842-04, Liu's meeting with Bhutto, March 2, 1963.

44. FMPRC 105-01842-04, May 17, 1963. That the PRC would frame things this way makes one wonder if there was, yet again, an untaken hint that Pakistan should broker a rapprochement with the United States. Advocating China's cause could lead to such an outcome. Public diplomacy suggests that the PRC's grand strategy at this point was far more reasonable than generally believed.

45. The idea of a leftward turn in Chinese foreign policy around this time seems to be gaining ground; see, for example, Niu Jun, "1962: The Eve of the

Left Turn in China's Foreign Policy." Certainly, one can discern a greater degree of ideological extremism in Chinese policy toward the Soviet Union—but third world policy seems to have been cold and calculating.

46. See Chen Jian, "China and the Bandung Conference," for the use of the five principles beyond 1962.

47. The best guide to these events is the redoubtable Radchenko, *Two Suns in the Heavens*; see also Mastny, "The Soviet Union's Partnership with India," and Luthi, *The Sino-Soviet Split*. Chen Jian makes the case that Tibet contributed to the Sino-Soviet split; see Chen Jian, "The Tibetan Rebellion and China's Changing Relations with India and the Soviet Union." It is worth emphasizing, as it was when considering China's third world policy, that Tibet did not necessitate a Sino-Soviet rupture. Had China not criticized the Soviet Union for its Cuban policy, or had the Soviet Union avoided military aid to India after the cease-fire, Tibet would have continued as a force unifying the two communist countries, instead of becoming a bone of contention. The fourth world provided the third world with a challenge, but it did not determine the measures that the PRC would take in response.

48. For an insightful account of the Pakistan-Afghanistan borderlands, see Johnson and Mason, "No Sign until the Burst of Fire." For a superb account of the Hmong, see Fadiman, *The Spirit Catches You and You Fall Down*.

Bibliography

ARCHIVES

Archives of the Foreign Ministry of the People's Republic of China (FMPRC)
Archives of the Ministry of Foreign Affairs of the Republic of China at
  Academia Sinica, Taipei
Chongqing Municipal Archives (CQA)
Guangxi Zhuang Autonomous Region Archives
Jilin Provincial Archives
Hoover Institution Archives, Chiang Kai-shek Diaries (CKS)
National Archives, Kew, Britain

WEBSITES

Berzin Archives, berzinarchives.com
Cold War International History Project, cwihp.org
Foreign Affairs Office, Sichuan Provincial People's Government, scfao.gov.cn
UN Yearbook, unyearbook.un.org

PUBLISHED PRIMARY SOURCES IN CHINESE

Dangdai Zhongguo congshu bianji bu, Dan, Zeng, Zhang, Xiangming,
  eds. *Dangdai Zhongguo de Xizang.* 2 vols. Beijing: Dangdai Zhongguo
  chubanshe, 1991–2009.
Haiwai chubanshe bian. *Gongshehua xia de qiaoxiang linzhao.* Taipei:
  Gaishe, 1958.
Han, Huaizhi, Tan, Jingqiao, Liu, Kai, eds. *Dangdai zhonggguo jundui de
  junshi gongzuo.* 2 vols. Beijing: Dangdai Zhongguo chubanshe, 2009.
Ji Youquan. *Bai xue.* Beijing: Zhongguo wu zi chu ban she, 1993.
Mao Zedong. *Jianguo yilai Mao Zedong wengao.* Beijing: Junshi Kexue
  Chubanshe, 2010.
Xizang Zizhiqu dangshi ziliao weiyuanhui and Xizang junqu dangshi
  ziliao lingdao xiaozu, eds. *Heping jiefang Xizang.* Lhasa: Xizang renmin
  chubanshe, 1995.
Xizang Zizhiqu dangshi ziliao zheng ji weiyuanhui. *Zhonggong Xizang
  dangshi dashi ji.* Lhasa: Xizang renmin chubanshe, 1995.
Xizang Zizhiqu difang zhi bian zuan weiyuanhui. *Ali Diqu Zhi.* 2 vols.
  Beijing: Zhongguo zang xue chu ban she, 2009.

Yang Gongsu. *Cang sang jiu shi nian: yi ge waijiao teshi de huiyi.* Haikou: Hainan chubanshe, 1999.

Zhang Yuxin, ed. *Heping jiefang Xizang 50 zhounian jinian wenji.* Beijing: Zhongguo zang xue chubanshe, 2001.

Xizang Zizhiqu zhengxie wenshi ziliao yanjiu weiyuanhui. *Xizang wen shi zi liao xuan ji.* 18 vols. Beijing: Renmin chubanshe, 1991–2004.

Zhonggong Qinghai difang zuzhi zhi bian zuan weiyuanhui. *Zhongguo gongchandang Qinghai difang zuzhi zhi.* Xining: Qinghai Renmin chubanshe, 1999.

Zhonggong Xizang zizhiqu weiyuanhui. *Xizang geming shi.* Lhasa: Xizang renmin chubanshe, 1991.

Zhonggong zhongyang tongzhan bu, ed. *Minzu wenti wenxian huibian.* Beijing: Zhong gong zhongyang dangxiao chubanshe, 1991.

Zhonggong zhongyang wenxian yanjiu shi, zhong gong Xizang zizhiqu weiyuanhui, zhongguo zang xue yanjiu zhongxin, eds. *Mao Zedong Xizang gongzuo wenxuan.* Beijing: Zhongyang wenxian chubanshe, 2001.

Zhonghua renmin gongheguo waijiaobu, zhonggong zhongyang wenxian yanjiu shi. *Zhou Enlai waijiao wenxuan.* Beijing: Zhongyang wenxian chubanshe, 1990.

PUBLISHED PRIMARY SOURCES IN ENGLISH

Gompo Tashi Andrugtsang. *Four Rivers, Six Ranges: Reminiscences of the Resistance Movement in Tibet.* Dharamsala: Information and Publicity Office of H.H. the Dalai Lama, 1973.

Chiang Kai-shek. *China's Destiny.* Translated by Wang Chung-hui. New York: Macmillan, 1947.

Dalai Lama. *Freedom in Exile.* New York: Harper Collins, 1990.

Harrer, Heinrich. *Seven Years in Tibet.* Translated by Richard Graves. New York: J. P. Tarcher, 2009.

India Ministry of External Affairs. *Notes, Memoranda, and Letters Exchanged between the Governments of India and China.* 9 vols. New Delhi: 1954–63.

SECONDARY SOURCES

Acharya, Amitav, and See Seng Tan, eds. *Bandung Revisited: The Legacy of the 1955 Asian-African Conference for International Order.* Singapore: NUS Press, 2008.

Akasoy, Anna, Charles Burnett, and Ronit Yoeli-Tlalim, eds. *Islam and Tibet: Interactions along the Musk Routes.* Burlington, Vt.: Ashgate, 2011.

Anderson, Benedict. *Imagined Communities: Reflections on the Origin and Spread of Nationalism.* London: Verso, 1983.

Ascherson, Neal. "The Borderlands" in *Granta 30: New Europe!* Spring, 1990. (Accessible at http://www.granta.com/Archive/30/The-Borderlands).

Beckwith, Christopher. *The Tibetan Empire in Central Asia.* Princeton: Princeton University Press, 1987.

Brown, Jeremy, and Paul G. Pickowicz, eds. *Dilemmas of Victory: The Early Years of the People's Republic of China.* Cambridge: Harvard University Press, 2007.

Brown, Melissa, ed. *Negotiating Ethnicities in China and Taiwan.* Berkeley: Institute of East Asian Studies, University of California, Berkeley, Center for Chinese Studies, 1996.

Bugakski, Janusz. *Fourth World Conflicts: Communism and Rural Societies.* Boulder, Colo.: Westview Press, 1991.

Bulag, Uradyn. *Collaborative Nationalism: The Politics of Friendship on China's Mongolian Frontier.* Lanham, Md.: Rowman and Littlefield, 2010.

Chen Jian. *Mao's China and the Cold War.* Chapel Hill: University of North Carolina Press, 2001.

———. "The Tibetan Rebellion of 1959 and China's Changing Relations with India and the Soviet Union." *Journal of Cold War Studies* 8, no. 3 (Summer 2006), 54–101.

Christensen, Thomas. *Useful Adversaries: Grand Strategy, Domestic Mobilization, and Sino-American Conflict, 1947–1958.* Princeton: Princeton University Press, 1996.

Craig, Mary. *Kundun: A Biography of the Family of the Dalai Lama.* London: Harper Collins, 1997.

Dai Chaowu. "Sino-Indian Border War of 1962 and China's Response to the Colombo Proposals." Paper presented at the India and the Cold War conference, Wilson Center, Washington, D.C., 2009.

Darwin, John. *The Empire Project: The Rise and Fall of the British World System, 1830–1970.* Cambridge: Cambridge University Press, 2009.

Dikotter, Frank. *Mao's Great Famine.* New York: Walker, 2010.

Dreyer, June Teufel, and Barry Sautman, eds. *Contemporary Tibet.* Armonk, N.Y.: M. E. Sharpe, 2006.

Dunham, Mikel. *Buddha's Warriors: The Story of the CIA-Backed Tibetan Freedom Fighters, the Chinese Invasion, and the Ultimate Fall of Tibet.* New York: J. P. Tarcher, 2004.

Elliott, Mark. *Emperor Qianlong: Son of Heaven, Man of the World.* New York: Longman, 2009.

Fadiman, Anne. *The Spirit Catches You and You Fall Down.* New York: Farrar, Straus and Giroux, 1997.

Ferguson, Niall. *Colossus: The Price of America's Empire*. New York: Penguin, 2004.

Fisher, Margaret W. "India in 1963: A Year of Travail." *Asian Survey* 4, no. 3 (March 1964): 737–45.

Fleming, Peter. *Bayonets to Lhasa*. New York: Harper, 1961.

Fravel, M. Taylor. *Strong Borders, Secure Nation: Cooperation and Conflict in China's Territorial Disputes*. Princeton: Princeton University Press, 2008.

Gaddis, John. *We Now Know: Rethinking Cold War History*. New York: Oxford University Press, 1997.

Garver, John. "China's Decision for War with India in 1962." In *New Approaches to the Study of the Chinese Foreign Policy*, edited by Robert Ross and Alastair Iain Johnston. Stanford: Stanford University Press, 2005.

———. *Protracted Contest: Sino-Indian Rivalry in the Twentieth Century*. Seattle: University of Washington Press, 2001.

Gao Wenqian. *Zhou Enlai: The Last Perfect Revolutionary*. Translated by Peter Rand and Lawrence R. Sullivan. New York: Public Affairs, 2007.

Goldstein, Melvyn. *The Calm before the Storm*. Vol. 2 of *A History of Modern Tibet*. Berkeley: University of California Press, 2007.

———. *The Demise of the Lamaist State*. Vol. 1 of *A History of Modern Tibet*. Berkeley: University of California Press, 1989.

———. *The Dragon and the Snow Lion*. Berkeley: University of California Press, 1997.

———. *The Storm Clouds Descend, 1955–1957*. Vol. 3 of *A History of Modern Tibet*. Berkeley: University of California Press, 2013.

Goldstein, Melvyn, and Cynthia Beall, *The Nomads of Western Tibet*. Berkeley: University of California Press, 1990.

Goldstein, Melvyn, Dawei Sherap, and William R. Siebenschuh, *A Tibetan Revolutionary: The Political Life and Times of Baba Phuntso Wangye*. Berkeley: University of California Press, 2004.

Guldin, Greg. "Anthropology by Other Names: The Impact of the Sino-Soviet Friendship on the Anthropological Sciences." *Australian Journal of Chinese Affairs*, no. 27 (January 1992), 133–49.

Ignatieff, Michael. *Empire-Lite: Nation-Building in Bosnia, Kosovo, and Afghanistan*. Toronto: Penguin, 2003.

Jasanoff, Maya. *Edge of Empire: Lives, Culture, and Conquest in the East, 1750–1850*. New York: Knopf, 2005.

Johnson, Thomas H., and M. Chris Mason. "No Sign until the Burst of Fire: Understanding the Pakistan-Afghanistan Frontier." *International Security* 32, no. 4 (Spring 2008): 41–77.

Kalinovsky, Artemy, and Sergey Radchenko, eds. *The End of the Cold War and the Third World: New Perspectives on Regional Conflict*. New York: Routledge, 2011.

Khan, Sulmaan Wasif. "Cold War Co-operation: New Chinese Evidence on Jawaharlal Nehru's 1954 Visit to China." *Cold War History* 11, no. 2 (May 2011): 197–222.

Khazanov, A. M., and Andre Wink, eds. *Nomads in the Sedentary World*. Richmond, Surrey, UK: Curzon Press, 2001.

Khoury, Philip S., and Joseph Kostiner, eds., *Tribes and State Formation in the Middle East*. Berkeley: University of California Press, 1990.

Knaus, John Kenneth. *Beyond Shangri-La: America and Tibet's Move into the Twenty-First Century*. Durham: Duke University Press, 2012.

———. *Orphans of the Cold War: America and the Tibetan Struggle for Survival*. New York: Public Affairs, 1999.

Kramer, Mark, ed. "Great-Power Rivalries, Tibetan Guerilla Resistance, and the Cold War in South Asia." Special issue, *Journal of Cold War Studies* 8, no. 3 (Summer 2006).

Krasner, Stephen. *Sovereignty: Organized Hypocrisy*. Princeton: Princeton University Press, 1999.

Lamb, Alastair. *British India and Tibet, 1766–1910*. London: Routledge and Kegan Paul, 1986.

Langer, William L. *The Diplomacy of Imperialism, 1890–1902*. New York: Knopf, 1965.

Li Danhui. "Dui 1962 nian Xinjiang yita shijian qiyin de lishi kaocha- laizi Zhongguo Xinjiang de dang an cailiao." *Dangshi yanjiu ziliao*, no. 5 (1999), 1–22.

Li Jianglin. *Dang tieniao zai tian kong fei xiang: 1956–1962 qingzang gaoyuan shang de mi mi zhan zheng*. Taipei: Lianjing chuban, 2012.

———. *Lasa! 1959!* Taipei: Lianjing chuban, 2010.

Lin, Hsiao-ting. *Modern China's Ethnic Frontiers: A Journey to the West*. New York: Routledge, 2011.

———. *Tibet and Nationalist China's Frontier: Intrigues and Ethnopolitics, 1928–1949*. Vancouver: University of British Columbia Press, 2006.

Liu, Xiaoyuan. "Entering the Cold War and Other 'Wars': The Tibetan Experience." *Chinese Historical Review* 19, no. 1 (May, 2012), 47–64.

———. *Frontier Passages: Ethnopolitics and the Rise of Chinese Communism, 1921–1945*. Stanford: Stanford University Press, 2004.

———. *Recast All under Heaven: Revolution, War, Diplomacy, and Frontier China in the Twentieth Century*. New York: Continuum, 2010.

Liu, Xuecheng. *The Sino-Indian Border Dispute and Sino-Indian Relations*. Lanham, Md.: University Press of America, 1994.

Louis, Wm. Roger. *Imperialism at Bay: The United States and the Decolonization of the British Empire, 1941–1945*. New York: Oxford University Press, 1978.

Luthi, Lorenz. *The Sino-Soviet Split*. Princeton: Princeton University Press, 2008.

Maier, Charles. *Among Empires*. Cambridge: Harvard University Press, 2006.

Manning, Kimberly Els, and Felix Wemheuer, eds. *Eating Bitterness*. Vancouver: University of British Columbia Press, 2011.

Manuel, George. *The Fourth World: An Indian Reality*. New York: Free Press, 1974.

Martin, Terry. *The Affirmative Action Empire: Nations and Nationalism in the Soviet Union, 1923–1939*. Ithaca: Cornell University Press, 2001.

Mastny, Vojtech. "The Soviet Union's Partnership with India." *Journal of Cold War Studies* 12, no. 3 (Summer 2010): 50–90.

Maxwell, Neville. *India's China War*. London: Cape, 1970.

Mazower, Mark. *Balkans: A Short History*. New York: Modern Library, 2000.

——. *No Enchanted Palace: The End of Empire and the Ideological Origins of the United Nations*. Princeton: Princeton University Press, 2009.

McCarthy, Roger. *Tears of the Lotus*. London: McFarland, 1997.

McGranahan, Carole. *Arrested Histories: Tibet, the CIA, and Memories of a Forgotten War*. Durham: Duke University Press, 2010.

——. "The CIA and the Chushi Gangdrug Resistance, 1956–1974." *Journal of Cold War Studies* 8, no. 3 (Summer 2006): 102–30.

——. "Empire Out of Bounds: Tibet in the Era of Decolonization." In *Imperial Formations*, edited by Ann Laura Stoler, Carole McGranahan, and Peter C. Perdue. Santa Fe, N.M.: School for Advanced Research Press, 2007.

Miller, M. C. *Wronged by Empire: Post-imperial Ideology and Foreign Policy in India and China*. Stanford: Stanford University Press, 2013.

Morgan, Michael Cotey. "The Seventies and the Rebirth of Human Rights." In *The Shock of the Global: The International History of the 1970s*, edited by Niall Ferguson et al. Cambridge: Harvard University Press, 2010.

Mullaney, Thomas. *Coming to Terms with the Nation: Ethnic Classification in Modern China*. Berkeley: University of California Press, 2011.

Mullik, B. N. *My Years with Nehru: The Chinese Betrayal*. Bombay: Allied Publishers, 1971.

Niu Jun. "1962: The Eve of the Left Turn in China's Foreign Policy." Cold War International History Project, Working Paper No. 48.

Perdue, Peter C. *China Marches West: The Qing Conquest of Central Eurasia*. Cambridge: Belknap Press, 2005.

Porter, Bernard. *The Lion's Share: A Short History of British Imperialism, 1850-1983*. London: Longman, 1984.

Radchenko, Sergey. *Two Suns in the Heavens: The Sino-Soviet Struggle for Supremacy, 1962-1967*. Washington, D.C.: Woodrow Wilson Center Press, 2009.

Richards, J. F. *The Mughal Empire*. Cambridge: Cambridge University Press, 1993.

Robinson, Ronald, and John Gallagher. "The Imperialism of Free Trade." *Economic History Review* 6, no. 1 (1953): 1-15.

Robinson, Ronald, and John Gallagher, with Alice Denny. *Africa and the Victorians*. New York: St. Martin's Press, 1961.

Rose, Leo. *Nepal: Strategy for Survival*. Berkeley: University of California Press, 1971.

Samuel, Geoffrey. "Tibet as a Stateless Society and Some Islamic Parallels." *Journal of Asian Studies* 41, no. 2 (February 1982): 215-29.

Scott, James. *The Art of Not Being Governed: An Anarchist History of Upland Southeast Asia*. New Haven: Yale University Press, 2009.

———. *Seeing Like a State: How Certain Schemes to Improve the Human Condition Have Failed*. New Haven: Yale University Press, 1998.

Shen Zhihua. *Mao Zedong, Sidalin yu Chaoxian zhan zheng*. Guangzhou: Guangdong Renmin chubanshe, 2004.

Shneiderman, Sara. "Are the Central Himalayas in Zomia? Some Scholarly and Political Considerations across Time and Space." *Journal of Global History* 5, no. 2 (2010): 289-312.

Smith, Warren W. *China's Tibet? Autonomy or Assimilation*. Lanham, Md.: Rowman and Littlefield, 2008.

Snyder, Sarah. *Human Rights Activism and the End of the Cold War: A Transnational History of the Helsinki Network*. Cambridge: Cambridge University Press, 2011.

Snyder, Timothy. *The Reconstruction of Nations*. New Haven: Yale University Press, 2003.

Spence, Jonathan. *The Search for Modern China*. New York: Norton, 1999.

Taylor, Jay. *The Generalissimo: Chiang Kai-Shek and the Struggle for Modern China*. Cambridge: Belknap Press, 2009.

———. *The Generalissimo's Son: Chiang Ching-Kuo and the Revolutions in China and Taiwan*. Cambridge: Harvard University Press, 2000.

Thucydides. *The Peloponnesian War*. Translated by Richard Crawley and T. E. Wick. New York: Random House, 1982.

Tsering Shakya. *The Dragon in the Land of Snows: A History of Modern Tibet since 1947*. London: Pimlico, 1999.

Tucker, Nancy. *Strait Talk: United States–Taiwan Relations and the Crisis with China*. Cambridge: Harvard University Press, 2009.

Tuttle, Gray. *Tibetan Buddhists in the Making of Modern China*. New York: Columbia University Press, 2005.

Van Schendel, Willem. "Geographies of Knowing, Geographies of Ignorance: Jumping Scale in Southeast Asia." *Environment and Planning D: Society and Space* 20, no. 6 (2002): 647–68.

Vogel, Ezra. *Deng Xiaoping and the Transformation of China*. Cambridge: Belknap Press, 2011.

Waley-Cohen, Joanna. *Sextants of Beijing: Global Currents in Chinese History*. New York: Norton, 1999.

Wang, Xiuyu. *China's Last Imperial Frontier: Statecraft and Locality in Late Qing Kham Tibet*. Lanham, Md.: Lexington Books, 2011.

Westad, Odd Arne. *Decisive Encounters: The Chinese Civil War, 1946–50*. Stanford: Stanford University Press, 2003.

———. *The Global Cold War: Third World Interventions and the Making of Our Times*. Cambridge: Cambridge University Press, 2007.

———. *Restless Empire: China and the World since 1750*. New York: Basic Books, 2012.

Whelpton, John. *A History of Nepal*. Cambridge: Cambridge University Press, 2005.

Whiting, Allen. *The Chinese Calculus of Deterrence: India and Indochina*. Ann Arbor: University of Michigan Press, 1975.

Winks, Robin. *Cloak and Gown: Scholars in the Secret War, 1939–1961*. New York: Morrow, 1987.

Yang, Jisheng. *Tombstone: The Great Chinese Famine, 1959–1962*. Translated by Stacy Mosher and Guo Jian. New York: Farrar, Straus and Giroux, 2012.

Zagoria, Donald. *The Sino-Soviet Conflict, 1956–1961*. Princeton: Princeton University Press, 1962.

Zhai, Qiang. *China and the Vietnam Wars*. Chapel Hill: University of North Carolina Press, 2000.

Zhang, Shu Guang. "Constructing 'Peaceful Coexistence': China's Diplomacy toward the Geneva and Bandung Conferences, 1954–55." *Cold War History* 7, no. 4 (2007): 509–28.

———. *Economic Cold War: America's Embargo against China and the Sino-Soviet Alliance, 1949–1963*. Washington, D.C.: Woodrow Wilson Center Press, 2001.

Index

and Dalai Lama's departure, 36;
and People's Republic of China's
transition to less flexible imperial
structure, 41, 50, 59, 62, 83–85, 88,
111, 114, 116, 125, 133, 135, 164 (n. 7);
and local autonomy, 135, 139
(n. 3); failure of, 145 (n. 77)
Everest, and Sino-Nepali relations,
67, 68, 77, 82

Ferguson, Niall, 141 (n. 23)
First world countries, imperialism
of, 55, 56, 59
Five principles of peaceful coexistence: and People's Republic
of China's third world policy, 4,
28, 84, 114, 119–20, 132, 133; and
People's Republic of China's occupation of Tibet, 26–27, 29, 139
(n. 4); origins of, 27, 144 (n. 54);
and Sino-Indian relations, 27–30,
84, 114, 119, 120, 122, 123, 124; and
Sino-Nepali relations, 28, 68, 84,
153 (n. 21); and Sino-Pakistani
relations, 28, 129–30
Fleming, Peter, 147 (n. 10), 150 (n. 59)
Foreigners: foreign students as intelligence agents, 44; security in
Tibetan frontier, 63–67, 83
Foreign Ministry of the People's
Republic of China (FMPRC), 6–7,
9, 29, 64, 78–79, 111–12
Fourth world: and non-state actors,
2, 3–4, 83, 88, 134, 137 (n. 2);
impact on third world states,
3–4, 6, 168 (n. 47); third world
states subsuming, 5, 44, 45, 50,
55, 114; and Cold War history,
5, 135; Tibetan plateau as, 11–12,
26, 37, 125; and multiple foreign
policies, 20, 45; third world states

distinguished from, 58; People's
Republic of China's ignorance
of, 97; and People's Republic
of China as multination state,
118–19; and Sino-Indian relations,
120, 123; and provincial governments, 134
Fox, Reginald, 99–100, 160 (n. 34)
France, 55–56, 58
Fravel, M. Taylor, 151 (n. 4)
Frontier: defining of, 137 (n. 2). *See
also* Tibetan frontier

Gaddis, John, 5
Gallagher, John, 6
Garver, John, 84, 157 (n. 4), 163 (n. 78),
164 (n. 14), 166 (n. 26)
Geneva Conference, 5
Ghana, 126, 127
Goldstein, Melvyn, 138 (n. 5), 139
(n. 4), 140 (n. 10), 145 (n. 71), 154
(n. 38), 161 (n. 60)
Goloks, rebellion of, 32, 145 (n. 70)
Great Leap Forward, 32–33, 89, 110,
111, 113
Griffons, Himalayan, 139 (n. 2)
Gross, Ernest, 47, 148 (n. 30)
Guldin, Greg, 142 (n. 35)
Guomindang: Chiang Kai-shek as
leader of, 1; and Chinese civil
war, 14; establishment of rival
Chinese regime, 15; as imperial
force, 16; and People's Republic
of China's liberation of Tibet, 17;
and Tibetan crisis, 48; legitimacy
of, 53; and Tibetan rebels, 71,
74–76, 95, 154 (n. 38); in India, 94.
See also Republic of China
Gyalo Thondup: and Central
Intelligence Agency, 38, 47, 146
(n. 1); opposition to Chinese

Communist Party, 38–39; and Tibetan statehood, 39–40, 47, 48, 54, 59; and Afro-Asian Convention on Tibet, 51, 54, 151–52 (n. 6); resistance led by, 62

Hamite (Tibetan Muslim), 99–100
Han: expulsion from Tibet, 13–14; Mao on Han chauvinism, 22, 31, 142 (n. 36); tension with Tibetan cadres, 24, 31, 34; and Panchen Lama, 43; and Hui, 160 (n. 37)
Han-Tibetan Alliance Against Communism, 51
Herter, Christian, 56
Himalayas: and contested borders, 6, 29, 30; pilgrims traveling through, 26, 66, 88; trade in, 86–87, 104
Ho Chi Minh, 126
Hong Kong: and Deng, 22; and Tsang, 38; and Afro-Asian Convention on Tibet, 51, 53, 54; and Republic of China, 51, 73, 95, 146 (n. 2)
Huang Mou, 95, 146 (n. 6)
Hui, 100, 101–2, 103, 160 (n. 37)
Human rights, and Tibetan issue, 46–48, 57
Hungary, 120
Hunxue'ers: and Tibetan frontier, 65, 66, 67, 83–84, 88, 98–99; nationality of, 65, 66, 67, 88, 99, 103, 114, 160 (n. 46); People's Republic of China's policy on, 67, 83–84, 135–36; in People's Republic of China's state apparatus, 152 (n. 15)

Ignatieff, Michael, 137 (n. 3), 139 (n. 3)
Imperialism: Chinese imperialism in Tibetan frontier, 2–3, 6,

10, 58–59, 62, 83–85, 88, 116, 133, 137 (n. 3), 139 (n. 3), 164 (n. 7); comparative histories of empires, 5; forms of, 5–6, 138 (n. 7); Mao on, 14–15; Zhou on, 15; People's Republic of China's anti-imperial imperialism, 16, 17, 141 (n. 23); of Britain, 17, 29, 56, 57, 99, 149 (n. 39), 150 (n. 53), 157 (n. 74); nation-states forming in former imperial holdings, 40; perpetuation of, 41–42, 56–57, 58; and challenges to borderlands, 50; China as former victim of, 54–55, 119–20; of first world countries, 55, 56, 59; in international order, 56; United States as informal empire, 56, 119; of Republic of China, 59; of Qing dynasty, 125, 132, 150 (n. 55), 165–66 (n. 25)
India: Dalai Lama's exile in, 2, 36, 39, 42, 44, 71, 92, 105, 116, 121, 136, 161 (n. 56); and non-state actors, 4; ties to Tibetan rebels, 4, 90, 93, 94, 95, 104, 112, 123, 124, 147 (n. 20); multiple ethnicities in, 6; response to Tibetan crisis, 7; United States' support for, 16; as nation-state, 26; and Pakistan, 29, 54, 100, 129, 166 (n. 25); and Soviet Union, 45, 134, 168 (n. 47); and Afro-Asian Convention on Tibet, 51, 52, 54; treaties with Tibet, 52; and independence of Tibet, 53–54; nationals imprisoned in China, 65; and Nepal, 68, 77; and Chiang, 94, 95; Zhou's visit of 1960, 95; imperialistic policies of, 150 (n. 53); as multination state, 166 (n. 25). *See also* Sino-Indian relations

Indian Communist Party, 51
Indonesia, 123, 126, 127
Intelligence. *See* Spies and
    intelligence
Ireland, 46-47
Ismail (Muslim working with Ma
    Tengbiao), 70-71, 72, 74, 75, 76, 80

Japan, 52, 55, 150 (n. 53)
Jasanoff, Maya, 157 (n. 74)
Jinba, A Wang, 65

Kajis, 100-101, 102, 103, 120
Kalmyks, 42, 147 (n. 10), 152 (n. 12)
Kanting, 43, 44
Kashag, 12, 13-14, 20, 21, 31, 140 (n. 12)
Kashmir, 29, 54, 99, 100, 102
Kazakhs, 2, 141 (n. 16)
Kent, Sherman, 153 (n. 26)
Kenya, 54
Kham: Dalai Lama on land reform
    problems in, 24; low-intensity
    conflict in, 30-33, 38, 62, 144
    (n. 63)
Khambas: and Dalai Lama, 9, 31, 33,
    80, 139 (n. 9); and Long March,
    12; collaboration with People's
    Republic of China, 31; rebellion
    of 1956, 32, 33, 39, 62, 139 (n. 9),
    145 (n. 70); and Afro-Asian Con-
    vention on Tibet, 51, 151-52 (n. 6);
    rival Khamba groups in India, 62;
    and Sino-Nepali relations, 77, 82;
    abduction of Pamu, 90, 92-93;
    Pamu's information on, 92-93,
    94; Tibetans distinguished from,
    92-93, 158 (n. 12)
Khan, Ayub, 149 (n. 38)
Khazanov, A. M., 159 (n. 32)
Khrushchev, Nikita, 28, 51, 134
Kissinger, Henry, 140 (n. 10)

Knaus, John Kenneth, 47, 146 (n. 1),
    147 (n. 10)
Koirala, B. P.: and Sino-Nepali rela-
    tions, 68, 74, 75, 77, 79, 81-83, 155
    (n. 58); accusations of spying
    against, 83
Korea, 40, 41, 49
Korean War, 5
Krasner, Stephen, 146 (nn. 5, 7)
Kuomintang. *See* Guomindang

Latin America, 137-38 (n. 4)
Lenin, V., 72
Lhasa, Tibet, 33, 36, 39, 46
Lin, Hsiao-ting, 138 (n. 5), 140 (n. 15),
    154 (n. 38)
Liu, Xiaoyuan, 138 (n. 5), 142 (n. 35),
    164 (n. 7)
Liu Shaoqi, 132
Lobsang Jigme, 36
Long March, 12
Luthi, Lorenz, 148 (n. 24)

Ma Bufang, 14
Maier, Charles, 6
Malaya, 46-47
Manchukuo, 52
Manuel, George, 137 (n. 2)
Mao Zedong: territorial expansion
    of, 3, 16; rise to power, 12; on im-
    perialism, 14-15; minority policy
    of, 14-15, 22, 31, 142 (n. 36); and
    control of Tibetan plateau, 15-16,
    17, 20; long-term intentions for
    Tibet, 23, 143 (n. 40); and Sino-
    Indian relations, 27-28, 90; and
    five principles of peaceful coexis-
    tence, 28; and contested borders,
    29; and reform, 33; and Tibetan
    crisis, 34-35, 117; and Panchen
    Lama, 43; economic planning of,

69, 117, 118; and Pamu, 94; vision of, 114; on communes, 117; agricultural policies of, 163 (n. 4)

Martin, Terry, 142 (n. 35)

Ma Tengbiao: as Guomindang spy, 67, 69–70, 71, 72, 73, 75; and Ismail, 70–71, 72, 75, 76; and land reform propaganda, 72, 73; and Chou Shu, 74, 76; in Nepal, 80

McGranahan, Carole, 5, 137 (n. 3), 139 (n. 3), 140 (n. 10), 146 (n. 9)

McMahon Line, 29, 122

Miller, Manjari Chatterjee, 150 (n. 53)

Mimang Tibetan party, 70

Ming dynasty, 11

Mongols, 11, 152 (n. 12)

Mughal Empire, 150 (n. 55)

Mullaney, Thomas, 142 (n. 35)

Murville, Couve de, 56

Narayan, Jayprakash, 50, 53, 57–58

Nationalist Party, 12, 15, 140 (n. 15)

Nation-states: definitions of, 39, 146 (n. 5), 166 (n. 25); formation of, 39–40, 146 (n. 6); imperialism of, 55; sovereignty of, 58, 146 (n. 7)

Nehru, Jawaharlal: on People's Republic of China's occupation of Tibet, 26–27; and Sino-Indian relations, 27–28, 29, 46, 82, 87, 90, 120, 123–24, 125, 128, 133; and Zhou, 33, 120, 123, 125; and Tibet as election issue, 50; and Afro-Asian Convention on Tibet, 51; and Nepal, 77; vision of, 114

Nehru, R. K.: and Sino-Indian relations, 90, 96, 105, 121, 130, 159 (n. 26); and Taring, 95–96

Nepal: and non-state actors, 4; politics within, 7; Tibetan refugees in, 60–62, 80–81; diplomats on Tibetan frontier, 63–64; nationals imprisoned in China, 65, 152 (n. 13); citizenship of, 66; and balance-of-power politics, 68; and India, 68, 77; People's Liberation Army's counterinsurgency operation in, 77–80, 81, 83, 84, 155 (n. 58); Tibetan rebels in, 80–81, 84, 128–29; food crisis in, 109; and Sino-Indian relations, 127, 128, 165 (n. 20). *See also* Sino-Nepali relations

Nepali Communist Party, 69–70

Netherlands, 56

Ngabo Ngawang Jigme, 21

Nomads: and territorial claims for Indian government, 6, 97, 127; in Tibetan frontier, 10, 88, 112, 114, 116, 128; and border crossings, 60, 97; intelligence reports from, 81; citizenship of, 97, 104; and People's Republic of China's counterinsurgency tactics, 98; and People's Republic of China's land reform, 116–17; impact on sedentary society, 159 (n. 32)

Non-state actors: of Tibetan frontier, 1–4, 88; and fourth world, 2, 3–4, 83, 88, 134, 137 (n. 2); and Cold War, 2, 4, 5; and Sino-Nepali relations, 80, 83; as national security problem, 88; and Sino-Indian relations, 93, 95, 96–97, 98; and border crossings, 135

Norbu, Thubten Jigme, 48–49, 51, 149 (n. 36)

Norbulingka (Dalai Lama's summer residence), 34–36

Nyasaland, 56

Oman, 56, 57

Ottoman Empire, 17

Pakistan: and Zhou, 28, 129–30, 132,
144 (n. 56), 167 (nn. 39, 40); and
India, 29, 54, 100, 129, 166
(n. 25); and Sino-Indian relations, 96, 128, 129–30, 132, 159
(n. 26), 165 (n. 20); and United
States, 120, 167 (n. 44). *See also*
Sino-Pakistani relations
Pamu, Sangzheng Duojie, 90, 92–94
Panchen Lama (ninth incarnation),
20
Panchen Lama (tenth incarnation):
recognition of, 20, 21–22; negotiations with People's Republic
of China, 22; and reforms of
People's Republic of China,
24, 166 (n. 25); Dalai Lama's
relationship with, 25, 43; support
for People's Republic of China,
42–44, 47; Beijing visit for May
Day celebration, 43–45
Panchen Lamas, Dalai Lamas'
recurring disputes with, 11, 20, 42,
140 (n. 10)
Pan Zili, 79, 82, 95–96, 159 (n. 25)
Peng Dehuai, 17
People's Liberation Army (PLA):
invasion of Lhasa, 1, 16; invasion of Ali, 17, 141 (n. 25); and
Tibetan chieftains, 20; invasion
of Chamdo, 20–21; Khambas' co-
operation with, 31; and Norbulingka, 35, 145 (n. 78); and Tibetan
crisis, 36–37, 43, 125; Panchen
Lama's support for, 43; conflict
with Khambas, 62; and Tibetan
rebels, 62–63, 79, 152 (n. 7); inef-
fectiveness of, 64; counterinsurgency operation in Nepali territory, 77–80, 81, 83, 84, 155 (n. 58);
and center/periphery gap, 81, 156

(n. 67); and People's Republic of
China's state-building, 83
People's Political Consultative Conference, 86
People's Republic of China (PRC):
effect of non-state actors on, 1–2;
foreign policy of, 2, 5, 7, 10, 21, 22,
37, 48–49, 51–52, 83, 119, 132–34,
165 (n. 20), 167 (n. 45); weakness
in border regions, 2, 5, 35, 37, 40,
61–62, 145 (n. 77), 151 (n. 4); counterinsurgency tactics, 2, 6, 33, 44,
77–80, 83, 84, 88, 98, 104, 155
(n. 58); sovereign claims of, 2, 26,
29, 33, 37, 42, 47, 49, 50, 52, 58, 59,
64, 87, 93, 124–26, 164 (n. 7), 165
(n. 24), 165–66 (n. 25); imperial
approach of, 2–3, 4, 5, 6, 16–17, 51,
56, 58, 125, 137 (n. 3), 138 (n. 7),
139 (n. 3), 142 (n. 35), 165–66
(n. 25); as multination state, 3,
16–17, 118–19, 125, 132, 164 (n. 7);
foreign relations of, 3–4, 5, 114, 138
(n. 5); five principles of peaceful
coexistence, 4, 26–30, 68, 84, 114,
119–20, 122, 123, 124, 129–30, 132,
133, 139 (n. 4), 144 (n. 54), 153
(n. 21); and third world policy,
4, 28, 84, 114, 119–20, 129, 132, 133,
137–38 (n. 4); and domestic politics, 5, 138 (n. 5); multiple ethnicities in, 6; and minorities, 15,
31, 32, 44, 142 (n. 35), 145 (n. 69);
territorial claims of, 15–16, 51, 88;
and anti-imperial imperialism,
16, 17, 141 (n. 23); "one country,
two systems" model, 22, 143
(n. 40); and diplomatic rights, 26,
144 (n. 50); boundary commission of, 29–30; and Tibetan cartography, 30–31; and gradualism,

31, 145 (n. 71); watchful restraint policy of, 34; diplomacy of, 44, 45, 49, 50, 58–59, 76, 82, 84, 126, 134, 135, 146–47 (n. 9), 147 (n. 20), 148–49 (n. 36), 149 (n. 39), 167 (nn. 40, 44); support for Tibet as act of aggression against, 48, 49, 50, 96; and Afro-Asian Convention on Tibet, 50–51, 54; Soviet Muslim republics compared to, 51; propaganda on Tibet, 52, 61; neocolonialism of, 53; and center/periphery gap, 62, 83, 89, 106, 114, 134, 151 (n. 4), 156 (n. 67), 158 (n. 4); and factions of Tibetan rebels, 62–63; land reform in Tibet, 72–73; and propaganda against land reform, 72–73; exclusion policy, 83; delegation policy, 84; grand strategy of, 89, 98, 167 (n. 44); agricultural policies of, 89, 111, 112, 113, 116–17; and ethnic cleansing, 111; propaganda on communes, 118; and intra-Asian tensions, 129. *See also* Sino-Indian relations; Sino-Nepali relations; Sino-Pakistani relations; Sino-Soviet relations; Tibetan frontier

Pilgrims, in Tibetan frontier, 26, 66, 88, 114

Poland, 120, 150 (n. 53)

Porter, Bernard, 6, 149 (n. 39)

Portugal, 56

Prasad, Damodar, 70

Qiangba Luozhuo, 65, 66

Qing dynasty: territorial limits of, 3, 16, 17; and Chinese control of Tibet, 11; republican cause against, 12; and trade, 104;

imperialism of, 125, 132, 150 (n. 55), 165–66 (n. 25)

Qinghai, 20, 31, 32, 33, 70

Raghavan, Nedyam, 27

Republic of China: connections with Tibet, 7; and McMahon Line, 29; and Tsang, 38; and genocide in Tibet, 48; as enemy of People's Republic of China, 49; and Hong Kong, 51, 73, 95, 146 (n. 2); and Tibetan collaboration, 52; and neocolonialism of People's Republic of China, 53; and self-determination of Tibet, 53, 54, 71, 72; imperialism of, 59; spies of, 74–76, 95. *See also* Guomindang

Rhodesia, 57

Robinson, Ronald, 6

Roosevelt, Franklin D., 12, 140 (n. 12)

Rose, Leo, 151 (n. 4), 155 (n. 58)

Rowe, William, 150 (n. 55)

Samuel, Geoffrey, 140 (n. 10)

Sautman, Barry, 162 (n. 69)

Scott, James C., 140 (n. 10)

SEATO (South East Asia Treaty Organization), 28, 49, 129, 130, 131

Seventeen Point Agreement, 36

Shigatse Work Committee, 43

Sichuan, 27, 31, 32, 33, 110, 117

Sikkim, 23, 26

Simla Convention, 28–29

Sinha, S., 108, 111, 161 (n. 60)

Sino-Indian relations: tensions in, 2, 84, 121–22, 164 (n. 13); trade agreement in Tibet, 4, 27, 84, 88, 89, 104–11, 112, 113, 114, 115, 119, 120, 122, 128, 162 (n. 61); and Tibetan crisis, 4, 45–46, 88, 105, 120–21, 122, 123, 128, 130, 133, 138

(n. 5), 147 (n. 20), 148 (n. 27), 149 (n. 40); and third world unity, 4, 123, 165 (n. 20); and control of Tibetan plateau, 15-16, 26, 27; and Dalai Lama, 25, 46; and People's Republic of China's conduct in Tibet, 26-27, 45-46, 68, 90; and trade on Tibetan plateau, 27, 86-88, 100, 104, 105-6, 108, 110, 111; and five principles of peaceful coexistence, 27-30, 84, 114, 119, 120, 122, 123, 124; and contested borders, 28-30, 51, 52, 86, 87, 89-90, 92-97, 98, 99, 104, 105, 106, 110, 111, 114-15, 120, 122, 123, 124-27, 130, 133, 157-58 (n. 4); and Soviet Union, 45-46; and People's Republic of China's commune system, 69; and Nepal, 69-70; and Guomindang, 94; and Tibetan Muslims, 100-102; and Sino-Indian War, 114, 115, 120, 157-58 (n. 4), 163 (n. 78), 164 (n. 14)

Sino-Indian War (1962): political warfare prior to, 96; and Dalai Lama, 107; and Sino-Indian relations, 114, 115, 120, 157-58 (n. 4), 163 (n. 78), 164 (n. 14); and Colombo conference, 126-27, 166 (n. 29); and Sino-Soviet relations, 134, 147 (n. 20)

Sino-Nepali relations: and third world unity, 4; and control of Tibetan plateau, 26; and five principles of peaceful coexistence, 28, 68, 84, 153 (n. 21); and contested borders, 29, 30, 61-62, 67-68, 76, 77, 79, 80, 81-83, 88, 89, 99, 114, 151 (n. 4), 155 (n. 58), 156-57 (n. 72); and

People's Republic of China propaganda activities, 61; and Tibetan rebels, 64, 128-29; and foreigners' security in Tibetan frontier, 64-65; and Zhou, 67, 68, 69, 74-77, 78, 81-82, 109, 153 (n. 21); and People's Republic of China's commune system, 69, 72; and People's Liberation Army's counterinsurgency operation in Nepali territory, 77-80, 81, 83, 84, 155 (n. 58); and India, 106, 109-10, 112; and trade, 108-10, 112, 113, 128; and Tibetan crisis, 133

Sino-Pakistani relations: and third world unity, 4, 130, 132; and five principles of peaceful coexistence, 28, 129-30; and Pakistan's support for resolution on Tibet, 49, 149 (n. 38); and contested borders, 89, 96, 100, 130, 159 (n. 26); and Tibetan crisis, 133

Sino-Soviet relations: border in Xinjiang, 2; split in, 5, 44, 73, 147 (n. 20); and Tibetan crisis, 44-47, 49, 51, 59, 134, 138 (n. 5), 147 (n. 20), 168 (n. 47); and India, 45-46; and five principles of peaceful coexistence, 120

Smith, Warren W., 163 (n. 4)

South Asia, and Tibetan frontier, 10, 17, 26

Soviet Muslim republics, 51

Soviet Union: and struggle with United States for China, 13; and five principles of peaceful coexistence, 28; and Panchen Lama, 44-45; and India, 45, 134, 168 (n. 47); and Sino-Indian relations, 45-46; support for People's Republic of China in

United Nations, 46–47, 49, 55, 134; Pamu in, 93; minority policy of, 142 (n. 35); Poland as victim of oppression, 150 (n. 53). *See also* Sino-Soviet relations

Spies and intelligence: and PRC archival material, 6; Ciren, Asuo, and Chenbo from Dingri, 60–61, 83, 84, 157 (n. 77); and border crossings, 62, 88, 98; straightforward nature of spying, 69, 153 (n. 26); of People's Republic of China, 72, 76, 80, 81, 83, 93, 95, 155 (n. 53); and Republic of China, 74–76, 95; and Sino-Nepali relations, 74–76, 128; and Pamu's information on Khambas, 92–93, 94; and Hamite's multiple identities, 100; and Sino-Indian relations, 112; and Sino-Soviet relations, 134

Stalin, Joseph, 142 (n. 35)

Stewart, Michael, 57

Sukarno, 123–25

Sun Yat-sen, 12

Suonan Daji, 86–87, 111, 114–15

Sweden, 48, 148–49 (n. 36)

Taiwan. *See* Republic of China

Tang Dynasty, 11, 125

Tanzania, 127

Taring, G. N., 95–96

Taylor, Jay, 154 (n. 38)

Thailand, 47

Third world states: fourth world cutting across, 3–4, 6; and Cold War, 4, 26, 37, 137 (n. 4); unity of, 4, 123, 127, 129, 134, 137–38 (n. 4), 165 (n. 20); imperial subsuming of fourth world, 5, 44, 45, 50, 55, 114; emergence of, 6, 166 (n. 25);

People's Republic of China's policy toward, 10, 119–23, 126, 129, 132–34, 165 (n. 20), 168 (nn. 45, 47); and five principles of peaceful coexistence, 28; sovereignty of, 40; nationalism of, 41; and perpetuation of imperialism, 41–42; People's Republic of China fostering cooperation among, 52, 68; and decolonization, 55; fourth world distinguished from, 58; and Sino-Indian relations, 126–28, 165 (n. 20)

Three Antis, Two Reductions campaign, 60

Tibet: as multinational entrepôt, 3; religious freedom in, 3, 47; and neighboring states, 3–4; People's Republic of China's governance of, 3–4, 9–10, 15, 17, 21–22, 23, 42, 141 (n. 22), 143 (n. 44); Republic of China's connections with, 7; and sky burials, 9–10; difficulty in functioning as nation-state, 10–11, 20, 26, 39, 140 (n. 10); chieftains of, 11, 20, 31, 44, 140 (n. 10); statelessness of, 11–12, 26, 39, 125, 140 (n. 10); Chinese expelled from, 13, 14; and Chinese civil war, 13, 140 (n. 15); People's Republic of China's liberation of, 15, 16, 17, 21; and local collaboration with People's Republic of China, 17, 20, 21, 23, 25, 34, 42, 142 (n. 35); multiple foreign policies of, 20, 21; independence of, 20, 39, 40, 41, 47, 52–54, 93, 125; safeguards for Tibetan culture and religion, 21, 22, 23, 42, 47, 143 (n. 40); factions within, 21–22, 43, 44, 62; People's Republic of China's sovereignty over, 29, 33, 37, 42, 47, 49, 50, 52, 58, 59, 64, 87, 93, 124-26, 164 (n. 7), 165 (n. 24); cartography of, 30-31; People's Republic of China's reform in ethnically Tibetan areas, 31; and genocide case, 38, 40, 48; and Tibetans' competing foreign policies, 39; and People's Republic of China's diplomacy, 44, 45, 126, 146-47 (n. 9); treaties signed by, 52-53; People's Republic of China's land reform in, 72-73, 116, 117-18, 135; famine of 1962, 89, 111-15, 117, 118, 158 (n. 5), 162 (nn. 69, 73); asymmetric warfare in, 101; violence in, 102; food scarcity in, 110; People's Republic of China's commune system in, 117; communes in, 117-18

Tibetan Buddhism, 11, 13-14, 42

Tibetan frontier: non-state actors of, 1-4, 88; People's Republic of China's state weakness in, 2, 4, 35, 37, 40, 49, 50, 59, 61-64, 79, 83, 88, 96, 98, 114, 126, 134, 145 (n. 77), 151 (n. 4); Chinese imperialism in, 2-3, 6, 10, 58-59, 62, 83-85, 88, 116, 133, 137 (n. 3), 139 (n. 3), 164 (n. 7); cosmopolitanism of, 3, 26, 37, 65, 67, 118; crisis in, 4, 7, 34-36, 43, 45-46, 47, 48, 49-50, 59, 88, 117, 120-21, 122, 123, 125, 128, 130, 133, 138 (n. 5), 147 (n. 20), 148 (n. 27), 149 (n. 40); and Sino-Indian relations, 4, 28, 138 (n. 5); conditions of, 7-8, 59, 62; geography of, 9, 10-11; People's Republic of China diplomats in, 9-10, 63-64; and local autonomy, 10, 21, 22, 117, 139 (n. 3); People's Republic

of China's state-building in, 10, 26, 41, 45, 52, 59, 83, 98, 116-17, 163 (n. 4); and People's Republic of China's foreign policy, 10, 26, 139 (n. 4); ethnic tension in, 12, 31, 88, 117, 141 (n. 16); and Britain, 14; People's Republic of China's recovering of, 25-26; trade in, 26, 27, 28, 100, 104-6, 107, 135; and contested international borders, 28-29; low-intensity conflicts in, 30; and border crossings, 60, 62, 85; and Nepali diplomats, 63-64; foreigners' security in, 63-67, 83; and hunxue'ers, 65, 66, 67, 83-84, 88, 98-99

Tibetan Muslims, 6, 12, 100-103, 104

Tibetan plateau: as fourth world, 11-12, 26, 37, 125; People's Republic of China's control of, 15-16, 17, 20, 40, 42, 122; trade on, 27, 86-89, 100, 104-6, 108, 110, 111; cartography of, 30-31; food supplies for, 88-89

Tibetan rebels: Indian government's ties with, 4, 90, 93, 94, 95, 104, 112, 123, 124, 147 (n. 20); CIA links with, 33, 38, 138 (n. 5), 146 (n. 1); and People's Republic of China's state weakness, 40, 64-65; Panchen Lama on, 43; fragmented nature of resistance, 62-63; and Sino-Nepali relations, 64, 128-29; and Guomindang, 71, 74-76, 95, 154 (n. 38); in Nepal, 80-81, 84, 128-29; and non-state actors, 88; and Hamite, 100

Tibetan refugees: in Lhasa, 33; Dalai Lama advocating for, 39; in Nepal, 60-62, 80-81; in India, 94, 120, 121, 122; People's Republic of